CW00660789

WORK AND THE FAMILY

Edited by
PETER MOSS &
NICKIE FONDA

Work and the Family

Temple Smith
London

First Published in Great Britain in 1980
by Maurice Temple Smith Ltd
37 Great Russell Street, London WC1

© 1980 Anna Coote, Peter Elias, Nickie Fonda,
        Patricia Hewitt, Sheila Kamerman, Peter
        Moss, Rhona Rapoport, Robert Rapoport

ISBN 0 85117 1990

Photoset in 10pt Times by
Robcroft Ltd, London
Printed in Great Britain by
Billing and Sons Ltd
London, Guildford, Worcester and Oxford

Contents

THE CONTRIBUTORS

Anna Coote — Deputy Editor, New Statesman.

Peter Elias — Senior Research Fellow, Manpower Research Group, University of Warwick.

Nickie Fonda — Course Convenor, Brunel University Management Programme.

Patricia Hewitt — General Secretary, National Council of Civil Liberties.

Sheila Kamerman — Co-Director, Cross-National Studies of Social Service Systems and Family Policy, Columbia University School of Social Work.

Peter Moss — Research Officer, Thomas Coram Research Unit.

Rhona Rapoport — Co-Director, Institute for Family and Environmental Research.

Robert Rapoport — Co-Director, Institute for Family and Environmental Research.

1

Introduction
Peter Moss and Nickie Fonda

Most people, if pressed to consider the matter, would acknowledge
the strong impact work life has on family life and vice versa. This
relationship between work and the family shows itself in many ways in
everyday life – a mother unable to work or another unable to get a job
that does justice to her experience and qualifications, because of the
demands made on them by home and children; a father unable to see
much of his children or do as much to help at home as he should
because of long working hours; another father moving his family
repeatedly, through a succession of houses, schools and communities,
as the price of promotion; or, to take two final examples, some family
upset distracting a parent's attention at work, reducing performance
and increasing mistakes, or heavy work demands making a parent
tired, irritable and preoccupied at home. Such examples could be
multiplied by most readers. Most would probably dwell on the
limitations and disruptions that work and family impose on each
other; the work–family relationship is, too often, one of tension and
strain.

Occasionally, as for instance when some pundit accuses working
mothers of harming their children, the relationship, or one part of it,
gets temporary, emotive and ill-informed publicity. But most of the
time it is ignored and taken for granted. The possibility of improving
the relationship, and dispelling much of its attendant tension, receives
little attention, either from society at large or from politicians,
employers, trade unionists and those working with children and their
families.

The relationship between work and the family, and the possibilities
for change, have acquired new significance with the growing acceptance of the principle of equal opportunities, and the incorporation of
this principle into recent legislation. Any assessment of the work–
family relationship must now include its impact on equal opportunities as one of the major criteria, just as evaluation of the implications
of movement towards equality of opportunity must include its likely
impact on work and the family. Like it or not, and many people still
don't, equal opportunities will play an important part in the future
evolution of employment and home life.

This book is the end product of a seminar held in September 1979.
Its purpose was to examine the relationship between work, the family

and equal opportunities. Our starting point in organising the seminar was that the present relationship between work and the family had damaging consequences not only for work and the family, but also for the chances of attaining genuine equality of opportunity. Among these consequences, the following are most serious.

1 Many women with children who wish to work are unable to do so.
2 Women with children who do work are a very disadvantaged group of workers, measured in terms of job status, pay, other conditions of employment, prospects, etc.
3 As well as these short-term effects, having children has a massive detrimental effect on women's long-term employment prospects and income, up to and beyond retirement age.
4 Many women and probably some men with children face undue tension, strain and other difficulties in attempting to combine work and family life, which detract from their enjoyment of and contribution to both of these important areas of life.
5 Because of their heavy involvement in work, men with children often have insufficient time, energy or inclination to take a full share of family responsibilities and activities.
6 Some children of working parents are cared for in unsatisfactory conditions, for lack of adequate care being available.
7 These problems penalise not only parents and children, but employers and society as a whole, by wasting the employment potential of women and the domestic potential of men and reducing standards of performance in work and family life.

Each of these points is discussed at greater length later on in the book. For the moment, we wish to emphasise that none seem to be intrinsic problems. They are not, in our view, the inevitable results of people combining the two roles of worker and parent. Working mothers, or indeed working fathers, are not *the problem*. That lies in the failure of family life, work life and society in general to have yet developed the means to enable these roles to be comfortably combined, without penalising one or more of the participants, be it fathers, mothers, children or employers. These problems could be greatly diminished if a relationship between work and the family evolved which acknowledged the needs and importance of both these aspects of life and of all the participants in the relationship.

Origins of the current relationship between work and the family

With only twenty-four hours in a day and finite amounts of energy and goodwill, reconciling the demands made on these limited resources is one of the major dilemmas of adult life. Employment, child care and the domestic chores and duties of everyday life are three of the most time-consuming and insistent of these demands.

During the first 150 years of industrialisation in Britain, there emerged a new relationship between work and home, based on the increasing separation of employment on the one hand and parental and domestic tasks on the other. The separation was in part physical. Employment came to be concentrated in factories, offices and other workplaces completely apart and at increasing distance from the home. This process reached its culmination in the evolution of the suburb and long-distance commuting. The separation was also one of scale and organisation, the routine and discipline of factory life and the vast numbers involved contrasting with the intimacy and informality of family life. But the most striking aspect of the new relationship between work and family was the increasing division of labour based on sex – men and fathers going out to work, women and mothers increasingly confined to domestic chores and child-rearing.

The actual process was, of course, more complex. There was neither a complete nor a sudden break with the past. There had always been a degree of separation between work and the family: even before the Industrial Revolution, not all work was done in or near the home, and women did much of the day-to-day work involved with the care of home and children. One of the first consequences of factory development was, paradoxically, the growth of home working, as the expanding output in one newly mechanised sector of an industry required increased capacity in other unmechanised sectors. In textiles, for instance, the new spinning mills initiated a dramatic, if brief, period of expansion and prosperity for the handloom weaver, working from home with the help of his family. Even when industrialisation was well established, some women, especially in areas where local industry showed a high demand for women workers, refused to conform to their allotted domestic role. Reporting to the 1904 Interdepartmental Committee on Physical Deterioration about conditions in the Potteries, an area with a high level of female factory employment, a woman factory inspector commented:

> It is impossible not to be impressed by the universal preference amongst women for factory over domestic life and how depressed and out of health they become if obliged to remain at home . . . . At 13, a majority of these women begin to work in factories, to handle their own earnings and to mix with a large number of people, with all the excitement and gossip of factory life. Thus in most cases they grow up ignorant of everything pertaining to domesticity. After marriage, therefore, it is hardly probable that they would willingly relinquish this life to undertake work of which they are in so large measure ignorant and which is robbed of all that is to them pleasant and exciting.

Having made such allowances, we are still left with the fact that industrialisation did bring a significant shift in the relationship between work and the family. The new relationship, with its increased separation between these two areas of life, came to be incorporated in the 'cognitive maps' of ordinary people. The world of work was perceived increasingly as a man's world – tough, competitive, heartless – while the home was woman's territory – emotional, warm, supportive. Though separate, the two worlds came to be seen as complementary, home providing a haven of comfort and peace for menfolk, who in turn provided the economic means to enable women to service this haven and to develop healthy personalities in growing children. Such an arrangement apparently minimised conflict within the family and between work and the family, made no demands on government or employers and appeared to reflect a natural order, making best use of the assumed innate talents and inclinations of each sex.

The prevailing relationship thus came to acquire ideological legitimation. Most people came to accept it as the right and necessary way of doing things. But, as later events were to show, it was no more than one alternative, attaining temporary predominance from the interplay of economic, social, demographic and political forces, themselves liable to change.

The post-war change

The Second World War was a watershed in the relationship between work and the family. In none of the three Censuses prior to the outbreak of war – in 1911,[1] 1921 and 1931 – had more than 10 per cent of married women been economically active[2] (Halsey, 1972: Table 4.7): marriage virtually ended women's involvement in the labour force. The numbers of married women in paid work increased in the 1930s, but just before the war 'the proportion employed was probably little above 1 in 7' (Beveridge, 1942). In his *Report on Social Insurance and Allied Services*, published in 1942, Sir William Beveridge felt able to assume that 'In any measure of social policy in which regard is had to the facts, the great majority of married women must be regarded as occupied on work which is vital though unpaid, without which their husbands could not do paid work and without which the nation could not continue ... *during marriage most women will not be gainfully employed.*' [Our italics]

Beveridge's assumption proved wrong. Changes in labour market supply and demand produced a large-scale movement into the workforce by married women, both with and without dependent children. Between 1931 and 1951, the economic activity rate for married women more than doubled to 22 per cent, then nearly doubled again to 42 per cent by 1971; by 1978, it was expected to have reached 51 per cent (Central Statistical Office, 1978: Table 5.3). For married women below pension age, the economic activity rate passed the 50 per cent mark sometime in the early 1970s.[3]

Ideology also showed signs of change. The post-war women's movement developed a comprehensive and cogent critique of the inferior position of women in society and of the ideology used to legitimise this position. Although there may be no consensus about what specific model of work–family relationship is most valued, there is consensus in the movement about the inequitable nature of a rigidly defined sex-segregated model. There have also been signs of a more general concern in society, albeit less urgent and comprehensive, about the disadvantaged position of women, leading to legislation in the 1970s against some of the worst and most obvious discrimination faced by women in fields such as education and employment. This legislation marked a national acceptance, at least on paper, of the principle of equal opportunities. One of the purposes of the 1975 Sex Discrimination Act was to 'promote equality of opportunity between men and women generally', and the Act established a new body – the Equal Opportunities Commission – to further this end.

Movement has begun, but its extent should not be exaggerated, nor has it run its course: we are still very much in the throes of change. The evidence, discussed by Peter Moss and Peter Elias in Chapters 2 and 3, points to a substantial reservoir of currently non-employed married women who would like to work; to growing numbers likely to seek entry to the labour force in future years; to continuing growth, if at a much slower rate, in the numbers actually at work; and to the probability that the number involuntarily unemployed will also grow, as it did in the 1970s.

Women, including those with dependent children, are in the labour force to stay, but most of the post-war increase and projected future growth are accounted for by part-time employment. As Peter Moss shows in Chapter 2, the full-time employment rate for women with children has hardly changed in the last twenty years, while the part-time rate has nearly trebled. This part-time work has been heavily concentrated in jobs with poor status, poor pay and poor prospects. There still remains a wide gap in the quantity and quality of employment undertaken by mothers and by fathers.

A similar gap exists in the quantity and quality of work done in the home. A number of international studies undertaken in the 1960s, all pointed to the same conclusion:

. . . that husbands and children, when they help at all, tend to assist with only selected, often self selected tasks and for a very small fraction of the total hours devoted to housekeeping. As the recent multinational time budget research in 19 countries demonstrated,

the husband spends little more time assisting the wife and mother
with household tasks when she works outside the home, than when
she does not. (Cook, 1978)

Recent American research, such as the studies by Katharine
Walker referred to by the Rapoports in Chapter 7, indicate that
significant, if small, changes have occurred there in the last decade,
mainly in the amount of time men give to child-care. But, as Ann
Oakley (1972) has pointed out, increased involvement by fathers with
children is often confined to the more enjoyable tasks – play and
outings, for instance – leaving mothers with the bulk of the remaining,
less enjoyable jobs. Moreover, whatever the changes that are
beginning to stir, responsibility for child-rearing and the home
remains primarily with the mother, and she still does most of the work,
whether or not she also has a paid job.

Ideologically, change has also been slower than might at first seem
apparent. The women's movement in Britain remains a weak force
politically and its ideas are not widely understood or accepted.
Beneath the wider acceptance of the rhetoric of equal opportunities
and sex equality, there is less agreement and awareness about the
meaning and implications of the concept. Does it simply require the
removal of the most visible and blatant discrimination? Or does it
require a wide range of positive measures to actively promote equality
and remove all obstacles to women having a genuinely equal chance in
education, employment and other aspects of life? What are these
obstacles? How far, if at all, does equality of opportunity require
change in the attitudes, behaviour and position of men? What effects
can or should it have on marriage and family life? Central to these and
other questions is whether equality of opportunity can be achieved by
a few, fairly painless, reforms, restricted to a limited number of
defined areas, or whether it requires a major revolution in all aspects
of life, affecting both sexes, that cannot simply be grafted onto the
existing state of affairs.

Political response to the change

Despite these qualifications, there can be little doubt that the
relationship between work and the family is undergoing substantial
change. The outcome of this affects not only individual parents and
children but the economy and welfare of society as a whole.

A major influence on the relationship and the way it evolves is the
part taken by government in its regulation. Governments in the
nineteenth and early twentieth centuries left strictly alone, with the
important proviso that in a range of policies they assumed and
reinforced a sex-based division of labour and the prevailing ideology
about the proper roles of men and women. How far has this position

changed in post-war years?

The answer is hardly at all. A wide range of social policies, in fields such as income maintenance and services for children and elderly and handicapped people, continue to be based on an assumption that the primary role and responsibilities of men should be in the field of paid work, while women's should be in the home and in care of other family members, be they elderly or young, disabled or able-bodied (e.g. husbands) (Land, 1978). The continuing acceptance of this assumption also helps to explain the reluctance of successive post-war governments, of whatever party, to actively intervene in regulating the relationship between work and the family and to respond to the changes occurring in it. As Nickie Fonda shows in Chapter 5, successive administrations have done virtually nothing, except close large numbers of day nursery places after the war and introduce a modest maternity leave entitlement in 1976.

Work and the family also continue to be seen as totally separate policy areas, dealt with in isolation by separate departments, even though the relationship between the two areas should be a prime candidate for the joint approach to social policy urged some years ago by the Central Policy Review Staff (1975). Because of this separation, maternity leave could be introduced as part of employment legislation, under the aegis of the Department of Employment, without any discussion about, let alone provision of, necessary supportive child-care services by the Department of Health and Social Security. The example of maternity leave also illustrates the restricted interpretation that governments have placed on their responsibilities for furthering equal opportunities. A blatant cause of discrimination, job loss due to pregnancy and childbirth, has been legislated against. But nothing has been done either to support women who exercise their right to continue at work, through for instance the provision of good-quality child-care facilities, or to encourage men to take a greater share in the care of their babies, both necessary if the impact of parenthood on employment opportunities and prospects is to be equalised between men and women.

The political failure has gone deeper than just inadequate action. Both main political parties, either in government or in opposition, have failed to provide any encouragement or direction to informed public discussion about change – actual or potential – in the relationship between work and the family, or about the meaning, implications and possibilities of equal opportunities. Patricia Hewitt and Anna Coote show, in Chapter 6, how neither the Labour nor Conservative Party has begun to produce a coherent and comprehensive position on equal opportunities or on the needs of working parents, and how both have been hampered by a nostalgia for the 'ideal' family, based on clearly defined and immutable sex roles. The

main difference has been a greater readiness by Labour to accept a
mother's going to work, as long as, in Jim Callaghan's words, 'her
influence at the centre of the family is not weakened', and to concede
that something should be done 'to make the burden of the working
mother more bearable'. The Conservatives have been less ready to
give any support to the idea of mothers working, viewing the problems
faced by working mothers as essentially private ones, to be sorted out
mainly by women themselves as best they can. Neither party has
discussed men's roles in the family, or how these might or should
change in the future.[4]

The shallowness and lack of interest shown by the main political
parties in considering the relationship between the family and equal
opportunities, and their unwillingness to face up to the implications of
change in this area, have contributed to widespread public ignorance
and a low level of awareness about the issues involved. Nor is it easy
to see how this situation will change. At the centre of the whole issue
are the interests of a relatively powerless group – women with
dependent children – yet change must affect relatively powerful
groups, notably employers and working men. As Patricia Hewitt and
Anna Coote point out, while the TUC has impressive policies on
paper, little happens because 'male trade unionists collude with
employers . . . and women [trade unionists] wield insufficient power
to overcome men's resistance and the male-dominated trade union
movement is in no hurry to take the positive steps that would enable
them to do so'. As well as confronting powerful adversaries, change
arouses anxiety and uncertainty. The ultimate political failure has
been an unwillingness to confront these doubts and offer people a
positive view of what a new relationship between work, the family and
equal opportunities could offer all concerned and how it might be
achieved.

Definitions

Before introducing the contributors to the book, some common terms
need defining and assumptions spelling out.

'Work' covers an interest both in those actually in paid employment
and those wanting a job but unable to get one, for whatever reason.
Among those actually in employment, work is not assumed to be a
uniform or consistent experience. There is a great diversity of work
situations each with potentially different implications for family life.

Discussions about 'working mothers' foster the misleading notion
that women with children can be divided into two groups – those who
work and those who don't. In practice, there is much movement into
and out of the labour force by mothers, especially among those with
younger children: this means, for instance, that although about a
quarter of women with pre-school children are employed at any one

time, over half work at some stage in their children's first five years. Today's non-working mother is tomorrow's working mother. More-over, as Peter Moss discusses in Chapter 2, periods out of the labour force while children are young have a major and *permanent* bearing on future employment and earnings prospects.

The use of 'work' in this book as synonymous with paid employ-ment runs the risk of devaluing various sorts of unpaid work, especially those concerned with the care of home and children, which are predominantly undertaken by women. To note this is more than a ritual acknowledgement of a touchy issue. It provides a convenient point to emphasise that such forms of unpaid work are hard, demanding and time-consuming, and that an important part of the work–family relationship concerns the distribution of responsibility for such work. Changes in women's involvement in paid work imply the need for redistributing unpaid work with others, both inside and outside the family: in other words, women spending more time in employment, men spending more time on child care and housework.

'Family' is used as shorthand for parents with dependent children. As with work, there is room for considerable diversity of circum-stances and experience within this basic definition – single-parent families, two-parent families, families where the parents are married, others where they are not, different ways of organising the social, economic and domestic requirements of family life. Also, as with work, family circumstances are, increasingly, likely to change over time: to take a very simple instance, today's two-parent family may become tomorrow's lone-parent family, then via remarriage become a two-parent family again. Any discussion of the relationship between work and family life must take account of this diversity, and should not assume any one arrangement of family life to be superior: each will have its good and bad points. We have no wish, and indeed see no need, to focus exclusively on only one style of family life or attempt to place the various styles in some order of desirability.

The term 'dependent children' also requires some definition. The 'working mother' debate has tended to be mainly concerned about families with very young children, especially those under three. The great majority of children with working mothers, and indeed with working fathers, are over five, and their needs and those of their parents tend to get overlooked. This is particularly true of adol-escents: the recent report by the Central Policy Review Staff (1978a) on services for children of working mothers, for instance, was concerned only with children up to the age of eleven. Yet the needs of adolescents are real and considerable, and the heavy financial and emotional demands they make on parents deserve wider recognition (by researchers and policy makers anyway – presumably most parents have long recognised them!). Although needing much less physical care and supervision than very young children, adolescents require parental time and attention in other forms. Parents 'just being around' seems to be an important factor in maintaining some sort of equilibrium through the period of adolescent turmoil. 'Families with dependent children' must therefore be taken to include all those with children up to school-leaving age, and in many cases beyond.

Finally, though the contributors to this book have been concerned primarily with families with dependent children, the relationship between work and the family is also of particular importance to other families, notably those with other dependent or semi-dependent members, such as elderly or disabled relatives. Much of what is said in this book, it is hoped, has wider application to these families.

'Equal opportunities'

As should be apparent by now, in our view 'equal opportunities' must involve more than just the removal of the most blatant discriminatory practices. If it is to be a reality, the whole range of obstacles that have hindered women achieving equality of opportunity in education, work and other spheres of life must be identified and tackled. Legislation against blatant discrimination and active enforcement of the law are certainly needed, but so too is positive and wide-ranging action, including the sort of benefit–service package on employment advoc-ated in Chapter 4 by Sheila Kamerman, and also in the concluding chapter.

As with any other disadvantaged group, improving the position of women depends on major changes among those who benefit from their disadvantage. The achievement of equal opportunities requires the position of men to be subject to scrutiny and change. The corollary of equal employment opportunities and responsibilities for women is equal responsibilities and *opportunities* in family life for men: work and family both involve burdens and pleasures, which more equally shared would benefit both sexes, adults and children. In Sheila Kamerman's words,

> . . . a more important problem [than making it possible for women to achieve wage and occupational equity with men] . . . is to make it possible for men as well as women to have satisfactory family lives with adequate time and energy for parental and marital activities and responsibilities. Children need the attention and interest of both parents. Adults need the opportunity to participate in the two worlds of work and family, if they are to lead full lives.

Without this 'parental perspective', the issue of work and the family can all too readily be defined as a 'woman's problem' or 'a woman and child care problem', requiring solutions that only take account of women and children. Men can sidle innocently away from any controversy, leaving women on the defensive, to face alone the criticism, guilt and anxiety aroused by the whole emotive issue of work and parenthood. This is exactly the position in Britain today, with 'working mothers' conveniently the problem, and men, employers and society at large avoiding any responsibility. In many countries, however, as Sheila Kamerman points out,

> . . . the debate suggests some recognition that [the needs of women, children and society can only be satisfied if men are part of the solution]. What was discussed in the 1960s as a problem resulting from the changing role of women in society and was debated in the 1970s as the problem of the changing roles of men *and* women, now, as we enter the decade of the 1980s has been redefined. There is growing awareness that the fundamental issue is not just the changes in gender roles but the nature of the relationship between work and family life in the society in which all adults are likely to work; yet they want children and the society needs children and needs them to be well cared for if the society is to survive.

Finally, on the subject of equal opportunities, we do not see the concept as requiring everyone, male and female, to behave identically in work and family life or in any sphere of human activity. Genuine equality of opportunity between the sexes is compatible with a considerable degree of individual variation in each of these spheres, as long as this variation reflects genuine choice freely entered into, a genuine individuality rather than sex-based roles imposed by financial, cultural or other sanctions.

Overview of the book

The chapters that follow examine the current relationship between work and the family, the recent changes that have occurred in it, responses to these changes both at home and abroad, and possible future trends as we move into a new decade with a new technology.

In Chapter 2, Peter Moss brings together a range of statistical material, to review the current circumstances of, and recent trends in, parental employment – though the assumptions underlying most studies and major statistical sources mean that there is less material available on fathers than on mothers. The post-war increase in employment rates for mothers has been in predominantly part-time jobs. This has minimised the need for new child-care arrangements beyond the family and school (which continue to care for most children of working parents), but has maximised employment disadvantages, concentrating working mothers increasingly into poorly paid, low-skilled jobs, with few benefits or prospects. In the same period, fathers' work hours have continued to be long – averaging 43 a week excluding travel and unpaid overtime – and their employment position has improved, as an increasing proportion occupy professional and managerial jobs, leaving fewer in those least skilled occupations where mothers are heavily represented. The post-war history of parental employment demonstrates clearly that an increase in mothers' employment is not, by itself, likely to produce any significant progress towards greater equality in the workplace or in the home.

The chapter also considers the motives of mothers in seeking work, and mothers' attitudes to working. The reasons given by mothers themselves for working cover a broad spectrum of needs and benefits. The actual mix and weight attached to each reason varies from woman to woman: as well as money, which after all figures in the reasons most people would give for working, a majority of mothers also have other, non-financial reasons for taking a job. Evidence from several sources suggests that most employed mothers prefer working to being full-time housewives. Moreover, the number of non-employed mothers who would rather work substantially outnumbers those employed mothers who would rather leave the labour force. Not surprisingly, this latter group are mostly found among women working the longest hours in the worst jobs.

In Chapter 3, Peter Elias sets the trend of increased employment among mothers into the context of general employment and unemployment trends in the last two decades, using analyses by type of industry to identify areas of employment growth and decline for both men and women. He also considers some of the underlying factors which have led to increased labour force participation by married women, especially increased demand for part-time workers by certain service industries and the upward trend in women's real earnings, contributing to a parallel increase in labour supply. He looks finally at future employment prospects for men and women and at the factors likely to affect these, including the impact of microprocessor technology. The prospects, for both sexes, are gloomy, with a doubling of unemployment likely over the next five years: 'without a major reversal in the Government's economic policies, the transition to a high unemployment economy is likely to occur over the next 2 to 3 years'. The added impact of the new technology on unemployment remains an open and highly contentious issue. Peter Elias argues that the net employment effect may be considerably less than the massive unemployment predicted and that, in any case, the transition period for the full introduction of the new technology could be as long as fifteen to twenty years.

Unemployment – male and female – will make an increasing impact on the family in the 1980s. Growing unemployment will not, however, actually reduce the number of married women in employment. The female labour force will continue to grow, albeit at a slower rate than in the past and below the rate calculated in recent government projections. Some of this increase will go to swell the unemployment register, but there will also be job growth in a few sectors, mainly those where women traditionally form most of the workforce. In short, we can expect more married women at work and more unemployed over the next five years or so.

The next three chapters deal with some of the ways in which governments, political parties and other interest groups have responded to the concept of equal opportunities and to the work–family relationship and the changes occurring in it. Sheila Kamerman takes an international perspective in Chapter 4. She outlines five alternative policy options which industrial countries can theoretically adopt in response to developments in women's employment, using actual examples to illustrate each one. Each option implies values and assumptions about family life, work and the nature of society. Each has a range of implications and costs, as well as benefits, for all family members and for society as a whole.

One of the five options, pursuing a policy in which personal choice and parental preferences are the dominant values, is the most popular option in discussions in those countries yet to develop a distinctive, or indeed any policy, such as the UK. However, Sheila Kamerman casts serious doubt on the feasibility of this option. Her own preferred approach, illustrated with examples from Sweden, is to make it possible for both parents (or a sole parent) to manage family and work responsibilities simultaneously. To achieve this without undue stress for parents or children requires individual flexibility, which family members have already shown their capacity and willingness to provide. It also requires a government-backed 'benefit–service package' covering good-quality child-care, employment measures (e.g. entitlement to periods of leave, to care for sick children and for one year after childbirth, open to either parent), and social insurance benefits to compensate for loss of earnings arising from 'take-up' of these measures.

Britain is one of the few countries which still serve as an example of Sheila Kamerman's first policy option – to reject the idea of a specific policy response, preferring that individuals work out their own solutions in the market-place or through personal arrangements. In Chapter 5, Nickie Fonda outlines briefly, for there is little to tell, the response of post-war governments to the changes under way in the relationship between work and the family. The only response of any substance has been a statutory maternity leave, which is considered in detail in the main part of the chapter, including its background, its passage through Parliament, the provisions of the agreed legislation and their rationale, and the response of employers and women. In Chapter 6, Patricia Hewitt and Anna Coote describe the current positions taken by the two major British political parties, and also the

Confederation of British Industries (CBI), the Equal Opportunities Commission (EOC), the Trades Union Congress (TUC) and some individual unions, on equal opportunities and the needs of working parents. As already noted, the picture is a bleak one.

In Chapter 7, Rhona and Robert Rapoport, pioneers in the study of work–family relationships, consider the impact of work on the family. Research findings have failed to show any direct, intrinsic relationship between mothers working and negative outcomes for other family members, including children. In fact, generalisations (e.g. mothers at work = harmed children) cannot be safely made about the impact of work on the family, and attempts to isolate single variables (e.g. working mothers) to which overriding causal effect can be attributed only prove simplistic. In practice, work and family interact in many ways. Influences flow in both directions and produce good and bad effects, costs and benefits; a proper analysis of the impact of work on the family must assess and weigh both sets of outcomes.

The actual outcome in any one family will be the product of complex processes, involving the interplay of a number of variables. These include occupational circumstances, family structure and patterns of relating to work, formal and informal support systems and other resources available to families, levels of family stress and problems and group, family and individual values and expectations. Finally, the Rapoports suggest that two types of work impact on the family need to be distinguished – *structural impact*, the product of patterns of relating to work that are relatively stable over longer periods, and *event impact*, where the effects observed are the consequences of critical events in the world of work, such as unemployment or injury, usually of shorter-term duration. Both types of impact are illustrated with examples.

Finally, in Chapter 8, we review some of the major social, economic, demographic and technological changes in prospect over the next ten to fifteen years, and consider some of their possible implications for work–family relationships and equal opportunities. We argue, though not very hopefully, that government should take a more positive role in mediating the relationship between work and the family, to improve the welfare of parents and children and to discharge the commitment to equality of opportunity which requires positive action if it is to be properly met. More active government intervention might involve several roles, including the encouragement of innovation and good practice by employers – and here, the government as a major employer itself could provide a clear lead – and the provision of a basic benefit–service package (covering child care, employment measures and insurance benefits) to help parents to manage work and family responsibilities without undue stress for them and their children.

We also tackle some difficult issues that might arise from any attempt to improve the present relationship between work, the family and equal opportunities: for instance, ways in which a government intervention programme might be funded; how far parents could be provided with real choice in combining work and family involvement; and whether attitudes and behaviour of men could be altered to produce a significant increase in their involvement in the home, to balance women's greater involvement in the world of work. We ask whether government is likely to do anything positive and conclude that the prospects are poor. Despite this, we take the opportunity to set out the package of measures that are needed to bring about a better and more equal relationship between work and the family.

A better deal for all

The theme of this book is the need to give new and explicit direction to the changing relationship between work and the family. The goal, in our view, is a relationship that encourages greater equality of opportunity between the sexes; helps parents manage work and family life more easily, so reducing the tension that often exists at present; and maximises the benefits and enjoyment to be gained from both activities. The prospect of change in this relationship has been, and continues to be, a source of anxiety and concern to many, who see it leading down the slippery slope to social disorganisation and moral decline. We see it in a different light. Change will occur whether we like it or not; the trick is to ride and guide it, not to be run over by it. If this can be done, then a new relationship between work and the family based on equality could offer a better deal for all concerned – mothers, fathers, children, employers, society at large – with greater variety of experience, better use made of talents and more control by the individual over his or her life. It might even alter the present anomalous situation where many hundreds of thousands would like to work but can't, while many hundreds of thousands of workers have difficulty in finding enough time and energy in the day to fit in all the demands of work and home.

But if these potential benefits are to be realised, society must face up to change and examine carefully the possible ways of responding to it. We hope this book makes some contribution to this task.

2

Parents at Work
Peter Moss

Introduction

This chapter attempts to answer some important questions about parents' involvement in the world of work. How many work? How much work do they do? When do they work? What sort of work do they do? What are their conditions of work? Which parents work? How are children cared for while their parents are at work? It also attempts to tackle two other familiar questions – why *do* mothers go out to work? Wouldn't they rather stay at home?

Answers to these questions provide a starting point for any assessment of the relationship between work, the family and equal opportunities. But before seeking these answers a few notes of caution are necessary. This is not a comprehensive overview of the field: some questions, which could probably have been raised, are ignored and those that are dealt with often get incomplete answers. To some extent, this is my own fault. Useful sources have, doubtless, been missed and others may have been inadequately digested and appreciated. But the incompleteness of the answers is also due to inadequacies in existing statistical sources. Three inadequacies deserve special mention. First, although I have attempted to answer most questions for both parents, there is usually less to say about fathers than about mothers. In research and statistics, fatherhood and working fathers have received much less attention than motherhood and working mothers. As a result, the sources for men are fewer and the data very limited.

Secondly, most of the sources used here are cross-sectional, that is, they present information on the situation under study at one point in time. Family circumstances and parental behaviour do not stand still. They are constantly changing: the current situation may differ considerably from last year's, and may indeed only be fully understood in terms of what has occurred over the intervening year. Cross-sectional studies cannot portray these changes. The picture they give, while not in any sense false, may by itself mislead or encourage oversimplification of complex issues; it is also of limited value in understanding the dynamics of family behaviour and work–family interactions. What is needed are sources which show not only the current circumstances of families but also the experience of family members in work and other related areas over time.

Finally, much of the data used in this chapter comes either from analysis of 'one-off' surveys or from 'one-off' analysis of annual government surveys. Having been done only once, and often several years ago, such surveys or analysis rapidly assume historical rather than current significance. What is needed – especially in a period of rapid economic, technological, social and demographic change – are published statistical time series, to provide, on a regular basis, a wide range of data on the relationship between work and the family, which could be used to plot developments in the relationship. Currently, the only such time series are provided by the General Household Survey (GHS), a large-scale annual survey undertaken by the Government's Office of Population Censuses and Surveys (OPCS). Though confined to mothers only and limited in scope in other ways too, [1] the published GHS Tables are a valuable innovation, permitting trends in mothers' employment in the 1970s to be followed in a way that is impossible for earlier decades.

Given these limitations, it is necessary to fall back on the patchwork of sources used here, which vary considerably in origin, methods, coverage, purposes and adequacy – and which often use different definitions, making comparisons between studies difficult, if not impossible. As far as possible, I have tried to stick with data from the 1970s and to national studies using large samples. This has the drawback of glossing over the considerable local variations that can and do occur, some of which are discussed later. While it is important that the probability of area differences should always be borne in mind, the main focus for this chapter is the situation nationally.

How many parents work?

Mothers

Mothers shared in the post-war movement of married women into the labour force described in Chapter 1. The return to work began among women with older children. In the 1950s, economic activity rates grew faster among women whose children were mostly of secondary school age. But in the 1960s, the employment trend became firmly established among mothers with younger children, the fastest increase being among women with primary school children: for women with pre-school children, the rate of increase went from a mere 6 per cent in the 1950s to 45 per cent in the next decade[2] (see Fig. 1).

By the 1960s, employment rates were rising faster for women with children than for married women in general[3] (see Fig. 2). This faster pace was maintained during the 1970s. Between 1971 and 1977, the employment rate for all married women went up from 42 to 49 per cent, and for women with children from 41 to 52 per cent. Nearly all of this increase occurred in the first half of the decade, the employment rate for mothers reaching 51 per cent by 1975 and changing little over

FIGURE 1   ECONOMIC ACTIVITY RATE OF MARRIED WOMEN WITH
DEPENDENT CHILDREN BY DURATION OF MARRIAGE
(GREAT BRITAIN)

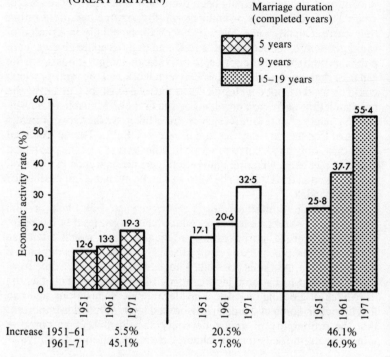

Increase 1951–61   5.5%   20.5%   46.1%
        1961–71   45.1%   57.8%   46.9%

Source: Britton, 1975, Table 6

the next two years.

To estimate increases in employment in the 1970s for mothers with
children of different ages is less straightforward. It involves comparison
of data from two sources, the 1971 Census and 1977 GHS, which
probably overestimates the rate of increase.[4] The trend, however, is
still clear. Employment rates increased for women with children of all
ages, but rose twice as fast among mothers of pre-school children as
among other mothers (see Fig. 3).

The statistics summarised so far seem to give a clear picture of the
extent of mothers' employment. By 1977, just over half (52 per cent)
were at work; by comparison, 58 per cent of all married women and 67
per cent of all women without dependent children had jobs, *including
in both cases only women under sixty* (OPCS, 1979a: Table 4.4,
4.5). But these figures should be treated with caution. Different
official statistical sources come up with rather different results. Most
of the 1970s figures quoted in this chapter are taken from the General

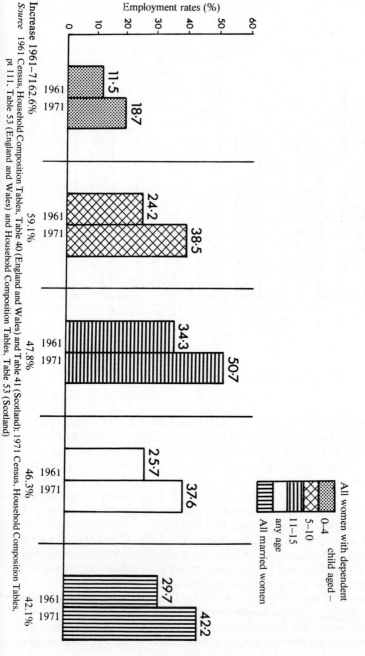

FIGURE 2 EMPLOYMENT RATES FOR WOMEN WITH CHILDREN AND ALL MARRIED WOMEN, 1961–71 (GREAT BRITAIN)

FIGURE 3   EMPLOYMENT RATES FOR MARRIED WOMEN AND
WOMEN WITH CHILDREN, BY AGE OF CHILDREN, 1971 and
1977 (GREAT BRITAIN)

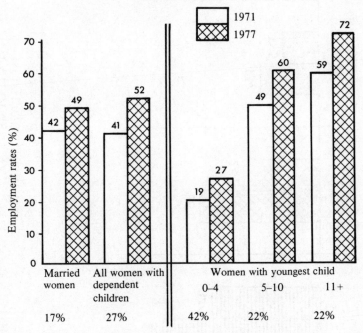

Source   1971 Census, Table DT 0677; 1973, Table 6.3; OPCS, 1979a, Tables
4.2,4,4

Household Survey. This annual survey draws on a relatively large
sample (the 1977 survey, for instance, included some 4,400 women
with dependent children); its results in 1971 were in general similar to
those derived from the Census of that year. But when compared with
results drawn from the Family Expenditure Survey (FES), another
annual government survey also with a relatively large sample,
considerable differences emerge. To take just one example, the 1977
GHS shows an employment rate of 27 per cent for married women
with pre-school children. But in the 1977 FES, 45 per cent of married
women with pre-school children were able to record 'hours per week
usually worked' and 54 per cent actually gave details of earnings[5] – in
other words, more mothers of pre-school children appear to be
employed, according to the FES. The GHS/FES difference is
considerably less for women with older children, but still exists.

One reason for these differences – though not explaining them all –
is that the two surveys are not in fact measuring quite the same thing.

The GHS, and indeed the Census, give a picture of the number of people working or seeking work at one point of time, i.e. during the week before interview. They do not, and cannot, give a picture of employment over a period of time. The FES does, at least to some extent. Among employees, the FES picks up anyone who has earned anything at any time *in the thirteen weeks prior to interview,* including people who have stopped work by the time of the interview itself. The FES earnings data also include anyone who has had any income from self-employment at any time *in the twelve months preceding the survey,* again even if that person no longer works. A substantial difference between the FES and the GHS might therefore be expected for any group whose members were particularly likely to work intermittently, dropping into and out of the labour force fairly regularly. The proportion of that group working at some stage in a given period of time (e.g. thirteen weeks or twelve months) would then be significantly higher than the proportion working at any one time; and a survey like FES measuring employment over that given period would produce higher figures for the group than a survey like GHS which only measured employment at one point in time.

Women with children seem to be just such a group of intermittent workers. Other studies support this conclusion. In the 1977 GHS, for instance, 51 per cent of married mothers were currently employed, but a further 8 per cent were recorded as having worked at some stage in the twelve months preceding interview (OPCS, 1979a:Table 4.22). These figures cover women with dependent children of all ages. Intermittent working is, however, more likely, the younger the age of the children concerned, and especially among mothers of pre-school children. In a large survey of pre-school children in the 1950s, 26 per cent of mothers had worked at some stage during the child's first five years, though never more than 14 per cent were employed at any one time (Douglas and Blomfield, 1958). Twenty years later, in the Child Health and Education in the Seventies (CHES) study, a national survey of 13,100 five-year-old children, 37 per cent had a mother currently employed, 4 per cent had a mother employed occasionally on a seasonal basis (e.g. fruit picking, tourism, temporary shop work) and a further 13 per cent had a mother who, though neither currently nor occasionally employed, had worked at some stage since the child's birth. Less than half (45 per cent) of the mothers, therefore, had *never* worked during their child's first five years – compared to 74 per cent who had never worked in the earlier Douglas study (Butler *et al.*, forthcoming).

A final factor in the FES/GHS differential on employment rates concerns self-employment. As already mentioned, the FES earnings data include anyone who has been self-employed in the preceding year, and the number of self-employed workers appears to be particularly high among mothers of pre-school children. In the 1974 FES, for instance, 34 per cent of all employed mothers with children of this age were classified as self-employed, the proportion falling away to 13 and 7 per cent of employed mothers with a youngest child aged 5–10 and 11–15. For mothers with young children, therefore, self-employed status and intermittent working are common and probably related.

Part of the difference between levels of employment reported in the General Household and Family Expenditure Surveys must be due to differences in definitions and criteria. But it seems unlikely that it can be wholly accounted for in this way. Especially for women with young children, the GHS figures should be regarded as a minimum estimate of employment, probably missing more marginal and intermittent employment activities which are particularly common among younger mothers.

The extent of unemployment among women with children is harder to determine than their level of employment. Many mothers seeking work will not register as unemployed, and registered unemployment statistics do not, in any case, distinguish women or men with children. In the 1971 Census, 1.9 per cent of women with children were economically active but not employed, and between then and 1978 the number of unemployed women (both registered and unregistered) grew by 280,000, to nearly three-quarters of a million, an increase of 63 per cent. This growth was entirely due to a steep rise in registered unemployment – where the numbers quadrupled in these seven years – and includes a substantial increase among married women. Their share of total registered unemployment (male and female) rose from 5 per cent in 1971 to 11 per cent in 1978 (Elias, 1980). In addition to mothers who are seeking jobs, there is a further group who would like to work but do not seek it because of child care or other difficulties: this group is discussed in more detail later in the chapter.

Fathers

Among the age group of men most likely to have dependent children, i.e. 25–44-year-olds, economic activity rates have been very high and consistent over recent years, the levels for 1951, 1961, 1971 and 1977 varying only between 97.8 and 98.5 per cent (Central Statistical Office, 1979: Table 5.3). An analysis of the 1975 GHS data showed 96 per cent of fathers actually *working,* compared to an economic activity rate of 98 per cent for the year for men aged 25–44 (Layard *et al.,* 1978: Table 7.10). The gap between work and economic activity reflects the level of unemployment among men with children. But as with mothers' employment, so with fathers' unemployment it is important to examine its extent over a period of time, as well as at a given point. GHS data, for instance, show that the proportion of men unemployed at some stage in the twelve months preceding interview is approximately double the proportion unemployed at the time of interview. In 1977, 8.4 per cent of married men with dependent children were unemployed for all or part of this twelve month period. The level for men with three or more children was twice that for other fathers or childless married men (14.7 and 6 per cent respectively), while overall the highest levels of unemployment were among single men (19 per cent) and widowed, divorced and separated men (16 per cent) (OPCS, 1979a: Table 4.17, 4.20).

Integrating the evidence for mothers and fathers, we can estimate the part played by parents in the labour force, using 1977 GHS data for the purpose. Assuming that 94 per cent of fathers living with their children were actually working in 1977 – a figure which allows for some increase in unemployment since 1975 – and with 52 per cent of mothers employed, then parents made up 43 per cent of the labour force and 75 per cent of all parents were employed.

How much do parents work?

Mothers

The post-war growth in the employment of married women has been largely due to an increase in part-time work. Between 1950 and 1970, the proportion of female employees in manufacturing industry who worked part-time rose from 12 to 20 per cent: in the 1960s alone, the number of part-time female workers in this sector grew 21 per cent despite a decrease of 16 per cent in full-timers (Department of Employment, 1973). Although the position in the service sector – where the majority of part-time jobs are found – cannot be established with similar accuracy, 'between 1961–1971, almost all the growth in service employment was due to growth in the numbers of female workers by nearly 1.2 millions and the indications are that nearly all this growth has been in part-timers' (Department of Employment, 1975a).

More precise and comprehensive statistics are available from 1971. They show a continuing strong growth in women's part-time employment, numbers rising by 41 per cent (1.16 million) between 1971 and 1978. During this time, the number of full-time women employees fell 4 per cent (208,000), and the part-timers' share of the total female labour force increased from 30 to 38 per cent (Elias, 1980). These general trends in female employment are discussed in more detail by Peter Elias in Chapter 3.

Most of the increase in mothers' employment has also been due to part-time jobs. The proportion of *all* mothers in full-time employment changed only from 14 per cent in 1961[6] and 1971 to 16 per cent in 1977, while part-timers increased from 12 per cent of all mothers in 1961 to 24 per cent in 1971 and 35 per cent in 1977. In 1961, therefore, working mothers were equally divided between part-time and full-time jobs, but by 1977 there were more than twice as many in part-time as in full-time work. At this later date, 69 per cent of all working mothers had part-time jobs – compared to 27 per cent of women without children – and mothers accounted for two-thirds of all part-time women workers (OPCS, 1979a: Table 4.5).

The chances of a mother working full-time increase as her youngest child gets older. Only 5 per cent of all women with a pre-school child have full-time jobs, compared to 28 per cent with a youngest child over ten. Despite this increased likelihood of full-time employment, part-time work still accounts for nearly two-thirds (62 per cent) of all working mothers in this older age group (see Fig. 4) (OPCS, 1979a: Table 4.5).

The growing number of mothers working part-time has lowered the average hours worked per week for this group of women as a whole and especially for mothers of pre-school children. Table 1 illustrates this trend, for the first half of the 1970s: it gives the proportion of *children* – aged nought to two, three to four and five to ten years old –

TABLE 1 CHILDREN OF MOTHERS IN PAID EMPLOYMENT BY AGE OF CHILD AND HOURS MOTHER WORKS, 1971 and 1974-6 (GREAT BRITAIN)

Hours per week	Percentage of children in age group					
	aged 0–2		aged 3–4		aged 5–10	
	1971	*1974–6*	*1971*	*1974–6*	*1971*	*1974–6*
1–12	23	37	22	33	18	24
13–21	29	27	31	32	29	30
22–30	13	12	14	17	20	23
31+	30	21	28	17	29	24

NB Percentages do not add to 100 as some mothers did not state hours
Source Central Policy Review Staff 1978a; Annex 2, Table 5

whose mothers worked 1–12, 13– 21, 22–30 or 31+ hours a week, and shows how these proportions changed between 1971 and 1974–6.[7] For all groups, there was a downward shift in hours between the two dates. In 1971, the largest group of children under three were those whose mothers worked more than 30 hours a week, followed by those with mothers working 13–21 hours; for three- and four-year-olds, this order was reversed. By the mid-1970s, the largest group for both these pre-school ages was children whose mothers worked 12 hours or less a week. The hours of working mothers for children aged five to ten were more evenly spread at both dates, and the trend to shorter average hours was less marked, but still apparent; at both 1971 and 1974–6, the largest group were those with mothers working 13–21 hours.

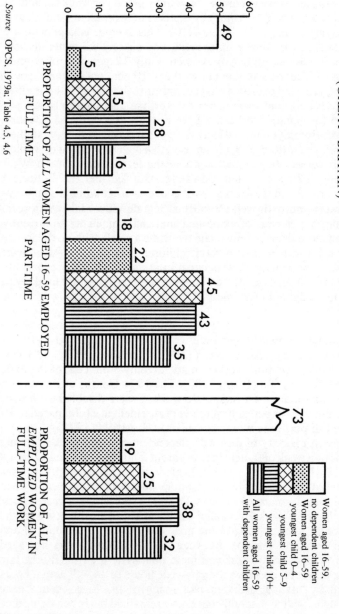

FIGURE 4 PROPORTION OF ALL WOMEN AGED 16–59 EMPLOYED FULL-TIME AND PROPORTION OF ALL EMPLOYED WOMEN IN FULL-TIME WORK BY AGE OF YOUNGEST CHILD, 1977 (GREAT BRITAIN)

Source OPCS, 1979a: Table 4.5, 4.6

In 1975, the average number of hours worked per week (including basic hours and paid overtime) by mothers in two-parent families was 23[8] (Layard *et al.*, 1978: Table 7.10). This average is kept down by high levels of part-time employment, and also by the generally low level of overtime worked by women. Only 12 per cent of women workers (17 per cent of manual workers, 10 per cent of non-manual workers) received overtime pay, according to the 1978 New Earnings Survey (NES), and their hours of overtime averaged only 4.4 per week (6 for manual workers, 3.3 for non-manual workers) (Department of Employment, 1979a). A recent OPCS survey studied shiftwork and attitudes to it in areas with a high proportion of women manual workers (e.g. Inner London, the textile areas of the West Midlands, Lancashire and Yorkshire, Dundee and the Potteries) (Marsh, 1979). In these areas with above-average women's employment rates and with well-established female industrial workforces, less than 5 per cent of employed married women were currently working more than six hours paid overtime a week, with no difference between those with and without children (see Fig. 5). Moreover, because of the generally low occupational status of women, especially those with children (discussed in detail later on), they are unlikely to work much unpaid overtime.

Fathers

The number of men in part-time work has also increased considerably, with a rise of 26 per cent (150,000) between 1971 and 1978. Despite this, part-time workers made up only 5 per cent of the male labour force in 1978 (Elias, 1980). The 1971 Census of Production showed that many part-time male workers were disabled or in poor health and that 40 per cent were over retirement age (compared to 10 per cent of part-time women workers) (Hurstfield, 1978).

The vast majority of men with dependent children work full-time, the working week of fathers in two-parent families averaging 42 hours in 1975[9] (Layard *et al.*, 1978: Table 7.10). This average disguises substantial differences in basic hours and *paid* overtime between manual and non-manual workers. Despite a shortening of *basic* hours, *actual* hours of work for manual workers have changed little over the last twenty years, owing to the post-war growth of substantial and regular overtime working. Between the wars, basic hours averaged 47–48, with overtime adding a mere half an hour extra. By the late 1950s, however, despite a drop in basic hours to 44–45, actual hours worked by manual workers had reached 49. Basic hours have continued to fall, but actual hours have remained fairly constant since falling back to 46–47 in the early 1960s (National Board of Prices and Incomes, 1970). In the 1978 NES, the average week for a male manual worker was 46 hours, made up of 39.9 basic hours and 6.1

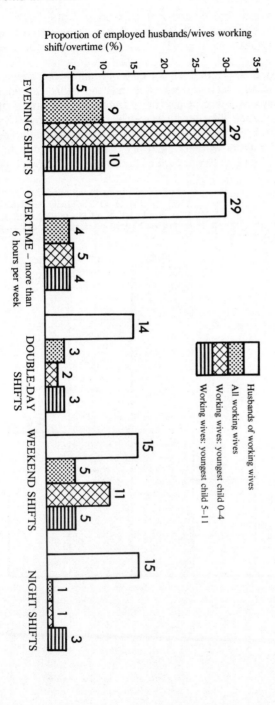

FIGURE 5 PROPORTION OF EMPLOYED MARRIED WOMEN AND THEIR HUSBANDS WORKING EVENING, DOUBLE-DAY, WEEKEND AND NIGHT SHIFTS AND OVERTIME, 1977 (areas with high proportion of women in manual occupations)

Proportion of employed husbands/wives working shift/overtime (%)

EVENING SHIFTS

OVERTIME – more than 6 hours per week

DOUBLE-DAY SHIFTS

WEEKEND SHIFTS

NIGHT SHIFTS

Husbands of working wives
All working wives
Working wives: youngest child 0–4
Working wives: youngest child 5–11

Source   Marsh, 1979, Tables 2.6, 3.5

hours of paid overtime. For non-manual workers, total hours were more than 7 hours less, at 38.7, which included a shorter basic week (37.3) and much less overtime (1.4) (Department of Employment, 1979a).

The 1978 NES shows that 41 per cent of male workers received overtime pay in the survey week, but that the figure for manual workers (56 per cent) was nearly three times that for non-manual workers (20 per cent). Those getting overtime pay averaged 10 hours of overtime a week, but again there is a large occupational difference – 10.2 hours for manual workers against 6.5 for non-manual. In the OPCS shiftwork study, 29 per cent of husbands of employed wives

FIGURE 6   AVERAGE PAID AND UNPAID OVERTIME HOURS IN PREVIOUS WEEK FOR MEN BY MARITAL STATUS AND PRESENCE OF CHILDREN, 1970 (LONDON AND HOME COUNTIES)

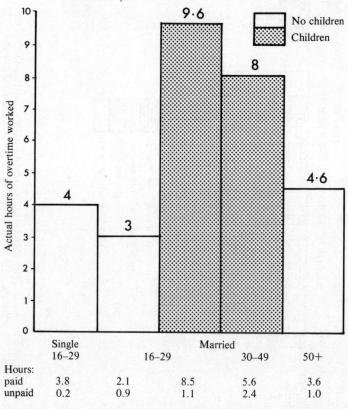

Hours:	Single 16–29	16–29	Married 30–49	50+
paid	3.8	2.1	8.5	5.6	3.6
unpaid	0.2	0.9	1.1	2.4	1.0

Source Young and Willmott, 1973; Table 19

(and 35 per cent of husbands of non-employed wives) worked more than six hours overtime a week (see Fig. 5).

A number of studies have shown that paid overtime is most common among younger married men, especially those with dependent children whose 'financial commitments and hence the incentive to work overtime tend to be greatest . . . Older men tend to have fewer commitments and tire more easily, while single young men often prefer more leisure' (National Board of Prices and Incomes, 1970). Fig. 6 shows the effect of children on overtime – both paid and unpaid – for a sample of men in London and the Home Counties (Young and Willmott, 1973): for instance, married men under thirty with children worked four times as much paid overtime as similarly aged but childless husbands. A similar pattern, for a national sample, occurs in the 1975 FES, married men with children being more likely than other married men to work 45 hours or more a week (see Fig. 7).

FIGURE 7 PROPORTION OF MARRIED MALE EMPLOYEES WORKING 45 HOURS A WEEK BY AGE OF WIFE AND PRESENCE AND AGE OF CHILDREN, 1975 (GREAT BRITAIN)

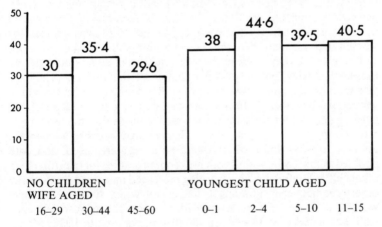

NB excludes self-employed

Source DHSS (SR3) analysis of 1975 FES

The extent of *unpaid* overtime, and trends in its working, can only be guessed at, because of the difficulty of incorporating it into regular employment statistics. Fig. 6 suggests that it is most common among fathers over thirty. Willmott and Young also found it most commonly worked by men in professional and managerial jobs. This, plus longer journey-to-work times, were the main reasons why this group of male workers had the longest weekly working hours (including travel).

They averaged a 57-hour week, compared to 51 hours for other non-manual workers and 52 hours for manual workers.

Although the average working *week* (including travel and unpaid overtime) may be fairly static, or even increasing slightly as more fathers move into professional and managerial jobs, the actual length of the working *year* has probably decreased as a result of a sharp increase in paid holiday entitlement, at least among manual workers. In 1961, 97 per cent had only two weeks entitlement and none had more than three weeks: by 1978, the proportions were none and 82 per cent respectively. Most of this turn-round occurred by the middle of the 1970s, and there has been little change in recent years[10] (Central Statistical Office, 1979: Table 5.11).

When do parents work?

Mothers

An important employment trend in post-war years has been an increase in shiftwork. In 1954, 12 per cent of manual workers in manufacturing industry worked shifts (616,000)[11]: by 1978, this had increased to 30 per cent (1.47 million) with a further increase to 38 per cent anticipated by 1982. The rate of increase in shiftwork in manufacturing industry between 1964 and 1978 was greater for women than for men. Women, however, are still less likely to work shifts. In 1978, they made up over one quarter of all manual workers in manufacturing, but only 14 per cent of all shiftworkers. They are also largely confined to two types of shift – doubleday (i.e. two shifts worked per day, usually from 6 a.m. to 2 p.m., 2 p.m. to 10 p.m.) and evening (i.e. a part-time shift, such as 5 p.m. to 9 p.m., sometimes referred to as the 'twilight' shift). This is partly because women are unlikely to work shifts where overtime is regularly used, and both doubleday and twilight shifts offer less opportunities for overtime than other shifts. Doubleday shiftworking increased more rapidly than any other type between 1964 and 1978, during which time the numbers working it (male and female) trebled. It is now the most widely used shift, accounting for 34 per cent of all shiftworkers: in 1971, 30 per cent of doubleday shiftworkers were women. By contrast, twilight shiftworking only increased from 67,000 to 81,000 between 1964 and 1978, and became relatively less important during this period, accounting by 1978 for only 5 per cent of shiftworkers: however, virtually all these workers are women, three-quarters being concentrated into just four industrial groupings – engineering, vehicles, textiles and food, drink and tobacco (IFF, 1978).

With the exception of twilight or evening shifts, women with children show very similar shiftworking patterns to women as a whole. Fig. 5 shows the situation in the industrial areas covered by the OPCS shiftwork study. Only 2–3 per cent of working wives, whether with or without children, worked doubleday shifts and only 1–3 per cent did night shifts[12]: the position for unmarried women, not shown in Fig. 5, was very similar. The main difference comes with evening shifts. These were worked by 29 per cent of employed wives with pre-school children, but only 10 per cent of employed wives with children five to ten and 5 per cent of all other women. Manual workers were much more likely to work this shift; 37 per cent of employed mothers of pre-school children in manual jobs worked evenings compared to 11 per cent in non-manual jobs. The extent of evening shiftwork would be considerably lower in areas with less manufacturing industry and a smaller proportion of women in manual occupations than in the OPCS survey areas. While women with children, and especially young children, are more likely than other women to work evenings, the majority – probably at least four out of five – work during the day.

Figure 5 also includes 'weekend shifts' (i.e. working after 1 p.m. on Saturdays and/or on Sundays). These were worked by 11 per cent of working mothers with pre-school children, twice the level for other married women including those with older children.[13] Taking *all* employed women in the survey together, 17 per cent worked on Saturdays and 5 per cent on Sundays, compared to 7 per cent doing 'weekend shift', implying that most Saturday working was mornings only. In the 1975 CHES study of five-year-olds, 72 per cent of employed mothers worked weekdays only, 3 per cent weekends only and 25 per cent both weekdays and weekends; the mothers most likely to work at weekends were home workers, 47 per cent of whom did so.

As with twilight shifts, weekend working varies considerably between areas. In a 1970 OPCS survey of five local authorities – Dundee, Dorset, Glamorgan, Haringey and Halifax – the proportion of employed married mothers working Saturdays varied from 16 (Haringey) to 35 per cent (Dundee) while for employed lone mothers the variations were even greater, from 14 (Halifax) to 48 per cent (Glamorgan). Sunday working was at a lower level, but equally varied, from 5 to 23 per cent for married mothers and 6 to 22 per cent for lone mothers (Hunt *et al.*, 1973). Stepping back again to national level, the best estimate would be that 20–30 per cent of employed mothers work for all or part of the weekend, but mostly on Saturday only, and that this proportion is highest among mothers with younger children.

Fathers

Men with children, and especially those in manual and less skilled jobs, are more likely than other men to work shifts. In a 1970 survey by the National Board of Prices and Incomes of factories in three areas, 62 per cent of shiftworkers had children, compared to 38 per cent of regular day workers. Increased levels of shiftworking have been accompanied by changes in the relative popularity of different types of shift. Among manual workers in manufacturing industry, three shift arrangements and permanent nights showed a relative decline between 1954 and 1978, falling from 45 to 30 per cent and 10 to 7 per cent of all shiftworkers respectively (with an absolute decline in numbers for permanent nights); alternating day and night shifts have held a constant 24–25 per cent; and doubleday shifts have more than doubled their position from 16 to 34 per cent (IFF, 1978). The evidence suggests that shiftworking fathers are probably now spread fairly evenly between doubleday, alternating day and night, and rotating three shift systems (Equal Opportunities Commission, 1979a).

There are no national data on weekend working. Fifteen per cent of husbands in the OPCS shiftwork study worked a 'weekend shift' (Fig. 5), but this included men with and without children.

What sort of work do parents do?

Mothers

Working mothers are heavily concentrated in low-paid, low-status jobs in a narrow range of industries. Fig. 8 is based on 1974 FES data and shows the type of jobs done by employed married women with

FIGURE 8   PROPORTION OF EMPLOYED MARRIED WOMEN WITH PRE-SCHOOL CHILDREN, THEIR HUSBANDS AND CHILDLESS MARRIED WOMEN AGED 16–45 IN HIGH AND LOW-STATUS OCCUPATIONS, 1974 (GREAT BRITAIN)

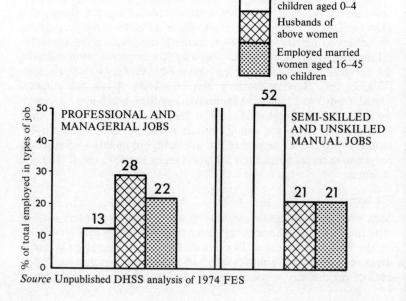

Source Unpublished DHSS analysis of 1974 FES

pre-school children; it also compares their position with that of (i) married women of childbearing age (i.e. 16–45) who have *no* children, and (ii) employed married fathers with pre-school children and working wives. The contrast is clear. More than half of the mothers are in unskilled or semiskilled manual work, only 13 per cent in managerial or professional work. The CHES study shows a similar picture – 45 per cent of employed mothers of the five-year-old sample in unskilled and semiskilled jobs, only 17 per cent in managerial or professional jobs.

Job opportunities for women may improve slightly as their children get older, and work gets less intermittent. The scope for improvement, however, is limited by the high proportion of mothers employed part-time, even when their children are at secondary school (see Fig. 4). Part-time work, as currently constituted, includes a large number of low-status jobs with poor prospects. Even among women with children, part-time workers have worse jobs than full-timers. In the CHES study, 24 per cent of full-time working mothers had professional or managerial jobs and 35 per cent semiskilled or unskilled manual jobs; for part-timers, the figures were 15 and 50 per cent respectively.

A recent OPCS survey of management attitudes and practices towards women workers also shows the restricted job opportunities associated with part-time work. Ten per cent of surveyed firms employed part-time workers as managers, supervisors, foremen, salesmen or skilled manual workers. Nineteen per cent, however, employed them as unskilled manual workers, 43 per cent as office staff and 57 per cent in domestic and catering jobs. Part-time work also carried other disadvantages. Only 28 per cent of firms provided opportunities for part-timers to obtain further education and training, 17 per cent regarded part-timers as eligible for promotion and a mere 14 per cent allowed them to join pension schemes (Hunt, 1975). In another survey, of the retail trade, 72 per cent of full-time women workers were covered by an employer's sickness scheme, against 34 per cent of part-time workers (Hurstfield, 1978).

There is no information on the distribution of mothers' employment between different types of industry. All we can go on is the distribution for all women workers, and part-timers in particular. In December 1978, the three industries which employed most women – distributive trades, professional and scientific services and miscellaneous services[14] – accounted for 58 per cent of female employees (by contrast, the three major employers of men had only 28 per cent of male employees). The concentration of part-time women employees is even greater and has been growing steadily; 69 per cent were employed in the three main women's industries in 1971, 73 per cent by 1976.

FIGURE 9 PROPORTION OF EMPLOYED MARRIED MOTHERS WITH PRE-SCHOOL CHILDREN, THEIR HUSBANDS AND CHILD-LESS MARRIED WOMEN AGED 16–45 EARNING LESS THAN £30 A WEEK, 1974 (GREAT BRITAIN)

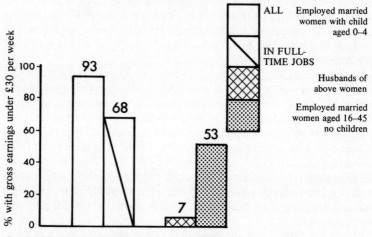

Source Unpublished DHSS analysis of 1974 FES

Working mothers are very low paid. Fig. 9, which again uses FES data, shows the proportion of married working mothers with pre-school children, in full-time and part-time jobs, earning less than £30 a week in 1974, compared to (i) their husbands, and (ii) childless married women of similar age.[15] Again, mothers do far worse than either of the other groups (though compared to occupational status, childless women do far worse than men). Part of the reason for the poor position of mothers is that most work considerably shorter hours than either the fathers of the childless women. But this is not the whole explanation. Women with children also have low *hourly* earnings. Fig. 10 shows 1975 hourly earnings for full-time and part-time male and female workers and for mothers and fathers in two-parent families. Mothers earned 61 per cent of male full-time earnings, owing to the lower earnings of women in general and of part-time workers in particular, part-time women workers being the lowest paid group of all. In 1977, 74 per cent of women in part-time employment earned less than 120p an hour,[16] compared to 47 per cent of full-time women workers and only 13 per cent of men in full-time jobs[17](Hurstfield, 1978).

The impact of children on women's earnings is not confined to the years when their children are dependent. It affects earnings potential throughout their adult lifetimes. In a study drawing on data from the *1967 American National Longitudinal Survey of Work Experience for Females 30-44 Years of Age,* Solomon Polachek (1975) argues that one of the major reasons for women's lower earnings is their discontinuous labour force participation, as they first drop out entirely from employment for a period after their first child is born (averaging ten years in America at the time of the Survey), then return intermittently to work (another four years on average in mid-1960s America), before a final and permanent return to work. This discontinuous participation lowers women's earnings in three ways. First, levels of training and education before having a family are reduced in anticipation of future employment disruption; secondly, 'on the job' experience, the length and continuity of which strongly influence earnings, is severely curtailed: and thirdly, there is a net depreciation of skills during periods out of the labour force. Women either enter occupations requiring less training or else, in jobs typified by much 'on the job' training, train less 'on the job' than men. As a result, they are concentrated in lower-paying occupations and in lower-paid jobs in higher-paying occupations. For women with at least one year of college education, five years out of the labour force in 1960s America resulted in a drop of more than 30 per cent in earnings

FIGURE 10 HOURLY EARNINGS FOR MEN AND WOMEN, WHETHER IN FULL-TIME OR PART-TIME WORK, AND FOR MOTHERS AND FATHERS IN TWO-PARENT FAMILIES, 1975 (GREAT BRITAIN)

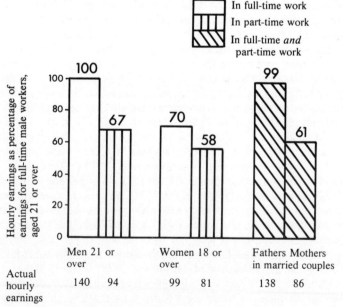

Source Layard *et al.,* 1978: Table 4.14; 7.10

potential; even this may be an underestimate, since anticipation of leaving the labour force may well affect earlier education and training decisions. Finally, Polachek calculates that assigning male experience to females (i.e. continuous labour force participation *and* no reduction in earlier education and training in anticipation of parenthood) explains up to 50 per cent of the male-female difference in hourly earnings.

While the precise results from Polachek's study are specific to a particular time and country, his general conclusions have wider applicability. The direct and indirect consequences of women's discontinuous labour force participation on their occupational status and earnings are long-term and massive. They far outstrip earnings lost during the years when they actually stop work to care for children.

Fathers

Men with children are more likely to be found in higher-status jobs than other men. In 1971, 26.4 per cent of fathers were in professional or managerial jobs compared to 23.8 per cent of childless married men and 15.9 per cent of single men; the proportions in unskilled and semiskilled manual jobs were 20.8, 26 and 28 per cent respectively (1971 Census, Household Composition, Pt 111, Table 48; England and Wales only). These proportions for all fathers are very similar to those for fathers of pre-school children shown in Fig. 9, and for fathers of five-year-olds in the CHES study, where 25 per cent had professional or managerial jobs, 47 per cent had skilled manual jobs and only 18 per cent had unskilled or semiskilled jobs.

The occupational status of fathers has been shifting upwards in recent years, reflecting the general improvement in men's employment position. Using a rather different classification – socio-economic groups (SEGs) – the proportion of fathers in SEGs 1–4 (employers, managers, professionals) increased from 16.5 per cent in 1961 to 20.4 per cent in 1971, while the proportion in SEGs 9, 10, 11 and 15 (manual workers, including agricultural workers) fell from 58.5 to 52.3 per cent (1961 Census, Household Composition, Table 42; 1971 Census, Household Composition, Pt 111, Table 48). This upward trend has continued, at least for men in general, through the 1970s. (For women, however, the 1970s have seen a general decline in occupational status, related to the large increase of married women in part-time work. Between 1971 and 1976-7, the proportion of women in non-manual jobs fell from 59 to 56 per cent, while the proportion in semiskilled and unskilled manual work rose from 33 to 36 per cent (Central Statistical Office, 1979: Table 5.10).)

Finally, on earnings, Fig. 10 shows that hourly rates for fathers are almost identical to those for all full-time male workers. Amongst manual workers, it is probable that *weekly* earnings are higher for fathers than for other men, because of their greater propensity to work shifts and overtime. For non-manual workers, where earnings owe less to overtime and shifts and increase with age and experience, fathers probably earn less than older men without children, but more than younger childless men. There are, however, no published sources of weekly, monthly or annual earnings against which these assumptions can be tested.

Which parents work?

Numbers of children

The rise in births between 1977 and 1978 was the first annual increase since 1964.[18] Between then and 1977, annual births fell by two-fifths, and this steep decline in fertility was accompanied by important changes in family building. There was a compression of childbearing, especially into the third to seventh years of marriage, which accounted for 55 per cent of births in 1978, compared with 44 per cent in 1961. This compression occurred as couples waited longer after marriage before starting families and completed their families sooner. These trends have, in turn, been related to a reduction in family size, with families increasingly limited to two children: third and later births have fallen off, contributing 32 per cent of all legitimate births in 1961 but only 19 per cent in 1978, while between 1970 and 1978, the proportion of mothers with three or more children fell by nearly a quarter, from 26 to 20 per cent (Central Statistical Office, 1979: Table 2.14; OPCS, 1979b: Table 7).

These changes have had major implications for the period of time for which women have left the labour force because of childbearing.

> If we can show the 'typical' mother of today as marrying at 23, and having her first child at 25 or 26, and her second (and probably last) at 27 or 28, we have a very changed picture from that of the pre-1960 period with its leisurely progression of births over a relatively long period ... whereas a generation ago the vast majority of women were tied up in childbearing and rearing between 20 and 40, this period has now been more than halved. (Eversley and Evans, 1976)

The fact that there are fewer women with three or more children has also had a direct bearing on overall employment rates for mothers, since women with larger families (i.e. three or more children) are less likely to be employed. In 1978, 45 per cent worked and 13 per cent had full-time jobs. Among mothers with only one or two children, the figures were 54 per cent and 17 per cent respectively. (Overall employment levels were similar for one- and two-child mothers, but the former were more likely to work full-time.)

The lower employment rate for mothers with three or more children explains why the proportion of children with working mothers is lower than the proportion of mothers going to work. In 1978, for instance, 49 per cent of *children* had mothers in employment, compared to 52 per cent of *mothers* who had a job (Central Statistical Office, 1979: Table 3.3; OPCS, 1979b: Table 7).

As already noted, fathers with three or more children experience higher unemployment rates than men with smaller families. Layard, whose GHS analysis confirms that men with large numbers of children are more likely to be unemployed, suggests that this may reflect 'the higher social security benefits paid to large families and the lower wage rates commanded by fathers of large families'.

Ages of children

The age of youngest child has an important bearing on women's employment rates, which drop to only 27 per cent where the youngest child is under five. Even within this group, child's age has a considerable effect, less than a fifth of children under two having mothers at work, compared to over a third of four-year-olds (see Table 2). The impact of child age is most clearly quantified in Layard's

TABLE 2   PERCENTAGE OF CHILDREN IN EACH YEAR BETWEEN BIRTH AND 10 WITH AN EMPLOYED MOTHER, AND THE PERCENTAGE INCREASE IN EMPLOYMENT RATES BETWEEN YEARS, 1976 (GREAT BRITAIN)

	Child's age										
	0	1	2	3	4	5	6	7	8	9	10
With employed mother	11.8	18.9	23.3	26.4	34.4	43.0	42.5	47.1	53.1	50.4	54
Increase in employment rate compared to previous year		+60	+23	+13	+30	+25	-1	+11	+13	-5	+9

Source Central Policy Review Staff, 1978a; Table 2

regression analysis of factors bearing on women's labour force participation. He concludes that

> ... among women, otherwise similar, those with a youngest child under 3 have a participation rate 67% lower than [married] women with no child at home. Women whose youngest child is between 3 and 6 have a participation rate that is 42% lower ... Once the child is 6 or over, its presence in the house seems to have relatively little effect on the mother's work.

Layard's last point is illustrated in Fig. 11. Women with a youngest child at primary school have a slightly lower employment rate than

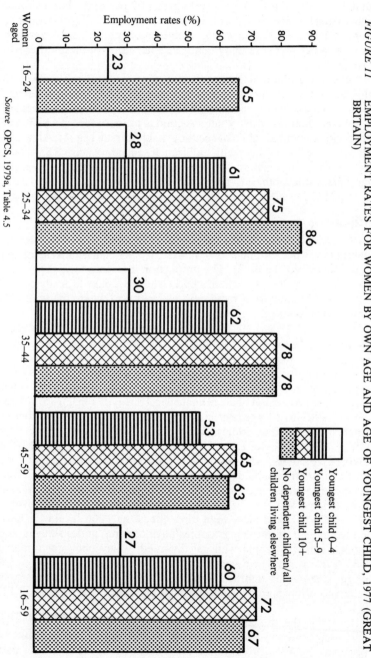

FIGURE 11 EMPLOYMENT RATES FOR WOMEN BY OWN AGE AND AGE OF YOUNGEST CHILD, 1977 (GREAT BRITAIN)

Source OPCS, 1979a, Table 4.5

childless women aged 16–59 (60 against 67 per cent), but a similar rate to that for all *married* women below retirement age (60 against 58 per cent). Women with a youngest child at secondary school actually have a rather higher employment rate than either of these other two groups.

School-age children, however, still have a considerable effect on the hours worked by employed mothers. Nearly three-quarters of employed childless women have full-time jobs, but only 25 per cent of employed mothers with a youngest child at primary school and 38 per cent with a youngest child at secondary school (see Fig. 4). Although less than half of mothers with children at secondary school have full-time jobs, they account for 61 per cent of all full-time working mothers, while mothers of pre-school children account for only 12 per cent (OPCS, 1979a: Table 4.5).

Marital status

11.6 per cent of families with dependent children are headed by a lone parent (10.3 per cent by a lone mother, 1.3 per cent by a lone father) (OPCS, 1979b: Table 3). The proportion increases from 8 per cent for families with a pre-school child (which account for only one in seven of all lone-parent families) to 12 per cent where the youngest child is five or over.

Between 1971 and 1976, the number of lone-parent families grew by about a third, from 570,000 to 750,000 (OPCS, 1978). This increase had two main causes. First, the number of single mothers, who account for about one in six of all lone mothers, grew by 44 per cent. Births outside marriage have not decreased as rapidly as other births – the proportion of illegitimate to all births increasing from 6 per cent in 1961 to 11 per cent in 1978 – and an increasing number of single mothers are deciding to keep their children (Central Statistical Office, 1979: Table 2.14, Chart 2.21). Second, the number of divorced mothers, who account for just over one in three of lone mothers, nearly doubled (92 per cent). The 1970s have witnessed an enormous increase in divorce. The 1977 figure for divorces granted in England and Wales (170,000) was more than four times the level in 1951 (38,000) and more than three times the 1966 level (47,000). Sixty per cent of divorcing couples have children under sixteen, and though half the people who get divorced in any one year remarry within five years, the recent surge in divorces has inevitably meant more lone-parent families – even if many remain as such for a relatively short period (Central Statistical Office, 1979: Table 2.11, 2.12).

In 1971, the overall employment rate for lone mothers was 10 percentage points higher than that for other mothers (47 against 37 per cent). By 1977 this difference had been reduced to only one point

(52 against 51 per cent). In families with pre-school children the rate for lone mothers was still slightly higher (32 against 27 per cent), but in families with older children the rates were actually slightly lower for lone mothers. The main difference that remains is in the level of full-time employment: half the lone mothers who go to work (and a quarter of all lone mothers, employed or not) have full-time jobs compared to 29 per cent of employed mothers in two-parent families (and 15 per cent of all mothers in two-parent families). The difference is greatest in families with pre-school children, where 44 per cent of employed lone mothers work full-time, as against only 19 per cent of other employed mothers (OPCS, 1979a: Table 4.6). Because lone mothers are more likely to work full-time, their weekly hours are higher than for other mothers, averaging about 31 in 1975. For similar reasons, their hourly earnings are also rather higher, averaging out at 94p in 1975, just below the 98.5p for full-time female workers (Layard *et al.*, 1978: Table 8.8 and Appendix Table 33).

Data from the 1975-7 GHS show how employment rates vary between *different types* of lone mothers. The lowest rate (39 per cent) was for single mothers and the highest (56 per cent) for divorced: the rates for widows and separated mothers were 53 and 46 per cent. The proportion working full-time also varied, ranging from 69 per cent of employed single mothers and 54 per cent of employed divorced and separated mothers to only a minority of widows (42 per cent) (Leete, 1978a).

There is some evidence that the occupational status of employed lone mothers is worse than that of other mothers. The OPCS study of five local-authority areas found that lone mothers' jobs were at a slightly lower level than those of other mothers, though this was obscured by the different part-time/full-time ratios for the two groups (Hunt *et al.*, 1973). Another study, based on data from the National Child Development Study, suggested that different groups of lone mothers had different employment prospects. Among mothers who had stayed on at school beyond minimum leaving age, *divorced and separated* mothers were twice as likely as those in two-parent families to have had manual occupations, and only half as likely to have had non-manual jobs. For *widows*, however, the trend was in the opposite direction. (Because of low numbers, single mothers were excluded from the analysis.) (Ferri, 1976)

Lone fathers are less likely to work than other fathers (86 against 96 per cent in 1975). In the National Child Development Study, one in six lone fathers had been out of work in the twelve months prior to interview compared to one in fourteen of other fathers. It also appeared that lone fathers were more likely to have been out of work for a long time, the proportion without a job for six months or more being five times greater among lone fathers than among those in two-parent families (Ferri, 1976). Nearly all lone fathers who are working have full-time jobs and their average hours per week, 41 in 1975, was only one hour less than those for fathers in married couples. Hourly earnings, at 146p, were above those for fathers in two-parent families (136p) (Layard *et al.*, 1978: Table 8.8, Appendix Table 33).

Social class

Certainly since the early 1960s and possibly before, there has been a slow but steady erosion of class differences (defined in terms of husband's occupation) in employment rates for married women with children. In 1961, 22 per cent of mothers whose husbands were employers, managers or in professional occupations were economically active. Ten years later, the proportion had grown by two-thirds to 36 per cent and their share of all economically active married mothers had gone from 14 to 19 per cent. This was due both to increased employment rates and to an increase in the proportion of fathers in these higher-status jobs. By contrast, economic activity among mothers with husbands in manual work, excluding agricultural workers, rose by just under a half from 27 to 41 per cent and their share of all economically active married mothers fell from 62 to 53 per cent. Finally, economic activity among mothers with husbands in other non-manual occupations (i.e. those who are not professionals, managers or employers) rose by just over half to 42 per cent, a rate of increase falling between the other two groups (1961 Census, Household Composition, Table 42; 1971 Census, Household Composition, Pt III, Table 48).

Working-class mothers are still more likely to out to work than their middle-class counterparts, but the gap is now small (1971 Census; Hamill (1978); Smee and Stern (1978); Butler *et al.*, (forthcoming)). Using a rather different occupational classification to the one above,[19] the difference between economic activity rates for mothers with husbands in manual and non-manual jobs was only 1.6 per cent in the 1971 Census (39.7 against 38.1 per cent); in the later CHES study, the difference in employment rates between the two groups of mothers was 3 per cent. Employment rates are lowest of all for Social Class 1 mothers (wives of men in professional occupations). Even here, though, the difference is not great. The extremes in the CHES study, for instance, range only from 31 per cent (for Social Class 1 mothers) to 39 per cent working (for mothers married to men in Social Class IIIM, i.e. skilled manual occupations). Among manual workers, mothers with husbands in unskilled jobs are *least* likely to work (1971 Census, Household Composition, Pt III, Table 48; Butler *et al.* (forthcoming)). In the CHES study, their employment rate was 34 per cent, and compared to the five other social class groups – three non-manual and two manual – only Social Class 1 mothers had a lower rate.

The CHES study also shows that middle-class mothers are more likely to be involved in seasonal, temporary or other occasional work and more likely to work at home. This last point is consistent with the findings of more local studies that the job status of mothers who work at home is not, overall, any worse than that of those who go out to work (Moss and Plewis, 1979); for instance, in a study of pre-school families living in Westminster, 55 per cent of homeworkers were in unskilled and semiskilled manual occupations, compared with 58 per cent of all employed mothers (Osborn, 1975).

Two other points relate to fathers' employment. First, as already mentioned, in Willmott and Young's study men in professional and managerial occupations had the longest working week, when travel and unpaid overtime were taken into account. Second, there is a much higher incidence of unemployment among manual workers and especially those normally employed in semiskilled or unskilled jobs. In the 1977 GHS they made up 37 per cent of men having one spell of unemployment in the twelve months before interview and 48 per cent of those having two or more spells, despite being only a fifth of the labour force (OPCS, 1979a: Table 4.18).

Income

The analysis by Layard and his colleagues (1978) of GHS data shows a strong inverse relationship between husbands' income and the participation of wives in the labour force. The equation suggests that, other things being equal, 'a rise of 1 per cent in the husband's wage will *lower* the proportion of women working by 0.11 percentage points'; or, put another way, if one group of husbands earns 10 per cent more than another, the employment rate for wives in the higher-earning group will be 1.1 per cent less than in the lower-earning group.

Of course, in practice, other things are rarely equal, and Layard's analysis identifies other variables affecting married women's employment and quantifies their likely impact. In particular, the level of a *wife's* earnings (actual or potential) has twice the impact of a husband's wage, but pulls in the opposite direction, i.e. a rise of 1 per cent in wives' wages will *increase* the proportion working by 0.22 percentage points. So, in the case of a wife with a high-earning husband, while his earnings act as a disincentive to her employment, her relatively high earnings potential (assuming that her educational and vocational qualifications are also likely to be relatively high) provides an incentive to her to seek work. Or, to take a real example, the disincentive effect on women's employment of the doubling of men's real wages between 1945 and 1973 was outweighed by the incentive effect of a doubling of women's real wages in this same period.

The result of these and other conflicting influences is that there is

only a modest relationship between mothers' employment rates and
levels of family income, *excluding* wife's earnings. Mothers with low-
paid husbands are more likely to be at work, but there are also plenty
of employed mothers with higher-paid husbands. In Layard's analysis
the average family income from sources *other than the wife's
earnings* was lower in families with a working mother: 46 per cent of
'working mother' families had an income, *excluding* her earnings, that
was 140 per cent or less of their Supplementary Benefit (SB)
entitlement, compared to 31 per cent of families with a non-working
mother. In the 1974 FES, employment rates for mothers of pre-
school children (excluding the self-employed) varied from 30 per cent
where the husband's income was less than £40 a week to 25 per cent
where it was £60 or over.

In the 1972 voluntary income survey, a follow-up to the main
Census, the relationship between husband's income and wife's
employment differed according to the age of youngest child. In all
cases, economic activity rates for mothers fell as husbands' income
increased. But this relationship was least marked when there was a
pre-school child in the family, where there was very little difference
between high and low income groups, and most marked where there
was a youngest child aged twelve or over[20] (see Fig. 12). This 'age of

FIGURE 12 PROPORTION OF MARRIED WOMEN WHO ARE ECONOM-
ICALLY ACTIVE BY AGE OF YOUNGEST CHILD AND
INCOME OF THE MARRIED COUPLE EXCLUDING
INCOME FROM WIFE'S ECONOMIC ACTIVITY, 1972
(UNITED KINGDOM)

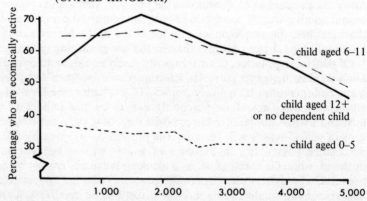

Annual income of married couples excluding income from wife's economic activity (£)
Source Banfield, 1978, Table 5

child' difference may mean that the level of husband's income has a
growing impact on the employment behaviour of mothers as children
get older and more costly; alternatively, there may be a generational
change, with younger mothers being less influenced by husband's

income and/or more influenced by other factors.[21]

In families with two working parents, mothers' earnings on average make up 20 per cent of family income. Mothers with older children contribute more (25 per cent where the youngest child is eleven or more compared to 14 per cent where there are pre-school children), as do mothers with fewer children, while the lower the husband's earnings the greater the wife's contribution (Hamill, 1978). The contribution of working mothers plays an important part in lifting families out of poverty. Layard's analysis shows that, without the earnings of working mothers, the proportion of families *with a working father* and an income below 140 per cent of their SB entitlement would have risen from 17 to 39 per cent. In 1974, according to the FES, without mothers' earnings the number of families *with a working father* and income at or below SB level itself would have risen from 62,000 to 154,000 (Hamill, 1978). More locally, in a study of Stockwell, the percentage of couples with children who were living in poverty was 24 where the wife was not working, 4 where she worked part-time and nil where she worked full-time (Shankland *et al.*, 1977).

Finally, GHS data show that 87 per cent of *lone*-parent families had an income below 140 per cent of their SB entitlement where the parent was not working, compared to 37 per cent where he or she had a job (GHS Unit, 1978).

Level of education

Over the last thirty years, there has been a marked rise in levels of education, at least as measured by such indicators as school-leaving age, qualifications attained and attendance at further education. In 1977-8, for instance, 28 per cent of people in their late twenties had at least one GCE 'A' level or its equivalent, nearly treble the 10 per cent in their parents' generation (i.e. men and women in their fifties) who had attained this level of qualification. Three-quarters of this older age group had left school at fifteen or under, compared to only two-fifths of their children's age group (Central Statistical Office, 1979: Chart 4.17, Table 4.10). Women have shared in these educational gains. The overall proportion of female school-leavers entering full-time further education has risen steadily to 26 per cent in 1977-8, despite a substantial recent decrease in the numbers going to teacher training. This rise is reflected in the numbers in further and higher education at any one time. Between 1966-7 and 1977-8, the number of women in higher education (i.e. doing degrees, teacher training and other advanced courses) increased by a third, to 196,000 for full-timers, and five-fold, to 67,000 for part-timers; in non-advanced further education, numbers increased by more than a quarter to 830,000 (Central Statistical Office, 1979: Table 4.10, 4.11).

There is some evidence that level of education affects women's employment behaviour if and when they have children. A government survey of women's employment, in the mid-1960s, suggested that more educated women were more likely to work, though the difference was not large – 51 per cent of married women whose education went on to nineteen or over, compared to 43 per cent whose education had stopped earlier (Hunt, 1968). Other pre-1970 studies provide further evidence. A re-analysis of data from the 1950s longitudinal study by Douglas and Blomfield showed that more educated middle-class mothers were more likely to work outside the home at some stage before their child was five (Young and Willmott, 1973), while in a study of managers and their wives, most of whom were in their thirties and with young children, the proportion of wives who either had a job or planned to get one was 73 per cent for those with two years or more higher education, 48 per cent for those with less higher education and 31 per cent for those with none (Pahl and Pahl, 1971). More recent evidence comes from the CHES study. Thirty-six per cent of mothers with 'O' levels only or no qualifications were currently employed, compared to 41 per cent with a vocational qualification, 45 per cent with a degree or teaching diploma and 47 per cent with an SRN training.

Ethnic origin

Mothers born outside the British Isles, with a child under five, are more likely to go out to work than those born within. The difference is due to ethnic minority mothers being more likely to take full-time jobs. In a recent study of families with pre-school children in two areas of Inner London, married mothers born outside the UK and Eire were less likely to work part-time but three to four times more likely to work full-time, depending on their children's ages: the difference for lone mothers was much less, but full-time work was still more common among those born outside the British Isles (Moss and Plewis, 1979). An earlier study, using 1971 Census data for four non-London local authorities with high ethnic minority populations, found similar results. Ethnic minority mothers of pre-school children had employ-ment rates that were well above average, and two-thirds or more of these mothers were working in full-time jobs, compared to less than a third of employed white mothers. In the most extreme case, Leicester, 85 per cent of ethnic minority mothers were employed: 87 per cent of these mothers worked full-time against only 32 per cent of white employed mothers (Lomas, 1975).

There are considerable differences between ethnic minority groups. In a 1974 Policy and Economic Planning (PEP) survey, the employment rate for West Indian women was well above that for the general population, while for non-Muslim Asians it was similar and for Muslim Asians much lower. This held true for all women aged 16–55 and for women at ages when they were most likely to have children: among 25–34-year-olds, for instance, the employment rates for West Indians, non-Muslim Asians, Muslim Asians and the general population were 73, 47, 17 and 44 per cent respectively. Within the Asian group, the difference between Pakistani women and others (Indians and African Asians) was even greater than that between Muslims and non-Muslims, Pakistani Muslims being less likely to work than other Muslims. The survey again showed that among women workers of all ages, West Indian, Muslim Asians and especially non-Muslim Asians were more likely to work full-time, the proportions being 73, 72 and 79 per cent, compared to 61 per cent for the general female labour force.

Finally, up to the age of fifty-four, the proportions of white and ethnic minority men in work were very similar (Smith, 1976).

Unemployment

Levels of unemployment (male or female) and married women's economic activity are inversely related – the higher the one, the lower the other. For instance, the results of one recent study of labour force participation of married women in 106 towns and cities indicate that a 1 per cent rise in local unemployment has the net effect of discouraging participation by 0.75 per cent (Greenhalgh, 1977).

A number of studies using FES and GHS data have found that wives of unemployed men are less likely to be in employment themselves. In the 1977 GHS, 52 per cent of mothers whose husbands had *not* been out of work in the previous twelve months had jobs, compared to 35 per cent whose husbands had been unemployed. An analysis of 1974 FES data showed that wives of employed husbands were twice as likely to work as wives of husbands who had not worked during the previous thirteen weeks (Hamill, 1978). A third study, using the 1971 Census and the 1971-3 GHS, confirms these results, 'the wife of a man out of work [being on average] only two-thirds as likely to have a job'. This finding held irrespective of numbers of children, age of husband and social class (Smee and Stern, 1978).

The authors of this last study suggest that the association of male unemployment and low economic activity for wives could be due to unemployed men having wives with less marketable skills and being concentrated in areas with poor employment opportunities for both men and women; and also to husbands' unemployment causing women to withdraw from the labour force, partly because of the work disincentive built into the social security system. They also add that the economic activity differential between wives of employed and non-employed husbands may close in periods of rising unemployment, as the increase 'catches families where the propensity of wives to work is higher than in families of the "hard core" unemployed'.

Wives, whose husbands are not working because of sickness, are also less likely to be employed themselves, especially where the husband's illness is long-term and he is not seeking work. The employment rate in the 1974 FES for married women with children and employed husbands was 56 per cent, compared to 24 per cent for mothers whose husbands were either unemployed or sick (Hamill, 1978).

Area variations

Reference has already been made to variations between areas in the extent of shiftwork and weekend working, and similar variations could be recorded for most of the other items discussed in this chapter. In this section, discussion of area variation is confined to overall and full-time employment rates for women.

We are immediately faced with the fact that several 'units of analysis' are available (e.g. regions, local authorities, districts within authorities, etc.), and that area differences can be found using any of them. Table 3 lists regional variations for employment rates for

TABLE 3   EMPLOYMENT RATES FOR MARRIED WOMEN BY REGION, 1977 (UNITED KINGDOM)

Region	Employment rate (%)	Region	Employment rate (%)
North	49.3 (9)	Rest of South-East	56.3 (4)
Yorkshire/Humberside	53.3 (7)	South-West	56.6 (3)
North-West	54.7 (6)	Wales	46.3 (11)
East Midlands	57.3 (2)	Scotland	52.2 (8)
West Midlands	55.7 (5)	N. Ireland	44.7 (12)
East Anglia	47.8 (10)		
Greater London	58.2 (1)	UNITED KINGDOM	54.1

NB Figures in brackets give rank order, 1 being highest.
Source Department of Employment, 1978a; Table 70

married women, taken from the 1977 FES. The highest levels are recorded in Greater London (58.2 per cent), the East Midlands (57.3 per cent), the South-West (56.6 per cent – presumably reflecting high seasonal employment in tourism) and the South-East (56.3 per cent); the lowest levels are in East Anglia (47.8 per cent), Wales (46.3 per cent) and Ulster (44.7 per cent).

Within regions, employment rates vary considerably between authorities. Fig. 13, based on the Census, shows full-time and overall employment rates (in a rather modified form) for women with pre-school children, in London and six other major English cities. There

FIGURE 13 EMPLOYMENT OF MARRIED WOMEN WITH PRE-SCHOOL
CHILDREN, 1971 (MAJOR ENGLISH CITIES AND GREAT
BRITAIN)

Source 1971 Census, unpublished tables

are considerable differences in overall rates and in the proportion of
mothers working full-time. In 1971, for instance, Manchester had an
overall employment rate 43 per cent higher than Sheffield's, and a full-
time rate that was double. Inner London boroughs had higher rates –
overall and for full-time work – than Outer London boroughs, with the
exception of Brent, Ealing and Haringey, which had the highest rates
of all.

The 1970 OPCS survey of five local authorities shows similar area
differences. Overall employment rates for mothers in two-parent
families ranged from 35 per cent in Glamorgan to 56 per cent in
Halifax. The greatest difference was for mothers of pre-school
children, going from 15 per cent in Glamorgan to 39 per cent in
Haringey: for mothers of older children (5–15), the rates ranged only
from 41 (Dorset) to 63 per cent (Halifax).

Area differences clearly reflect variations in local labour markets
and in the characteristics of local populations. They may also reflect
differences in expectation and attitude rooted in local traditions. In
general, low levels of mothers' employment are associated with areas
which traditionally have provided fewer job opportunities for women
– rural districts, seaports, centres of coalmining, engineering and iron
and steel production. A study of trends in women's work in the present
century, found that

... the factor most highly correlated with the activity rate of married women was a measure of the extent of women's work in each area in the past. The finding that the current activity rate of married women was more highly correlated with the tradition measure than with any of the measures of current industrial composition suggests that although the 'tradition' may have originated in the nature of the available jobs in the area, current practice in regard to women's work after marriage is less dependent upon current industrial composition than upon past employment practice. (Gales and Marks, 1974)

Why do mothers go to work . . . and would they rather not?

The large-scale post-war movement into the labour force by married women and the factors underlying it are considered further in the next chapter. Here we focus down on the individual woman, the reasons she has for working and how willingly or unwillingly she goes to work.

The reasons mothers have for going to work are many and varied. Some of the most common are to be found in the following comments by working mothers with pre-school children, living in two areas of Inner London (Moss and Plewis, 1979).

Independence – continuing with something. I'm interested in the work. It's good for me. Also, I'm not in a pigeon-hole as 'John's mother'.

Being able to afford to buy clothes for the children, being able to afford a holiday. It's nice to have a life of your own, to meet people. If you're a housewife, you haven't got much conversation with your husband.

Freedom of mind, independence, money, we've all benefited because I'm happier.

Not for money, but prestige and interest and to keep contact with professional life.

Complete freedom, feeling myself normal again. Stimulation, friendship, proving myself.

I couldn't bear not to – I adore what I'm doing.

It's purely financial . . . [but] it does give you something to do. If I was at home all day, I would get bored and depressed and have more financial problems. It's also a chance to meet people.

I feel it's fair to my husband that I work. A wife should participate [in the family business]. It gives my husband more freedom.

I like the entertainment value in the Civil Service – that's not really the word though. I couldn't just sit around. I like working, the people, the feeling you're getting somewhere.

I need that sense of self that work brings.

It's just nice to know there's something you can still do, even if it's watching children in a playground. I'm not just housebound all day.

Most studies that have tried to quantify the reasons given by mothers for working have come up with similar conclusions (Yudkin and Holme, 1969; Hunt, 1968; Moss *et al.*, 1973; Moss and Plewis, 1979; Butler *et al.*, forthcoming). Most mothers give finanical reasons, but the degree of financial urgency varies considerably. Attempts have been made to assess degrees of urgency. Yudkin and Holme distinguished between mothers who gave 'absolute financial necessity' as their main reason for working, and those who were working to 'improve their standard of living'. Thirteen per cent of working mothers were in the former group, 84 per cent in the latter. The later CHES study again distinguished two groups, but defined them differently – those who worked for 'financial necessity' (to contribute to housekeeping, rent, clothes, etc.) and those who worked for 'financial advantage' (e.g. for savings, household appliances, luxuries, car, to gain independence). The two CHES groups were virtually identical in size, 43 per cent giving 'financial necessity', 45 per cent 'financial advantage'. These two examples illustrate the difficulties of attempting to classify the financial motives for mothers working. Differing and rather general criteria make the meaning of the findings uncertain and comparison between surveys difficult: do the differences between the Yudkin and Holme and CHES studies, for instance, reflect real changes in the reasons mothers work over the decade or more that separates the two studies? And if so, are these changes because the financial position of families has deteriorated or because views about what constitutes 'essentials' and 'luxuries' have changed? Or are the differences simply due to changes in the definitions being used? More fundamentally, without 'hard' objective data on family income and expenditure, assessments of 'necessity' and 'advantage' must be highly subjective. One mother's 'extra' is another's 'necessity', and even attempts to define these terms according to expenditure items run into this problem: one mother may work to sustain levels of housing or clothing which she considers 'essential', but which appear 'luxurious' to another mother, while a car or financial independence may appear absolute necessities to many women. Finally, great care must be taken in the way in which such results are discussed. They may be used in conjunction with an assumption that for mothers to work because of financial necessity is a bad thing. But is it? Is it any different to or worse than fathers working for 'financial necessity', which most men would say they did? Should 'providing' or 'bread-winning' be a valued and praiseworthy role for men, but a suspect, even objectionable one when undertaken by women?

A majority of mothers – perhaps around two-thirds – give financial motives as their *main* reason for working, but this still leaves a substantial minority who give other reasons prime importance. Moreover, few mothers say they work only for money. Most mothers also give other non-financial reasons, along the lines of those already quoted. What might be broadly termed 'social' reasons (e.g. to meet people, get out of the house, an escape from boredom, to add extra interest to life, etc.) are most commonly given. Reasons related to career prospects or the intrinsic interest of the work done are mentioned by only a relatively small minority. Some mothers also explicitly refer to the importance of work in terms of self-esteem and its value in maintaining an adult identity.

These findings do not take us very far, most being fairly predictable. They show that mothers work for a variety of reasons, but that the actual combination of reasons varies between women, as indeed does the importance attached to each reason. In the CHES study, for instance, financial reasons (necessity and advantage) are given as the main reasons for working by 72 per cent of mothers doing unskilled and semiskilled manual jobs, by 71 per cent of mothers with no qualifications and by 85 per cent of lone mothers, compared to 44 per cent in professional and managerial jobs, 25 per cent with degrees and 61 per cent in two-parent families. Career and intrinsic job interests do not figure high overall, but this might be expected, given the low calibre of the jobs done by most mothers. Among the relatively few mothers in professional and managerial jobs, these considerations assume much more prominence; in the CHES survey, they were given as the main reason for working by 35 per cent of mothers working in these jobs, compared to only 4 per cent of those in unskilled or semiskilled manual jobs. In their study of women graduates, the Rapoports and Micahel Fogarty have shown the importance of attitudes to careers, especially commitment to the idea of women having careers and levels of career aspiration, in shaping the employment behaviour and expectations of this group of highly educated women (Fogarty, Rapoport and Rapoport, 1971).

Perhaps the main value of the survey data gathered so far is to emphasise that working women with children are not some strange and alien group whose practices and motives are hard to comprehend. But most surveys have left a lot uncovered, failing to pursue attitudes and feelings about work beyond one or two basic and rather crude questions on reasons for working. Such superficial questioning cannot really be expected to produce a clear picture of the meaning of work for any individual or of its relative importance and place in that

individual's life. More sensitive and extensive questioning is necessary to get a full understanding of mothers' attitudes to work. As
Susannah Ginsberg (1976) has pointed out, the whole issue of
working or being a full-time housewife and mother arouses strong
feelings of conflict for many mothers. To admit to seeking work
because of dissatisfaction with some aspect of the domestic role may
be difficult in some cases, and going to work for the money may
provide an easy and acceptable rationalisation, glossing over the full
complexity of a woman's feelings.

Even if most women give 'financial reasons' as their main motive
for working, there is a lot of evidence that a majority prefer to be
employed, irrespective of their financial situation. Table 4 (p.60) summarises some of this evidence, drawing on three studies – a 1975 survey
of two areas of Inner London undertaken at the Thomas Coram
Research Unit (TCRU), a 1974 national survey by OPCS of day care
needs and the 1970 OPCS survey of families in five local-authority
areas.[22] The first two surveys cover only women with pre-school
children, the third all women in two-parent families with children aged
0–15. The results from the three studies provide a very consistent
picture, from which a number of conclusions can be drawn:

1 Between a quarter and two-fifths of mothers are dissatisfied
with their employment status, i.e. currently work and would prefer not
to, or currently do not work but would rather have a job. The highest
dissatisfaction level is in the North Westminster area of the TCRU
study, being mainly due to the relatively high proportion who would
prefer to stop work. The highest level of satisfaction is in the same
study's South Camden area, being largely due to the high proportion
of satisfied employed mothers. This difference between the two Inner
London areas is returned to later.

2 The level of dissatisfaction with work is very consistent, 20–30
per cent of employed mothers preferring *not* to work. Although the
two Inner London areas *combined* fit into this pattern, there is a large
variation between the two areas; 18 per cent of working mothers are
dissatisfied in South Camden, 43 per cent in North Westminster. 30–
50 per cent of non-employed mothers say they would prefer to work,
dissatisfaction being less among mothers with pre-school children.

3 The number of non-employed mothers who would like to work
is two to three times greater than the number of employed mothers
who would rather stop work.

4 Except for the South Camden area, where the proportion is over
half, about two-fifths of mothers of pre-school children say they would
prefer to work; the figure for mothers of older children is rather higher
at just over 50 per cent.

A fourth survey, by Gallup Poll for *Woman's Own* (Sanders,
1979), provides very similar results, though the data are not

TABLE 4 SATISFACTION OF MOTHERS WITH EMPLOYMENT STATUS

	Study 1, 1970 (Hunt et al.)					Study 2, 1974 (Bone)	Study 3, 1975 (Moss and Plewis)		
	Dorset	Dundee	Glamorgan	Halifax	Haringey	Great Britain	South Camden	North Westminster	Two areas combined
Satisfied with Employment Status									
Works now and prefers to	27%	31%	27%	41%	34%	18%	36%	23%	29%
--- wants to cut hours		- - - no information - - -				no information	18	12	15
--- wants to keep same hours		- - - no information - - -				no information	17	9	13
Not working, does not want to	38	33	43	23	28	52	37	37	37
TOTAL SATISFIED WITH EMPLOYMENT STATUS	65	64	69	65	62	71	73	60	66
Dissatisfied with Employment Status									
Works now, wants to stop	7	11	8	13	13	7	8	17	13
Not working, wants to work	27	25	22	22	25	22	19	23	21
TOTAL DISSATISFIED WITH EMPLOYMENT STATUS	34	36	31	35	39	29	27	40	34
TOTAL–PREFER TO WORK	54	56	49	63	59	41	55	46	50
PREFER NOT TO	45	44	51	36	41	59	45	54	50

Sources Hunt *et al*, 1973, Vol. 1, Table 16; Bone, 1977, Table 4.3; Moss and Plewis, 1979, Table 4.5

sufficiently comparable to be included in Table 4. In the Gallup survey, only a fifth of all employed mothers (with children aged 0–15) would not want to go out to work 'in an ideal world where all financial pressure is removed'. The proportion varied from 31 per cent for mothers of pre-school children to 17 per cent for mothers of children at secondary school.

The two Inner London areas in the TCRU study had similar overall employment rates, but differed considerably in other respects. Both had full-time employment rates well above the national average, but North Westminster's was substantially higher than South Camden's; North Westminster also had more mothers in semiskilled and unskilled manual jobs and fewer in managerial and professional occupations. These area variations help explain the differences between the two areas shown in Table 4, especially the higher level of dissatisfaction with their employment status among working mothers in North Westminster.

Further analysis of the study data showed that dissatisfaction with working was independently related to two factors – hours per week worked and occupational status. A majority of full-time manual workers wanted to stop work altogether, compared to a minority of part-time manual workers and full-time non-manual workers and only a very small proportion of part-time non-manual workers. Most part-timers, in manual or non-manual occupations, wanted to continue work *and* not cut their hours, compared to only a small number of full-timers; more than half of full-time, non-manual workers wanted to reduce their hours but continue working (see Fig. 14).

In the initial analysis of the Thomas Coram Research Unit data, both lone mothers and ethnic minority mothers were found to be more dissatisfied with work than other mothers. Further analysis showed this to be because they were more likely to work full-time and ethnic minority mothers were also heavily concentrated in low-status manual jobs; in other words, there was no independent effect for country of origin and marital status once hours of work and occupational status were controlled for (Moss and Plewis, 1979). The 1970 OPCS study of five local-authority areas also showed lone mothers less likely to be satisfied with their employment status – whether employed or not – but more likely to prefer to work than mothers in two-parent families. A final point to make about the TCRU analysis is that it is based on the vast majority of mothers in the 'manual' group having unskilled and semiskilled jobs, the study areas being similar in this respect to the situation nationally. It is therefore possible that the attitude of employed mothers in *skilled* manual jobs would differ if looked at separately.

This discussion of mothers' satisfaction with their employment status again relies on the results of only one or two hypothetical

FIGURE 14 RELATIONSHIP BETWEEN SATISFACTION WITH WORK-
ING AND HOURS OF WORK AND OCCUPATION STATUS
AMONG WOMEN WITH PRE-SCHOOL CHILDREN, 1975
(TWO AREAS OF INNER LONDON) (percentages)

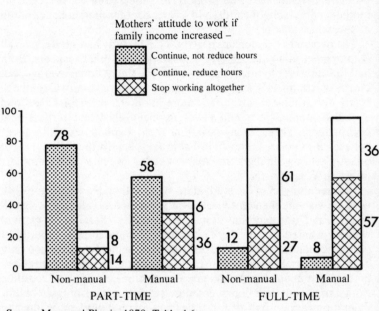

Mothers' attitude to work if
family income increased –

Continue, not reduce hours
Continue, reduce hours
Stop working altogether

Source Moss and Plewis, 1979, Table 4.6

questions from each of the studies reviewed. As with reasons mothers
give for working, so too the results for satisfaction with employment
status should be treated with caution; the whole field requires further
study. Taken together, however, the results seem to suggest that while
some mothers would rather not to go to work, most employed mothers
prefer to combine work and parenthood, though some, and especially
those in full-time work, would ideally like to reduce the hours they
work. The availability of better jobs would reduce the overall level of
dissatisfaction further. Finally, a substantial minority of non-employed mothers are at least strongly inclined to work, and might do so if job
or child-care opportunities arose or other circumstances changed.
Fathers' attitudes to and satisfaction with work remain unresearched.

How are children cared for while their parents work?

About half of all pre-school children with working mothers attend
some form of 'formal day care' (i.e. nurseries, playgroups, crèches
or minders), twice the rate for children with non-working mothers.
Some children of working mothers attend 'formal day care' either at
times when their mothers are not at work or for only part of their

mothers' work hours. Consequently this type of provision is the *main* form of care, while mothers actually work, for possibly only 25—30 per cent of pre-school children. It is, however, particularly important for the children of lone working mothers and full-time working mothers. Table 5, which draws on the results of the 1974 OPCS survey of day-

TABLE 5   PERCENTAGE OF PRE-SCHOOL CHILDREN USING 'INFORMAL' TYPES OF CARE WHILE MOTHERS ARE OUT AT WORK + PROPORTION OF CHILDREN ATTENDING 'FORMAL' DAY CARE BY MOTHER'S MARITAL STATUS AND WHETHER IN FULL-TIME OR PART-TIME WORK, 1974 (GREAT BRITAIN)

	ALL families	Family where mother EMPLOYED		
	(mothers employed + not employed)	Lone mother	Two Parents Works FT	Works PT
INFORMAL CARE WHILE MOTHER WORKS				
Mother, e.g. takes child to work	5	9	12	21
Father	10	2	22	48
Relative	8	57	33	29
Friend/neighbour	2	-	7	7
Other arrangement, e.g. nanny	1	2	2	2
FORMAL CARE AT ANY TIME IN THE DAY (whether mother at work or not then)[1]				
Playgroup	18	9	10	27
School (nursery, primary)	9	24	16	13
Day nursery (council, private)	2	11	11	2
Minder	3	22	21	5
TOTAL IN FORMAL CARE	32	61	56	46

Note: [1] The sum of individual types of provision may be more than the figure given in the 'total in formal care' row, where some children go, to more than one type of provision.

Source   Bone, 1977, Table 4.5 and 4.7

care needs, shows that more than a fifth of these children were at minders and 11 per cent at day nurseries (private and council), compared to a mere 3 and 2 per cent of all pre-school children.

The main types of care for pre-school children while mothers work are fathers (especially where mothers work part-time), relatives (mostly grandparents and especially for lone and full-time working mothers) and friends. Together, these 'informal' sources provide the *main* care for more than half of all pre-school children. Finally, around 15—20 per cent of mothers either work at home or take their children to work with them.

For older children, the child-care situation changes somewhat. School provides care for all children over five for six to seven hours a day – but only in term-time. This leaves gaps to be filled, before and after school and in holidays. The most common way to fill the after-school, term-time gap is for mothers to work only during school hours. This seems to account for between a third and a half of all working mothers, mostly, of course, those in part-time jobs. About 3 per cent of children are looked after by older siblings and 10–15 per cent are usually left on their own, the latter group mostly consisting of secondary school children; more will be left with siblings or on their own on occasion, when other arrangements prove temporarily unavailable. Fathers and relatives provide for most of the rest, more so for younger than older children; as with pre-school children, relatives are more commonly used by lone and full-time working mothers, accounting for 25–40 per cent of their children. Play schemes make little contribution overall, though they may be more important in a few areas where levels of provision are higher.

The same solutions are applied in school holidays, but with relatives playing a rather greater part. A substantial proportion of mothers – about 20–25 per cent, but lower for women in full-time work – are employed in term-time only, rather fewer than the proportion who work only during school hours. Relatives look after 25–35 per cent of children, but the numbers mainly looked after by fathers stay much the same as for after-school care, around 25 per cent. The number of children caring for themselves is probably higher, again with a big difference in the proportions for children under and over eleven: a substantial number of secondary school children, perhaps a quarter, are mainly left to their own devices, but less than 5 per cent of primary school children – though, again, more are left alone on occasion when other arrangements fall through. Play schemes are relatively unimportant, accounting for only 1–2 per cent while 2–3 per cent of children are looked after by minders and other paid help, much the same as for after-school care.

Considerable differences in care arrangements for school-age children were found to exist between the five local-authority areas in the 1970 OPCS study (see Table 6). Differences in the care of pre-school children were also substantial. In Haringey, for instance, 30 per cent of children under five whose mothers worked were with minders and only 12 per cent were cared for by their fathers, compared to 9 and 30 per cent respectively in Halifax. Such area variations reflect differences in work hours and other employment features, levels of service and availability of other sources of help, especially family.

One other aspect of child care has been missing so far – what happens when children are ill? The only study to tackle this is the

TABLE 6 CHILD-CARE ARRANGEMENTS FOR SCHOOL-AGE CHILDREN OF EMPLOYED MOTHERS IN TWO-PARENT FAMILIES, 1970 (FIVE LOCAL AUTHORITY AREAS, GREAT BRITAIN) (All figures are percentages)

Local Authority		Mother works school hours/ terms only	Mother works at home/takes child to work	Father	Relative/ Neighbour	Paid help	Child cares for self	Employment rate	
								Full-time	Part-time
DORSET	AS	53	6	11	14	2	15	10	31
	HO	25	18	9	24	4	23		
DUNDEE	AS	23	4	28	27	4	18	18	32
	HO	14	4	26	34	4	16		
GLAMOR- GAN	AS	38	7	29	23	4	7	16	26
	HO	30	9	25	32	4	9		
HALIFAX	AS	49	3	22	18	2	13	16	47
	HO	19	7	24	38	6	18		
HARINGEY	AS	31	14	20	16	10	19	17	32
	HO	10	15	24	28	11	20		

AS – After School Hours   HO – Holidays
Source Hunt *et al.*, 1973, Vol. 1, Tables 14 and 15

recent Gallup Poll for *Woman's Own*, and the most frequent answer, given by just over half of all mothers, was that they 'always' take time off, while a further 16 per cent 'sometimes' take time off; by comparison, 6 per cent of fathers were reported to take time off always or sometimes, though a further fifth would look after their children because they are at home in any case when their wives are at work. Finally, a third of the mothers referred to friends and relatives looking after sick children on occasion.

Apart from school itself, and the small proportion of children who are with their mothers while they work, the main form of care for children, over and under five, is the family; for older children, self-help is also important. These conclusions, and the estimates preceding them, are based on a number of studies (unpublished data from the OPCS survey on shiftwork; the OPCS study on day-care needs of pre-school children (Bone, 1977); the CHES study; and the Gallup Poll (1979) for *Woman's Own*). Although each attempts to cover child-care arrangements while mothers work, the results are not readily comparable – hence the rather imprecise nature of the estimates given. Moreover, none of the studies copes adequately with the frequent complexity of child-care arrangements, which often involve several care-givers. They either confine themselves to the *main* arrangements for each child or fail to link data on main and other types of care to provide a full picture. All focus on child-care while *mothers* work, rather than taking the broader parental perspective implied in the question at the beginning of this section, and none provides an answer to the most relevant and comprehensive question: 'how are children in our society cared for, and do these child-care arrangements vary between families with two, one or no working parents?'. Finally, we still know very little about the *quality* of care received by children under the many arrangements that do exist, though there is some evidence on child minding, which plays a particularly important part in the care of children under three with mothers working full-time: here standards are very variable, including a substantial minority of minders who are unsatisfactory, and a high proportion of parents who use child minders would prefer alternative forms of care if available (Bone, 1977; Mayall and Petrie, 1977; Hughes *et al.*, 1980).

'Plus ça change . . .'

Changes in work and family life since the war, and especially in the last two decades, have been many and widespread. Some have been touched on in this chapter, others are discussed elsewhere in the book. Yet, in many important respects less has changed in the relationship between work and the family than might appear at first sight. Many more women, and especially those with children, now go to work. But few have scaled the higher rungs of the occupational ladder, and especially the highest, to reach the professional and managerial positions of greatest reward, influence and standing. Notable exceptions only prove the rule; we may be entering the 1980s with the first woman prime minister in British history, yet the number of women MPs is at its lowest since the war. Most working mothers find themselves in the least skilled occupations, manual and non-manual, where they form the core of a secondary labour force that is unskilled, untrained, low-paid, with no prospects, easily taken on or laid off and predominantly female.

The number of fathers not at work may have grown, but only because of growing unemployment in recent years. Those who are employed overwhelmingly work full-time, and often full-time plus quite a bit extra in overtime: the place of many non-employed mothers in the home is still bought at the expense of their husband's absence, working long hours to support a one-income household. Apart from a greater propensity to work shifts and overtime, parenthood still has a minimal impact on men's employment circumstances and experiences.

Where mothers do work, responsibility for arranging child-care and meeting their children's other needs still falls largely on them and it is they, rather than fathers, who adapt their work lives, and especially their work hours, to meet these responsibilities. Apart from part-time work itself, and mothers stopping and starting jobs to cover school holidays and other difficult times, child care continues to be managed largely by traditional methods – school, family, friends, homework, taking children to work, leaving children to their own devices. The expansion of pre-school provision in the last ten to fifteen years, though substantial, has done little to change this picture. Most of the expansion has been in nursery education and playgroups, whose short, fixed hours and holiday closure make them of very limited value to working mothers, even those in part-time jobs.

Looking back on the post-war period, the most significant change in the relationship between work and the family is the greater diversity to have emerged in this relationship. The predominant family type at the beginning of this period – two married parents, mother at home and father at work – has contracted until it accounts for only a minority of families with children, perhaps only two out of every five, as more mothers go to work, more fathers find themselves unemployed and more families are headed by lone parents. Since all three of these trends are likely to continue in the foreseeable future, this 'traditional' form of family life will probably also continue to decline in numbers and significance.

3

Employment Prospects and Equal Opportunity
Peter Elias
Introduction

This chapter attempts to bring together information on past trends in
employment, unemployment and the labour force with recent projections of these trends.[1] The aim of the chapter is to present the economic
setting for policies designed to provide equal employment opportunities within the family. Ideally the information presented in this
chapter would, therefore, be classified in terms of family structure:
single men and women should, for instance, be distinguished from
married men and women, who would in turn be divided between those
with children and those without. Unfortunately, such classification is
not possible. Most employment data provide little or no detail on the
family characteristics of the workforce. Consequently, most of the
information presented in this chapter makes only a simple distinction
between men and women, with an occasional further division of
women into married and unmarried.

The chapter is presented in three parts. The first examines trends in
employment and unemployment over the last two decades. Changes
in the industrial composition of employment over the last decade are
studied to identify the main areas of employment growth and decline.
Some of the factors which have led to the rapid growth of female
employment are also considered in this section, together with
information on the occupational structure of employment. The
second part examines the changes that have occurred over this same
period in labour force participation, that is people available for work,
either in employment already or unemployed but seeking work. This
examination complements the information presented by Peter Moss
in Chapter 2 by providing information on some of the underlying
factors which could have brought about these changes in participation. The final section reviews the evidence presented in the previous
sections in conjunction with employment projections from the major
forecasting bodies in Great Britain. By this means it is hoped that a
clearer understanding can be gained of the various forces which are
shaping future employment prospects for men and women. Brief
consideration is given to the impact of technological change over the
next two decades, and the section concludes with an assessment of the
likely implications of these projections for employment opportunities
within the family.

Trends in employment and unemployment

Tables 7 and 8 indicate the scale of the structural change that has occurred in the labour market over the past twenty years. For males, there has been a substantial downward trend in full-time employment.

TABLE 7 CHANGES IN THE COMPOSITION OF THE MALE LABOUR FORCE, 1961-78 (GREAT BRITAIN)

	1961 (thousands)	Change as % of labour force			1978 (thousands)
		1961-6	1966-71	1971-8	
Employees: part-time[1]	144	1.0	1.8	1.0	753
full-time[2]	14,219	-1.2	-5.2	-3.5	12,622
Self-employed	1,385	-0.8	1.4	-0.8	1,341
Registered unemployed	231	-	2.2	2.4	978
Unregistered unemployed[3]	253	-0.4	0.6	-	283
Labour force	16,232	-1.5	0.7	-0.8	15,977

Notes   [1] For 1961 and 1966, the definition of part-time was self-descriptive and was not stated in terms of hours per week. From 1971 onwards the definition refers to those working 30 hours per week or less.
[2] Includes HM Forces. Excludes private domestic service workers from 1971 onwards.
[3] Derived as residual in 1961

Sources   1961, 1966 Census of Population; Department of Employment 1977b, 1979b; Manpower Research Group, University of Warwick, estimates of part-time employment, self-employment and unregistered unemployed for 1978

TABLE 8 CHANGE IN THE COMPOSITION OF THE FEMALE LABOUR FORCE, 1961-78 (GREAT BRITAIN)

	1961 (thousands)	Change as % of labour force			1978 (thousands)
		1961-6	1966-71	1971-8	
Employees: part-time[1]	1,815	10.5	1.4	12.3	3,867
full-time[2]	5,444	2.0	-1.3	-2.1	5,297
Self-employed	331	0.4	0.1	-	368
Registered unemployed	91	-0.3	0.4	3.4	403
Unregistered unemployed[3]	101	1.3	1.5	-0.4	300
Labour force	7,782	13.9	2.0	13.2	10,235

Notes and Sources As for Table 7

The part-time employment of men has increased considerably, but not on a scale large enough to absorb the decline in full-time employment. The net result has been an increase in the level of registered unemployment, despite a slight fall in the size of the labour force over this same period. This fall results from the reduced labour force participation of younger and older men, reflecting increased educational participation and earlier retirement respectively. This reduction in labour force participation more than offsets the increase in the male population of working age, resulting from the 'baby boom' of the late fifties and early sixties.

Table 8 shows that, from the mid-sixties onwards, female full-time employment has shown a similar, though smaller, rate of decline to that for males. In comparison with Table 7, the main contrasting feature of this table is the rate of growth of female part-time employment. While the level of 1.8 million part-time employees in 1961 might be an under-estimate due to recording error in the 1961 Census of Population, it is clear that the growth of the female labour force between 1961 and 1978 is primarily associated with the increase in part-time employment. Recently, the registered unemployment of women has risen sharply. In part this reflects the decrease in full-time jobs, although some of the increase must also be attributed to the fact that more women now register as unemployed upon being made redundant.

Some indication of the major changes in the industrial structure of employment can be obtained from Tables 9 and 10. These tables show changes in employment occurring between 1961, 1971 and 1978, by industry order for males and females respectively. While the industry orders are, in some cases, broad aggregates covering many different types of firms or activities, they are sufficiently distinct to enable the employment changes shown in Tables 7 and 8 to be located within certain sectors of the economy. From Table 9 it is clear that the primary, manufacturing and construction sectors have exhibited a strong downward trend in male employment in each of the last two decades. Within the manufacturing sector the engineering industries lost a considerable amount of employment between 1971 and 1978. Similar large rates of decline are found in textiles, clothing, bricks etc. and paper, printing and publishing. Within the service sector the picture is quite different. Insurance, banking and finance, professional and scientific services and miscellaneous services have all shown a considerable rate of employment growth in the 1961–71 and 1971–8 periods. This growth has not been sufficient to offset the decline in male employment in other sectors of the economy, leading to an overall decline of well over one million jobs between 1961 and 1978.

Table 10 shows that the general pattern of change for female employment is fairly similar to that for men. Employment in the primary and manufacturing sectors has fallen considerably in both periods, reducing the number of jobs held by women in these sectors by 600,000. For most industry orders the rate of decline is less than the comparable rate for men. The major exception is the textiles industry. For this industry the combined effects of improved technology and a high rate of import penetration have brought a major decline in employment. Because this industry employs predominantly female labour, these adverse trends have had a marked impact on female employment, with over 200,000 fewer women being employed in 1978 than in 1961. Offsetting these losses has been the rapid rate of expansion of female employment in insurance, banking and finance, professional and scientific services (which include the state education

TABLE 9   INDUSTRY ORDER CHANGES IN MALE EMPLOY-
MENT, 1961-78 (GREAT BRITAIN)

Industry Order[1]	1961	% change		1978
	(thousands)	1961-71	1971-8	(thousands)
1. Agriculture etc.	551	-43	-10	285
2. Mining, quarrying	704	-46	-14	327
3. Food, drink, tobacco	448	-	- 7	417
4. Coal, petrol products	47	-17	-18	32
5. Chemicals	309	1	- 2	306
6. Metal manufacture	569	-14	-18	406
7. Mechanical engineering	860	2	-11	780
8. Instrument engineering	98	8	-10	95
9. Electrical engineering	470	3	- 6	465
10. Shipbuilding	228	-25	- 6	161
11. Vehicles	756	- 7	- 4	671
12. Metal goods	376	7	- 5	386
13. Textiles	355	-13	-18	254
14. 15. Clothing, etc.	173	-21	-19	110
16. Bricks, pottery, etc.	253	- 6	-16	200
17. Timber, etc.	226	- 5	- 2	209
18. Paper, print, publishing	387	3	- 9	362
19. Other manufactures	176	19	-	209
20. Construction	1,376	-17	- 1	1,131
21. Gas, electricity, water	338	- 8	-12	273
22. Transport, communication	1,412	- 9	- 9	1,169
23. Distributive trades	1,303	-12	3	1,182
24. Insurance, banking etc.	371	28	17	551
25. Prof., scientific services	722	35	16	1,133
26. Miscellaneous	802	9	13	985
27. Public administration	892	9	-	972
Primary (Orders 1-2)	1,255	-45	-12	612
Manufacturing (Orders 3-19)	5,730	- 3	- 9	5,065
Construction (Order 20)	1,376	-17	- 1	1,131
Services (Orders 21-27)	5,841	3	4	6,264
TOTAL	14,202	- 6	- 3	13,072

Note   [1] The industry order classification is the 1968 Standard Industrial
Classification.
Source   Department of Employment 1975a, 1979c

system, private education, the national health and private health
services), miscellaneous services and public administration (other
local authority and central government employment). With the
exception of miscellaneous services, these industry orders all display
a lower rate of growth of female employment during 1971–8 than in
the 1961–71 period. The recent growth of female employment in
miscellaneous services has been remarkable, averaging over 4 per

TABLE 10 INDUSTRY ORDER CHANGES IN FEMALE EMPLOY-
MENT 1961-78 (GREAT BRITAIN)

Industry Order[1]		% change		
	1961	1961-71	1971-8	1978
	(thousands)			(thousands)
1. Agriculture etc.	140	-26	-12	92
2. Mining, quarrying	20	-25	- 7	14
3. Food, drink, tobacco	322	- 8	- 6	279
4. Coal, petrol products	7	-29	-20	4
5. Chemicals	134	- 8	-	123
6. Metal manufacture	73	-12	-17	53
7. Mechanical engineering	167	- 2	-12	145
8. Instrument engineering	59	-	-12	52
9. Electrical engineering	269	13	-10	274
10. Shipbuilding	11	9	8	13
11. Vehicles	120	-13	-11	93
12. Metal goods	188	-11	-11	150
13. Textiles	427	-37	-23	210
14. 15. Clothing, etc.	412	-17	-14	294
16. Bricks, pottery etc.	74	-12	- 3	63
17. Timber, etc.	55	- 9	-	50
18. Paper, print, publishing	205	- 7	- 9	174
19. Other manufactures	116	6	- 3	119
20. Construction	70	17	24	102
21. Gas, electricity, water	43	40	13	68
22. Transport, communication	237	8	-	257
23. Distributive trades	1,401	-	7	1,501
24. Insurance, banking etc.	304	61	19	583
25. Prof., scientific services	1,358	43	26	2,442
26. Miscellaneous services	986	5	34	1,379
27. Public administration	388	30	22	614
Primary (Orders 1-2)	160	-26	-11	106
Manufacturing (Orders 3-19)	2,639	-11	-10	2,096
Construction (Order 20)	70	17	24	102
Services (Order 21-27)	4,717	21	20	6,844
TOTAL	7,586	8	11	9,149

Note and Source As for Table 9

cent per annum between 1971 and 1978. In total, the service sector
has created an additional 2.1 million jobs for women between 1961
and 1978.

Changes in the level of female employment are not simply the result
of the fortunes of different industries and their general expansion or
contraction. Other influences include the changing pattern of working
hours (for example, the trend towards part-time and shift working)
and the impact of technological progress and its effect on occupational
structure within industries. Information on occupational trends in

employment is sparse. Apart from the Censuses of Population of 1961, 1966 and 1971 there are no reliable sources of information on occupational employment *by industry*. The New Earnings Survey provides some information, but its sample size is such that this information is only useful when aggregated to a simple 'manual/non-manual' occupational classification.

Some information on these occupational trends in employment is given in Table 11. This shows proportions of non-manual female

TABLE 11 CHANGES IN NON-MANUAL AND PART-TIME FEMALE EMPLOYMENT, 1970-8 (GREAT BRITAIN)

Industry Order	Non-manual female employees as % of all employees in industry		Percentage point change	Part-time female employees as % of all employees in industry		Percentage point change
	1970	1978	1970-8	1970	1978	1970-8
1. Agriculture etc.	3.9	4.5	0.6	7.9	9.2	1.3
2. Mining, quarrying	3.7	3.4	-0.3	0.8	1.4	0.6
3. Food, drink, tobacco	12.5	10.9	-1.6	14.3	14.2	-0.1
4. Coal, petrol products	11.4	12.8	1.4	1.7	2.8	1.1
5. Chemicals	13.4	12.6	-0.8	5.8	5.6	-0.2
6. Metal manufacture	6.2	6.0	-0.2	2.6	2.5	-0.1
7. Mechanical engineering	9.1	9.7	0.6	3.2	3.0	-0.2
8. Instrument engineering	12.8	13.7	0.9	7.0	6.1	-0.9
9. Electrical engineering	11.0	10.7	-0.3	8.2	7.1	-1.1
10. Shipbuilding	3.3	4.4	1.1	1.6	2.0	0.4
11. Vehicles	6.8	5.6	-1.2	2.0	1.6	-0.4
12. Metal goods	7.9	9.2	1.3	8.1	7.1	-1.0
13. Textiles	6.7	7.1	0.4	10.1	9.5	-0.6
14. 15. Clothing, etc.	8.9	8.0	-0.9	11.6	14.9	3.3
16. Bricks, pottery, etc.	7.2	8.2	1.0	3.4	4.8	1.4
17. Timber, etc.	7.0	9.0	2.0	4.0	6.6	2.6
18. Paper, print, publishing	12.7	13.9	1.2	6.8	6.9	0.1
19. Other manufactures	8.4	9.6	1.2	8.7	8.9	0.2
20. Construction	4.8	6.2	1.4	1.8	2.3	0.5
21. Gas, electricity, water	11.7	18.5	6.8	2.7	4.0	1.3
22. Transport, communication	11.7	12.7	1.0	3.0	3.6	0.6
23. Distributive trades[1]	43.9	45.3	1.4	19.5	21.8	2.3
24. Insurance, banking etc.[1]	43.0	45.9	2.9	12.1	10.3	-1.8
25. Prof., scientific services[1]	42.7	45.5	1.8	24.5	29.9	5.4
26. Miscellaneous services[1]	17.8	20.4	2.6	22.3	26.9	4.6
27. Public administration	22.3	32.4	10.1	12.7	7.4	-5.3
TOTAL	19.5	23.6	4.1	11.0	13.3	2.3

Note   [1] Part-time proportions from the New Earnings Survey shown for these industry orders are between 4 and 7 percentage points lower than those recorded in the Annual Census of Employment. This downward bias probably results from the lack of coverage of non-tax/national insurance payers by the New Earnings Survey and the additional coverage of double jobholders in the Annual Census of Employment.

Source   Department of Employment 1971a, 1979d

employees and part-time female employees to all employees in each
industry order, derived from the sample structure of the New Earnings
Survey, [2] for 1970 and 1978. Contrary to expectations, the growth in
the proportion of non-manual female employment within total
employment has been modest and, for some industries, has even been
in decline between 1970 and 1978. In the food, drink and tobacco
industries and in vehicle construction the proportion of non-manual
females has fallen by more than one percentage point in this period,
too large a fall to be accounted for by sampling error. Similar
downward trends in non-manual female employment are also in
evidence in the electrical engineering and clothing industries, both of
which are large employers of female labour. There are only two
industry orders – (a) gas, electricity and water and (b) public
administration – in which the occupational structure has moved
markedly in favour of non-manual jobs taken by women. This does not
imply that changes in occupational structure have had an insignificant
impact upon female employment opportunities. Manual semiskilled
and unskilled jobs might, for instance, have expanded at the expense
of craft employment. Similarly, within the non-manual occupations,
managerial and supervisory positions are held predominantly by men,
whereas clerical and secretarial jobs are almost exclusively considered female jobs. The expansion or contraction of one relative to the
other would lead to changing employment opportunities for men and
women, without producing any major movement of the workforce
from manual to non-manual jobs or vice versa. What Table II shows is
that, with the exception of the public utilities and public administration,
no such major trend occurred within the eight-year period.

Women tend to be highly concentrated within a few occupational
groups. The 1971 Census of Population indicated that 72 per cent of
all clerical, commercial and office occupations were held by women,
and that this occupational group alone accounted for about 30 per
cent of all women in employment. Similarly, women held 71 per cent
of all occupations in the health professions, although this group
comprised only 6 per cent of female employment. Between 1961 and
1971, female employment increased most rapidly in these occupational groups and in literary, artistic and sports occupations, sales
occupations and semiskilled jobs. Over the same period there was no
change, or even a decline, in the proportion of women employed in
managerial, scientific and engineering professions and skilled occupations requiring apprentice training. More recent evidence from
the occupational structure of registered unemployment shows that the
major increases in female unemployment have occurred in clerical
jobs and semiskilled occupations.

There is, therefore, little evidence of much occupational diversifica-
tion in female employment. Women are concentrated in semiskilled

occupations or a narrow range of professional jobs which are considered 'women's jobs'. It is the growth of these sectors of the economy in which these occupations are concentrated which has accommodated the rise in the numbers of women seeking work. Most of this growth is confined to relatively few industry orders within the service sector of the econmy (e.g. insurance, banking and finance; professional and scientific services).

Table 11 also includes information on recent trends in part-time female employment. As with non-manual occupations, it is evident that in some manufacturing industry orders there has been a decline in the proportion of part-time jobs held by women. But in the service sector, professional and scientific services and miscellaneous services both exhibit large increases in the proportion of female part-timers. These gains might be understated, given the incomplete coverage of the New Earnings Survey, but it is apparent that the marked overall increase in part-time employment shown in Table 8 is concentrated in the health and education sectors (state and private), other profess-ional services and miscellaneous services. The change in female employment in public administration (central and local government) shown in Table 10 has *not* been associated with an increase in part-time employment: it has been a consequence of the changing occupational structure of this sector, indicated by the strong growth in non-manual female employment shown in Table 11.

Valuable insight into the reasons for the growth of part-time employment comes from a recent survey of employers analysed by Bosworth and Dawkins (1979). Over three-quarters of all reasons given for an increase in part-time employment by firms in the manufacturing sector fell into demand-related categories (e.g. the need to meet particular workloads, the introduction of shiftworking). In the service sector, many establishments referred to the difficulty of finding full-time workers, suggesting that supply-side considerations play a larger role in the expansion of part-time employment in this sector. Conversely, 26 per cent of service sector establishments which reported a decrease in the proportion of part-time employment indicated that they had only taken on part-timers because they could not obtain full-timers.

This information suggests that in the manufacturing sector it is the value of part-time working to the employer which is the primary reason for the changing proportion of part-timers. In the service sector, shortages of suitable full-time workers have been a more significant factor. This reinforces the previous argument, that it is the growth of particular occupations in the service sector, which are predominantly 'women's jobs', that has led to the increase in female employment. This growth has been associated with a trend toward part-time working, as employers have had to accommodate the work preferences of married women.

The increase in part-time employment by firms and by the state is clearly one reason for the rapid increase in the participation of married women in the labour force. However, when analysing this increase in participation from the point of view of the family, as opposed to that of the employers, it becomes clear that other factors have facilitated this major change. The next section is devoted to an analysis of these factors.

Trends in labour force participation

As mentioned earlier, male labour force participation has declined over the last two decades as a result of two influences. More young men are now staying on longer at school and engaging in higher education. Table 12 shows a decrease in the rate of male labour force participation in the 16–24-year age group of only one percentage point between 1961 and 1978, but this broad age category conceals a significant decline in participation by 16–19-year-olds. At the other end of the age range, men are now retiring earlier than before. This shows up in Table 12 as a fall in labour force participation rates in the over-60 age groups. A steady decline in participation for the over-65-year-olds is in evidence since 1961. For the 1971–8 period a rapid decline in participation of 60–64-year-old males has also occurred. This may be a consequence of the high rates of unemployment experienced by this age group leading to an earlier withdrawal from the labour force.

For non-married women in the 16–24-year age group, participation has fallen by nine percentage points between 1961 and 1978, indicating a significant rise in the proportion of single women entering the higher education system. However, these changes for males and non-married females are dwarfed by the magnitude of the rise in the labour force participation of married women. Between 1961 and 1971 a rapid increase occurred in the participation of women in the 35–59-year ages, while between 1971 and 1978 the major increases have come from married women aged between 16 and 24. This finding agrees with the observation made by Peter Moss in Chapter 2 that the recent increases in labour force participation have come from mothers with very young children.

It is tempting to assume that the increase in provision of school places for young children has contributed to this rise in labour force participation. Between 1961 and 1977 the proportion of three- and four-year-old children in state nursery and primary schools rose from 16 per cent to 36 per cent of the age cohort, covering nearly 570,000 three- and four-year-olds by 1977. Some of this provision is made on a part-time basis and since 1977 there has been little increase in these figures. On the other side of this picture, the General Household

TABLE 12 CHANGES IN LABOUR FORCE PARTICIPATION (LFP) BY AGE AND SEX, 1961-78 (GREAT BRITAIN)

	LFP%	Percentage point change		LFP%
	1961	1961-71	1971-8	1978
Males				
16-24	83	-2	1	82
25-34	98	-	-1	97
35-44	99	-1	-	98
45-54	99	-1	-1	97
55-59	97	-2	-2	93
60-64	91	-4	-11	76
65+	24	-5	-5	14
Married Females				
16-24	41	5	15	61
25-34	30	8	14	52
35-44	36	19	15	70
45-54	35	22	12	69
55-59	26	20	6	52
60-64	13	12	-1	24
65+	3	4	-2	5
Non-married females				
16-24	78	-6	-3	69
25-34	88	-7	-8	73
35-44	82	-2	-11	69
45-54	76	2	-7	71
55-59	63	4	-5	62
60-64	32	2	-7	27
65+	7	-1	-2	4
All males	86	-3	-4	79
All females	37	6	5	48

Sources Department of Employment, 1971b, 1975b, 1977b; OPCS, 1979b

Survey indicates that the proportion of women in the sample who would work earlier than intended, were they not prevented from doing so by the need to look after children, has been constant at around 7 per cent of the female labour force.[3] This represents well over half a million women who would presumably be at work or seeking jobs at an earlier date than presently intended if suitable arrangements could be made for the care of their children. It appears therefore that the lack of provision of alternative care for young children continues to act as a constraint upon a decision by mothers to participate in paid work.

No consideration is given in the GHS to other, possibly more binding, constraints such as the availability of a suitable job at a wage sufficient to cover the costs of day care. As we have seen in Chapter 2, during the last decade, when the female labour participation of mothers with young children was increasing rapidly, alternative child-care arrangements were made principally within an informal network, relying heavily upon relatives. This suggests that it is the availability of jobs which is the principal factor in determining labour force participation and that child-care arrangements will be made after the decision to undertake paid work has been made. Where the State has not provided sufficient child-care places, the informal network of family and friends will take over, wherever possible, though its ability to do so may be diminishing. In a recent investigation of services for young children with working mothers (Central Policy Review Staff, 1978a) it was concluded that the traditional pattern of care of young children by grandparents could become less readily available, as a result of the increased number of older women returning to full-time employment.

In a recent study of the growth in married women's labour force participation (Elias, 1980), the author concluded that three factors are closely related to this increase. The growth in part-time employment in service-sector industries outlined in the previous section is undoubtedly a major factor. This must be considered alongside the strong upward trend in real earnings throughout the late sixties and early seventies and the decline in the birthrate. Some indication of the relevant strengths of these trends for married women of different ages can be gauged from Table 13. This table is based on all households participating in the Family Expenditure Survey (FES) in 1968 and 1975, in which there was a married woman whose husband was also present in the household. It compares averages in these two years for such households, for certain economic, demographic and employment variables. Households are divided into three categories, covering women in the 25–34, 35–44 and 45–54 year age groups respectively. The first row shows once again the remarkable increase that occurred in the labour force participation rates of married women, particularly the 35–44 age group, during the late sixties and first half of the seventies. It should be noted that these FES rates are higher than those recorded in Table 12, in that they are based upon a broader definition of labour force participation and include jobs undertaken on a casual and seasonal basis. Participation rates for husbands and other persons in the household over 16 years of age have changed little, or declined slightly, over the same period.

Some commentators have argued that the increase in the participation of married women is related to the increase in unemployment of male heads of households. It can be seen from Table 13 that this hypothesis cannot account for the scale of the increase in married women's labour force participation recorded in the FES between 1968 and 1975. Unemployment rates among husbands in the FES samples rose by only 1–1½ per cent in this period. Of much more

TABLE 13 SOME CHARACTERISTICS OF FAMILY EXPENDITURE SURVEY HOUSEHOLDS, 1968 and 1975

		Wife aged 25–34			Wife aged 35–44			Wife aged 45–54	
		1968	1975	% change	1968	1975	% change	1968	1975	% change
Labour force participation (%)	Wife	46.1	55.7	9.6	55.5	70.6	15.1	55.6	69.0	13.4
	Husband	99.5	99.1	-0.4	97.7	99.3	1.6	94.9	94.5	-0.4
	Others	60.6	62.3	1.7	77.9	77.5	-0.4	82.9	80.1	-2.8
Unemployment rate (%)	Wife	0.3	1.0	0.7	0.3	1.0	0.7	0.6	0.5	-0.1
	Husband	1.6	3.0	1.4	1.5	2.6	1.1	1.1	2.7	1.6
	Others	0.0	3.3	3.3	0.9	4.0	3.1	1.4	5.4	4.0
Net real earnings, employees (£/hr)	Wife	0.43	0.54	26	0.42	0.52	24	0.40	0.52	30
	Husband	0.69	0.80	16	0.73	0.80	10	0.69	0.75	9
	Others	0.40	0.49	23	0.32	0.40	25	0.38	0.46	21
Households without children (%)	children aged 0–1	67.3	75.0	7.7	91.0	95.4	4.4	98.6	98.8	0.2
	children aged 2–4	49.8	56.6	6.8	79.5	86.7	7.2	97.2	98.1	0.9
No. of households in sample		1,222	1,321	–	1,143	1,038	–	1,089	996	–

NB Net earnings are deflated by the annual average retail price index for 1968 and 1975 (15 January 1974 = 100).
The sample consists of households in which there is a married woman with husband present.
Source Department of Employment, Family Expenditure Survey Base Tapes, 1968 and 1975

relevance is the growth in employment opportunities and the increase in real earnings. Net real earnings of wives in the FES grew by about 25–30 per cent between 1968 and 1975, compared with increases of only 9–16 per cent for their husbands. This more rapid rate of increase for married women probably results from two factors. Between 1973 and 1975, the Equal Pay Act of 1970 was still in the process of implementation. There is evidence (Elias, 1980) to show that this created a once-and-for-all increase in the ratio of female to male earnings. Second, pay restraint policies operating in this period yielded higher percentage increases to the lower paid, proportionately more of whom are women. Consequently, there has been a substantial real increase in earnings for married women, which is likely to have acted as an inducement to participate in the labour market.

The data in Table 13 also show the effect of the decline in the birthrate which commenced in 1964. For married women aged 25–34 years there was a large increase in the number of households without children in the 0–1 age range, whereas for married women aged between 35 and 44 years, the principal increase has been in the proportion of households without children aged 2–4 years. For married women in these age groups this increase in the proportion of households without pre-school children must have had some significant impact upon their labour force participation decision. It is worth noting, though, the considerable rise in participation for married women aged 45–54 years, a group for which there is, of course, no corresponding change in the proportion of households with very young children.

With these influences in mind, it is worth considering the factors which underlie the projections of labour force participation made by the Department of Employment (1977). In making its projection, the DE lists the growth of part-time employment, the decline in the birthrate, the increase in the provision of day care for young children and the 'additional attraction of employment following equal pay' as factors which have influenced its forecasts. It is now apparent that some of these factors will evolve in a manner that could not have been anticipated when the projection was prepared in 1977.

Foremost among these will be the slow growth of employment in those sectors of the economy which are the major employers of women. Table 11 showed that part-time female employment expanded rapidly during the seventies in professional and scientific services, which include the health and education sectors, and miscellaneous services. The following section gives brief details of some recent work by the Manpower Research Group at the University of Warwick, which shows that employment in these services is expected to continue to grow to the mid-eighties, but at less than half the rate experienced over the 1971–8 period.

Other changes have also occurred which could not have been anticipated by the DE. After falling continually since 1964, the birthrate levelled out during 1977 and 1978 and has since begun to rise sharply. While the upturn in the birthrate might not signify the beginning of another 'baby boom', it does suggest that any increases in labour force participation rates of younger married women, projected on the assumption of a declining birthrate, will not be forthcoming. It is also unlikely that the provision of pre-school services will increase as rapidly as it did during the early seventies, owing to the present financial limitations surrounding most local-authority operations. Finally, married women's real earnings will not continue to grow relative to their husband's earnings as rapidly as they did during the sixties and early seventies. In part this is because, as mentioned above, earlier increases reflect a once-and-for-all rise in women's earnings. More generally, though, there will be little need for employers to attract women into the labour force, given the likely levels of unemployment that are expected to prevail through the eighties.

Another factor which complicates the task of projecting the labour force relates to the trend towards later marriage, the increase in the divorce rate and the subsequent increase in the population of single and divorced persons. The method of projecting the labour force used by the DE assumes that non-married women (single, widowed, separated and divorced) have rates of labour force participation which lie between the participation rates for married women and the rates for men. Any unforeseen trend in the proportion of non-married women in the economy could lead to substantial errors in projection.

To conclude, it seems likely that labour force participation rates for married women will not increase as rapidly as they did during the sixties and early seventies. Nevertheless, they will continue to increase, contributing to a rising male and female labour force in the early eighties. Most of this rise, however, will be due to the increase in the population of young people currently entering the labour market, the result of the 'baby boom' of the early sixties, an increase that will not peak until 1982. Until then, the employment problem facing young persons leaving school each year will be seriously heightened by this demographic effect.

Employment prospects

This section reviews some recent short- and medium-term projections of employment and unemployment. After discussing some of the problems associated with unemployment forecasting, some consideration is given to the possible impact of rapid technological change over the next two decades. The section concludes with a review of employment and unemployment prospects from the perspective of the family.

There is general agreement among economists that the 1979 oil price rise is creating a recession in world trade which might not recover until 1981-82. In conjunction with the 1979 increase in VAT in the UK, the strength of sterling despite continued import penetration, a strict monetary regime and rigid enforcement of cash limits in the public sector, there is every reason to expect unemployment to increase throughout 1980 and 1981. The London Business School's Centre for Economic Forecasting (1979) projects a level of registered unemployment of two million by 1982. The National Institute for Economic and Social Research (1979) projects a level of registered unemployment of 1.6 million by the end of 1980. An independent group of economists and businessmen, using the Treasury short-term model (*Guardian*, 15 October, 1979), forecasts a rate of decline of gross domestic product reaching 6 per cent per annum in the second half of 1981 and a consequential rise in the level of registered unemployment to 2.3 million persons.

For groups engaged in medium-term projections, the high levels of unemployment forecast for the mid-eighties and onward result from assumptions that import penetration will continue and that labour productivity will increase at rates which are moderate by past standards. The Cambridge Economic Policy Group (1979) assumes that, without import controls or a managed devaluation, the growth of the economy will be moderated by the need to constrain adverse trends in the balance of payments position. Given a continued rise in the labour force in the 1980s and a low rate of growth of gross domestic product, the Group suggests that unemployment could be over 2.5 million by 1985 and over 3.5 million by 1990. Leicester (1977) shows that, with a 2 per cent per annum rate of growth of gross domestic product and a 2.5 per cent annual increase in productivity, unemployment could reach 4 million by the end of the century, even after allowing for further growth in part-time employment and a decline in full-time hours of work. The Growth Project Group at Cambridge (Gibson and Barker, 1979) projects a loss of 1.2 million jobs between 1978 and 1985. The Manpower Research Group (Lindley, 1980) projects an overall decline in employment, based on present economic policies, of nearly 1 million by 1985 which, with an expected increase in the labour force of 1.2 million, could yield a level of unemployment above 3 million.

Beenstock (1979) is critical of these large forecast increases in unemployment. He argues that the labour market will adapt to a reduction in employment with a contraction in the labour force. He suggests that this will occur via the mechanism of a declining or constant real wage. As the previous section showed, the major factors contributing to the recent increases in female labour force participation have been rising real wages and the growth of part-time employment. If real wages remain constant or fall in the face of an inflationary spiral, then there will exist the possibility that women will not be attracted into the labour market in such large numbers as was previously forecast.

Countering this trend is the forecast expansion of employment in those industry orders which are predominant employers of female labour. The Manpower Research Group[4] projects a growth of employment in the national and private health services of about 14 per cent between 1978 and 1985, after allowing for the June 1979 budget measures and the effect of cash limits. Employment in miscellaneous services (sport and recreation, catering and personal services, community services) is expected to grow by about 10 per cent over this seven-year period. For these two sectors, an increase in employment in the region of half a million is projected. Since the proportion of women in miscellaneous services and the health service is between 65 and 75 per cent, employment growth in these areas could continue to offer significant job opportunities for women. In other service sectors, there will be a low rate of employment growth or, in some cases, such as the state education sector, even a decline. Overall, the MRG estimates that total service sector employment could grow by 2–2½ per cent between 1978 and 1985, providing a continuing if much slower increase in the level of female employment. The forecasts of employment decline are concentrated, by contrast, in the manufacturing sector of the economy, with the major impact on male full-time employment.

It seems unlikely that lack of growth of real wages will induce full-time male workers to withdraw from the labour force, given the present system of unemployment registration and benefit payment. However, there is some evidence from the General Household Survey that male labour force participation in the 60–64-year age group has been declining more rapidly than was anticipated by the Department of Employment in its latest labour force projection. As discussed in the previous section, this may be a result of earlier retirement decisions following a prolonged spell of unemployment. If such trends continue, it is possible that high levels of unemployment will reduce the forecast increase in the male labour force between 1978 and 1985 from half a million to 300,000. This does little to cushion the projected decline in employment in the primary and manufacturing sectors of the economy of about 1.5 million persons, over two-thirds of whom will be men. Given these trends in employment and the labour force, it seems likely that male unemployment will rise steadily over the next five years, approaching the two million level in the early eighties.

Official forecasts of the female labour force, particularly the married female labour force, have been notoriously unreliable. As indicated in the previous section, there is every possibility that the female labour force will *not* continue to grow at trend over the next decade. The projected growth in employment in miscellaneous services and the health sector will accommodate some further labour force expansion for women, but the low rate of economic growth will discourage many women from seeking jobs who would otherwise have been in employment. Taking this factor into account, along with the low growth of real earnings and the rise in the birthrate, it seems more likely that the female labour force will increase by about 700,000 between 1978 and 1985, not 850,000 as projected by the DE, although this figure could range between 500,000 and 800,000. The net result of these labour force and employment changes will be a level of registered female unemployment in the region of one million by the mid-eighties. Therefore, even after a substantial downward revision of the official labour force projection, the MRG forecast indicates a doubling of the levels of registered unemployment for both men and women over the next five years.

The forecast decline in employment in the manufacturing sector is derived partly from assumptions about productivity increases over the next decade. Most forecasters assume that productivity will grow fairly slowly in comparison with previous long-term trends. However, Barron and Curnow (1979) argue that the impact of microprocessor technology will lead to large productivity gains and massive unemployment. In producing such estimates they concentrate upon the displacement effects of such technology, largely ignoring the employment effects derived from the demand for new products which incorporate the technological developments.

It is, as yet, too early to assess with accuracy the implications of these developments, but some ideas can be gained by examining a related development, the introduction of large computer systems for data processing, management information and control purposes in the late 1960s. In a careful analysis of this technological change, Stoneman (1975) concluded that if an economy was saturated with this generation of computer technology, it would require 150,000–200,000 fewer employees in comparison with a non-computer economy. These estimates are net of the employment creation effects of computers, mainly in machine operating, programming and system analysis. The occupations most affected are, as one would expect, clerical and office jobs. Stoneman illustrates the transition process and suggests that the net employment effect may require at least twenty-five years to be fully realised.

A comparison with the introduction of microprocessor technology must be made cautiously. This technology represents not merely the advent of a new generation of mini-computing, but covers a wide range of applications, particularly in those areas where the consumer is provided with information; insurance, banking, finance, printing, publishing and distribution are key sectors in this respect. The occupations likely to be most affected are, once again, clerical occupations. Two parallels can be drawn with the introduction of large-scale computing. First, the transition period is likely to be fairly lengthy, taking at least fifteen and probably twenty years before saturation point is reached. Second, part of the implementation will take the form of improving product and service quality rather than pure saving of labour. The two major applications of this technology to date, calculating and timekeeping, have been mainly concerned with the former, and there is plenty of scope for improving the quality of information both within and from organisations, without reference to labour costs. Examples include the improvement in stock control and accounting information within organisations, more detailed bills, invoices and financial statements for customers, a better degree of control over machinery which is presently regulated electro-mechanically, an improved telephone service – but the list is almost inexhaustible.

The overall employment effects resulting from the introduction of microprocessor-based technology are unlikely to be as severe as Barron and Curnow suggest. For specific occupations, particularly clerical jobs, and within certain industries which process large amounts of information, the introduction of micro-electronics will have a significant effect upon the skills required, worker productivity and the nature of the job. Again, without more detailed analysis, it is impossible to predict the overall effect upon employment even in these specific areas, for an increase in the generation of information could offset the productivity gains derived from the new technology.

From the perspective of the family, the major impact upon family welfare will be the decline in full-time male employment throughout the eighties. Periods of unemployment, accompanied possibly by periods of retraining, will be increasingly commonplace for all family members, but especially for men. Young persons will find job entry difficult in late spring and early summer, given the large inflow to the labour force occurring at this time each year. Married women will no longer find it easy to obtain a job after a long period of withdrawal from the labour force and fewer will seek employment than was anticipated in the mid-seventies. Without a major reversal in the government's economic policies, the transition to a high-unemployment economy is likely to occur over the next two or three years. Obviously it is not possible to foresee how government, firms and families will react to such high levels of unemployment. Given that the areas of employment expansion are in those sectors and occupations in which women are heavily concentrated, it could be argued that women will suffer somewhat less than men in terms of the general increase in unemployment. Alternatively, more men might seek jobs in those areas of employment which have traditionally been held by women. In general, though, it seems unlikely that women will make much of an inroad into those jobs which have been the almost exclusive preserve of men (e.g. managerial positions, qualified engineers, skilled craft occupations) simply because the competition between men for such jobs will be high.

Little headway will be made within the broad meaning of the term 'equal employment opportunity' without a clearly defined programme designed to attract women towards craft and technical occupations, the engineering professions and managerial and supervisory positions in all branches of industry and to assist them in gaining the entry qualifications for those jobs, even when demand for such occupations might be in decline as a result of the poor state of the economy. Indeed, the limited progress made to date could easily be reversed in the face of poor employment prospects.

4

Managing Work and Family Life: A Comparative Policy Overview

Sheila Kamerman

Introduction

Most adults in industrialised countries spend a large portion of their daily lives at work, at home or commuting between the two. Whether the worlds of work and the family are complementary or conflicting has major consequences for the quality of their lives.[1] For most adults, thus far, these worlds are in conflict. The question addressed here is, to what extent this conflict can be attenuated, and how.

Work provides the primary source of economic support to families and is a major source of a variety of other satisfactions for family members. The family, in its turn, is the producer of future generations of workers-citizens and a major socialising force in imparting knowledge and skills to each new cohort of youth. Work, however, also operates as a severe constraint on family life, limiting the amount of time available for family tasks and activities and restricting the interaction of a worker with his or her family unit. At the same time, the family may act as a constraint on work performance.

Historically, concern about the work–family relationship has tended to focus on the negative consequences for families and children of (a) the physical separation of work and home, (b) the resulting absence of fathers from the home, and (c) the increased absence of mothers from the home as more women enter the labour force.[2] An implicit assumption has been that if some adaptation were needed, the family would adjust to the demands of the workplace; and, indeed, this has been the case thus far.[3] Furthermore, as long as one adult family member was prepared to remain at home fulfilling all family and home-related responsibilities, the tension between work and family life was tolerable, if sometimes only barely.

In recent years, the growth in female labour force participation rates in all Western industrialised countries has added a new dimension to the work and family relationship question. The rapid increase in labour force participation rates of married women with children (especially those with young children) and the growth in the numbers of lone mothers – who always have been in the labour force in significant numbers – have reduced the extent to which full-time participation in home work is available to support the family. As a consequence, the tension between family and work has become more severe, and far more visible, than previously.

There are those who view this increase in female labour force participation as contributing significantly to family stress and disorganisation: children are inadequately cared for or supervised while mothers work; family routines are disrupted or ignored; working women with independent incomes are more likely to dissolve unsatisfactory marriages; changes in women's roles inevitably lead to changes in men's – or to tension and conflict. An alternative hypothesis, which I have discussed elsewhere (Kamerman, 1979), is that, on the contrary, the growth in female labour force participation may provide the needed catalyst for changing the nature of the work–family relationship in ways which could have lasting and positive consequences for family life and for all family members – men, women and children. Indeed, it is only in those countries experiencing high rates of female labour force participation – where more than half

TABLE 14 LABOUR FORCE PARTICIPATION RATES FOR MEN AND WOMEN, 1975 (i.e. female and male labour force as percentage of respective male and female population aged 15–64)

Country	Women	Men
Australia	48.5	88.8
Austria	48.0	84.4
Belgium	43.9	83.8
Canada	50.0	86.2
Denmark	63.5	89.8
Finland	65.6	79.7
France	56.5	84.4
Germany	48.5	85.7
Greece	30.8	82.7
Iceland	45.1	93.9
Ireland	33.5	92.1
Italy	30.7	81.2
Japan	51.7	89.6
Luxembourg	31.1	85.5
Netherlands	26.9[1]	83.9[1]
New Zealand	39.0	88.0
Norway	53.3	85.9
Portugal	32.0	94.4
Spain	32.5	87.6
Sweden	67.6	89.2
Switzerland	54.6	94.6
Turkey	53.2	92.8
United Kingdom	55.3	91.5
United States	53.1	85.3
Yugoslavia	46.4	85.4
Average	46.2	87.7

Note   [1]Labour force figures expressed in man-years
Source   OECD 1978

the mothers of children under eighteen are in the labour force – that one can identify any real debate about the work and family intersect, and any constructive effort at dealing with the tension between these two domains[4] (see Table 14).

Regardless of whether the increase in the rate and numbers of working women is viewed as a positive or negative development, almost all analysts agree that the phenomenon is a fact of life in industrialised societies, and that in all likelihood, even if there is a temporary increase in unemployment rates, female labour force participation will increase over the next decade.[5] Even in Britain, where there is growing concern about the likelihood of unemployment rising over the next few years, it is generally agreed that female labour force participation rates will be high, probably higher than they are today. Moreover, there is a general consensus in all industrialised countries that if this trend to higher female labour force participation rates continues, the tension between work and family life will grow.

A debate, however, erupts when one explores what an appropriate policy response should be.

The theoretical policy options

There are five alternative policy options which industrialised countries can theoretically employ in response to this development. All involve taking a deliberate stance with regard to where the adaptation should occur (in the family, at work, or both) and who should make the adjustment (men, women, children or some combination; employees, employers or both). I have pointedly described these as 'theoretically distinct' options because, as I indicate later, no country supports a 'pure' policy position. Each position can be qualified or varied. Existing social, political and economic realities in each country, in their interaction, require a unique policy mix.

In so far as we can identify prototypical policy models, they are as follows:

1 A country can decide to reject the idea of a specific policy response, preferring that individuals work out their own solutions in the market-place or through personal arrangements.

2 A country can decide that all adults should work, and therefore, subsidise out-of-home child-care services so that children may be well cared for at reasonable cost to parents.

3 A country can decide that traditional gender roles represent the best way to minimise the strain between work and family life, and subsidise one or a lone parent to remain at home to concentrate fully on home and family responsibilities.

4 A country can decide to permit parents in a two-parent family to choose whether one or both parents will work, and leave a similar choice regarding work to a lone parent. However, parents would be assured of good-quality child-care if they made one choice and protection against economic penalty if they made the other.

5 A country can decide to make it possible for both parents (or a lone parent) to manage family and work responsibilities simultaneously. To achieve this without undue stress for children or parents, a country could enact measures to reorganise work and family life separately and in their relationship.

Needless to say, each option implies values and assumptions about family life, work, and the nature of society and each has implications – costs as well as benefits – for family members (men, women, children) as well as society generally.

In what follows, I discuss each option: (a) describing the types of measures developed in different countries to implement the preferred option in real world terms; (b) exploring where each of these measures is likely to lead, if employed as an exclusive strategy; (c) analysing how and why countries 'package' various measures into a policy and what may be the possible implications of this. Finally, I suggest what a preferred policy might be and how it might be developed, if the goal is to achieve a less conflict-ridden relationship between work and family without penalising families, family members or society.

The policy models

Individuals working out their own solutions

To identify this as a policy option raises a question as to whether the absence of policy is itself a policy choice. Certainly, the experience in several countries, including Britain, would suggest that this is so.

The United States provides a particularly interesting illustration of this position, because there has been much public debate about the consequences or implications of a rapidly accelerating and high female labour force participation rate. Yet no explicit national policy has been developed in response. In 1978, 60 per cent of United States mothers of school-aged children, 50 per cent of mothers of children aged three to five, and 40 per cent of mothers of children under age three were in the labour force; and about two-thirds of these women worked full-time. Despite this situation, widespread public concern about the role of government in society and national paranoia about 'government interference in the family' has led to repeated Congressional rejection of any explicit national policy supporting publicly operated child-care.

Instead of dealing with the fundamental question of how to ensure sufficient quantity and quality of child-care services to the children of working parents, United States policy continues to support the existence of two conceptually and operationally separate but parallel child-care systems: pre-school education and social welfare day-care services. Extensive public funds are spent through tax credits to subsidise a small portion of the private child-care expenses of working parents, while other public monies go to support federally funded day-care centres for the children of the welfare poor (regardless of whether their parents are working) and for the children of some of the working poor. Because there is no national child-care system, most working-class parents are neither eligible for the existing publicly subsidised programmes nor able to purchase high-quality care in the market. Yet, clearly, they must use some kind of care.

The lack of national provision goes well beyond the realm of publicly provided child-care services. The United States is unusual in its failure to provide any kind of statutory maternity benefits for employed women. Nor are there any other national measures directed at facilitating management of work and family life (although there is a policy to make it possible for one group of parents – single mothers on public assistance – to manage family responsibilities and not work, which will be discussed subsequently).

In effect, in every area in which work and family most clearly intersect – child-care for the children of working parents, income replacement for employed women at the time of childbirth, the organisation and structure of work schedules – the United States has opted for avoidance of public provision, and left the solutions to the market or to whatever personal arrangements individuals can make.

Because there is a real need, some market and individual responses have emerged. About 40 per cent of the female labour force is covered, by private insurance, with some form of maternity benefits (providing hospital care and about two to six weeks paid leave after childbirth at some portion of prior earnings). Close to 60 per cent of the children aged three to five are in some form of pre-school education programme (or are already in first grade of school) but most of this is part-day and much is private. Another large group of children are in day-care centres or in informally and privately arranged family day care (i.e. with child minders).

When interviewed, working parents with young children list the absence of good, reasonably priced child-care as their primary problem in coping with work and family responsibilities. Their solutions include: working different shifts so as to share child-care between them; depending on the help of relatives, friends, neighbours – often several in combination each week; organising a complicated package of nursery school, child minder, and one or more neighbours. As a result, the children of working parents may experience three, four or even more kinds of care in an average week, as they spend part of the day in a pre-school programme and another part with one or two child minders, and are brought to and from these services by a parent, a neighbour or still a different person.

Apart from the child-care problem, working parents complain

bitterly about the rigidity and unresponsiveness of the workplace. Few changes have occurred there, despite a labour force made up increasingly of women with children and the husbands of these women. Beginning hours at work often conflict with school opening times (and schools are equally rigid about when they open and close). Most jobs still do not provide maternity leave or paid time off if a child is ill. Talking to women who live this way makes it very clear that being a member of the labour force and a full-time parent in many communities in the United States means trying to manage against overwhelming odds in an unresponsive society.[6]

The result is largely one of great stress on working women with young children as they attempt to organise complicated and multiple child-care arrangements in an environment in which most women continue to be expected to bear primary responsibility for home and family even while working full-time. Neither the community nor the workplace has made any adaptation to the changed reality. Families manage in a variety of ways, at best only partially satisfactory. The long-term consequences for parents and children cannot be assessed as yet.

We turn now to an examination of those policy options in which the decision has been to develop specific measures directed at the work–family intersection.[7]

Subsidising out-of-home child-care services

Given the traditional view of women as carrying primary responsibility for child-care and child bearing, it is no wonder that women identify child-care as their major problem or need if they are to work outside the home. In most countries the growth in female labour force participation occurred first among older women and then among those with school-aged children. School still represents the most significant child-care institution outside the family, even though the caring function is secondary to that of providing a formal education. In general, women with school-aged children continue to have significantly higher labour force participation rates than those with pre-school children (see Table 15).

There are several reasons for this. Compulsory school, which begins at age five, six or seven depending on the country, includes provision for almost all children, thus ensuring supervised care while school is open. In some countries, there are extensive supplementary school programmes – either a long school day which includes a variety of special activities in addition to formal 'learning' programmes (such as in the German Democratic Republic) or supervised arrangements where children can do their homework after school (as in France) or supervised independent leisure-time centres (as in Sweden). Many women, in many countries, work part-time, so that their work day and

TABLE 15 LABOUR FORCE PARTICIPATION RATES OF WOMEN BY AGE OF CHILD, 1976 (percentages)

Country	Labour force participation rates for women with children		
	0-3 years	3-6 years	School-age
France	43	44	48
Federal Republic of Germany	32	34	41
German Democratic Republic	80	85	85
Great Britain[1]	21	31	57
Hungary	82[2]	75	75
Sweden	58	64	78
United States	35	48	56

Note [1]Figures for Great Britain refer to 1978, and to the proportion of *children* with working mothers. The second column is for children aged 3-4 years.
[2]Includes women home on child-care leave: 33% if these women are excluded.

Sources Kamerman and Kahn 1980: Central Statistical Office, 1979, Table 3.3

the school day coincide. Supplementary child-care services for school holidays may be organised separately, and are easier to arrange than all-day care for younger children.

Nevertheless, a large group of women – the largest group in many countries – work full-time and continue to use a variety of informal supplementary services, not because there is no recognition of the need for more formal arrangements but because these have not yet been developed. Where these services are concerned, the lag in development usually reflects the pressure from other priorities.

Establishment of pre-school education programmes, in particular those for children from age three to compulsory school entry, has received the highest priority during the last twenty years. Indeed, in those countries where most 3–6-year-olds attend pre-school programmes, their mothers work at about the same rate as women with older children. For example, despite the fact that female labour force participation rates are about 80 per cent higher in the German Democratic Republic than in France (87 per cent in the GDR; 48 per cent in France), there is relatively little difference in labour force participation rates between women with children aged three to six and women with school-aged children, in either country. Both countries are unusual, however, in that they have very extensive pre-school programmes, serving 90 per cent in the GDR and about 95 per cent of this age group in France (regardless of whether mothers work). Indeed, France has the highest proportion of pre-school places for this age group of any country in the world. Moreover, since the French programme is open to children from age two, 27 per cent of the two-year-olds attended in 1977, and provision is currently projected for 45 per cent of this age group within the next two years.

The French pre-school, the *école maternelle*, is a publicly funded programme (private programmes represent a very small proportion of the overall number of pre-school programmes) operated within a separate administrative structure under the auspices of the public education system. The basic programme covers the normal school day (8.30 or 9 to 11.30 or 12 and 12.30 or 1 to 3.30 or 4), with extensive supplementary care (before school opens, at lunch, after school closes, Wednesdays when schools are closed) available especially in schools located in working-class neighbourhoods. The basic programme is, of course, free. The supplementary programmes are heavily subsidised. Some observers have expressed concern about very large groups of children (thirty-five and often larger) with very few adult staff (a teacher and usually one assistant). However, the enthusiasm of French parents for the programme is quite clear from their use of it.

Only a few countries as yet have enough places in pre-school for all children whose parents want them to participate. In addition to France and the GDR, Belgium and Israel are among the few which now serve 90 per cent or more of this group. However, several Eastern European countries, as well as the Federal Republic of Germany (FRG), have places for 75 per cent or more of 3–6-year-olds.

Two other developments are especially noteworthy, with regard to out-of-home care for children of this age. First is that the predominant type of care, by far, is the group or centre-based programme. In all countries where a national child-care policy[8] has emerged the position taken is to support the development of group programmes (pre-school, as part of the overall school system, or freestanding and independent). Even in a country such as Sweden where pre-school programmes still do not exist in sufficient quantity to serve all children whose parents want them to participate, national policy stresses group, centre-based programmes, not family day care or child minding. Where child minding is extensive in such countries, it is seen as a stop-gap measure. The argument is: children develop better in group programmes, and need the peer stimulation, the facilities and the trained staff which can only be provided in a group setting. Only in those countries which have yet to develop a national policy in this field is there debate about expanding child minding for children aged three and older.

A second and closely related development, characterising the last few years, is the rapid increase in the number of two-year-olds entering these pre-school programmes. Here, it seems to be largely a situation in which demand and supply are converging quite happily. I mentioned earlier that the French *école maternelle* serves, by law, children aged two to six and that over one quarter of the two-year-olds (largely 2½-year-olds) now attend, with an expectation that almost half will participate by the end of 1980. Although the programme is open to children of non-working as well as working mothers, priority for two-year-olds is given to the children of working mothers. Given the labour force participation rates of these women, places for 45 per cent of all two-year-olds would probably mean that all such children of working mothers could be cared for. Several other countries are now lowering the age of entry into their pre-school programmes, as the demand for group care grows with the increase in working mothers, and as the birthrate declines in some countries making more space available in programmes previously serving a larger cohort of children aged three and over. Since child development theory underscores the absence of any good rationale for providing a group experience for children specifically at three – and there is some argument that *if* a distinction is to be made, age two could be more appropriate – some psychologists, too, support such a trend. Thus child development theory, demography, labour market trends and parental preferences all seem to converge on the expansion of pre-school group or centre-based programmes for children, beginning at the age of two.

In contrast, although there is a growing consensus in many countries regarding group care for children aged two and older, debate and lack of consensus continue around the question of what kind of out-of-home care is best for younger children, in particular those from about six months of age to two years. Here, too, services are increasing in all industrialised countries. Moreover, group care is expanding too, even for these children. However, child minding continues to be dominant in most countries, either because it is available, it is preferred by some parents, it is viewed as a cheaper form of care, or it is seen as closer to 'family' or 'mother' care.

The GDR is the country with the most extensive group care for children under three, serving 60 per cent of the children aged five months (when the paid maternity leave ends) to three years, but 80 per cent of the one- and two-year-olds, the ages for which the programme is especially designed. Some additional expansion is planned for these programmes, but only enough to serve about 70 per cent of the entire cohort. Here, a preference for group care is the dominant policy position and the dominant type of care. In contrast, although group care is the preferred method in Swedish policy, too, actual provision is nowhere near sufficient and family day care continues to be extensively used and supported.

France has the most extensive out-of-home care for children under three of any Western country, covering about one-third of the group. In contrast to others, it also has the most diversity. Two-year-olds are largely in group care, primarily the *école maternelle*, but also crèche (or day care). For the under-twos, however, out-of-home care is overwhelmingly some form of family day care, either licensed and supervised or informal and private. Only a very small number can be served in the limited places available in the crèches. France has the most extensive amount of licensed family day care of any country in the world and is placing growing stress on the significance of licensing, even where the child minder is a relative. The debate about family day care versus crèche continues in France, but it is carried on in a context in which the need for *more* out-of-home care continues to be acknowledged. In contrast to several other countries, such as the United States, the Federal Republic of Germany and the United Kingdom, the argument is only as to the type of care to be expanded – family day care or group care – not as to whether care should be expanded.

To summarise:

1 Growing attention is being paid to the need for services and programmes to supplement the standard school day for the school-aged children of working parents, but there is no systematic picture of what exists or what is preferred as yet.

2 There has been an extraordinary expansion in pre-school programmes for children from about age three to compulsory school entry during the past decade. Group programmes have clearly emerged as the preferred type of care. Although significant differences exist in the way in which these programmes are designed across countries, the similarities are greater than the differences.

3 There is a growing tendency for two-year-olds to participate in pre-school programmes regardless of whether the programmes were open to this age group previously or whether a decline in the size of the 3-6-year-old cohort has made more places available. In both cases it is the growing demand by parents that is now being met.

4 There is no clear pattern in the development of out-of-home care for children under two, but there is growing pressure for increased public provision. In some countries the preferred type of care is group and centre-based; in others, family day care is preferred; in still others, both.

5 Because of the paucity of services and the extent to which their children clearly need care, parents with children under age three are the ones who experience the greatest tension between work and family life, in most countries. Regardless of what other help is available, in the absence of help with child-care, one parent must be at home. Subsidised out-of-home care is still nowhere near adequate to meet the demands of working parents.

Subsidising parents at home

If one explores the extent to which countries subsidise women (or a parent) to remain at home, two questions are central: Are there full subsidies available – a full wage substitute – for parents with very young children in those countries which do not provide sufficient child-care services for this age group? Are there partial subsidies available for parents with somewhat older children, where child-care is not readily available for a full work day, and thus one parent can only work part-time?

Short-term wage replacement, covering a brief period of time before and after childbirth (and almost always for employed women), characterises almost all industrialised countries. This type of social insurance benefit was developed first as part of health or sickness insurance programmes in many countries after the Second World War. However, such benefits have been strengthened, extended – or first initiated – in several countries during the last ten to fifteen years, following the increase in female labour force participation. Begun initially as a form of health protection for mothers and children, the policy objective in several countries now includes support of the psychological adjustment of mother and child, as well as protection against loss of income as a consequence of childbirth. In recent years, there has been growing discussion of the need to define fathers as eligible for the benefit too, as child development research stresses the significance of fathers in children's lives, and as concern for male and female equality underscores the value of equal treatment for men and women in their parenting and family roles as well as in their work roles.

Sweden was the first country, in 1974, to change its maternity leave policy to a *parental* insurance benefit. It is also the country which provides the most extensive benefit. The most significant part of the parent insurance is its replacement of 90 per cent of full wage (up to the maximum wage under social insurance) for nine months following childbirth (or adoption), with up to six weeks to be taken if preferred, before expected birth. Parents may share the benefit, with either mother or father leaving work to remain at home to care for a child, and receiving temporary wage replacement. Moreover, the last three months of the benefit may be used at any time until the child is eight years old, either as full-time leave or as a proportionately longer period of part-time work, again by either or both parents. However important income replacement is, parent insurance in Sweden is designed to achieve still more. By permitting parents to share the benefit and to use it to subsidise part-time work, two other objectives are accomplished: (a) children spend a shorter day away from home when parents have more time to spend with their children; and (b) an explicit national policy has now been implemented, in support of male and female equality at home and at work. These are significant for both work and family life, as will be discussed subsequently.

When the parental insurance was first instituted in 1974, only 2 per cent of the eligible fathers used the benefit. Since then, however, the proportion has grown rapidly. In 1977 close to 11 per cent of the eligible fathers used the benefit for an average of forty days. Men with highly educated wives or with wives holding relatively high-level jobs are more likely to use the benefit, as are men who are governmental employees. In 1976, for example, over 11 per cent of fathers who worked in the public sector, but only 7 per cent of those who worked in the private corporate sector, used the benefit. The number is continuing to grow, although precise data are not yet available. Take-up for 1978 was estimated at close to 14 per cent.

Norway and Finland are the only other countries which now permit fathers to share the entitlement to post-childbirth leave and to the parallel work-related cash benefit. Each permits fathers to use up to two weeks of this benefit. (Norway, like Sweden and France, also provides an entitlement for parents to an extended unpaid supplementary leave. In Norway, this leave is available until the child's first birthday.)

There is growing discussion in many European countries regarding the need to increase the length of the post-childbirth leave, as well as to extend entitlement to fathers. Priority has been given, thus far, to lengthening the leave. Where three months was typical for most countries in the early 1970s, six months is now becoming the common period for paid leave. In most cases, the benefit level is equal to full wage replacement, up to whatever is the maximum covered wage. Pressure to extend the benefit still further continues; however, the terms of the debate are such that no one seems to be suggesting more than a maximum of one year for such social insurance protection for working parents.[9]

One immediate consequence of this benefit is that the age of entry into day care in different countries is in direct relation to the length of the paid leave. Thus, where the leave is relatively short, as in France, one sees much younger infants in day-care centres than in Sweden, or indeed the GDR, which offers a supplementary lower level maternity leave benefit covering an additional twenty-six weeks (making up one year in all) to mothers having a second and subsequent child, and a special cash benefit to a single mother who cannot find a place for her child in a day-care centre. Another long-term consequence may be that the future child-care debate in several countries will focus primarily on the one-year-olds, as fewer children under one need care, and more children aged two and older enter pre-school programmes.

Given current post-childbirth leave of about six months in most countries, the need for economic support for about two years still remains for many families, even in those countries where there are universal or close to universal pre-school programmes for children aged two and a half and older. What, if anything, is provided for these families? Here, Hungary is unique in its new 'social invention' – the child-care grant. This is a universal, flat rate, cash benefit, provided to women who have previously been in the labour force. The grant begins on completion of the twenty-week maternity leave following childbirth (the payment for which is wage-related) and lasts for up to thirty-one months, or until a child is aged three. In effect, the benefit represents leave from employment with full wage, fringe benefit and seniority protection, in addition to the uniform cash payment. The money part of the benefit, for one child, is equal to about 40 per cent of the average female wage (and more than twice this for a woman who has two children under three). Women who receive this benefit are defined as part of the labour force, but at home on child-care leave.

Certainly, one consequence of this benefit is to provide an incentive for young women to enter the labour market at an early age, as soon as they complete their schooling. Moreover, it practically guarantees return to active labour force participation, since the grant is terminated abruptly when a child reaches its third birthday. Although a pronatal incentive is built into this policy (and several others) by increasing the benefit for second and third children, it is not yet possible to determine whether there are any long-term fertility effects. Thus far, there seem to be only calendar effects, with births being spaced more closely together, and there is certainly no indication that more families are having more than two children, despite a goal of the policy being an increase in births and family size. There is some evidence that male and female roles tend to return to traditional models in families where women are at home on extended child-care leave, and that these are harder to change over time.

Initiated first in 1967 during a period of over-supply of unskilled female labour, this benefit has been modified and made more flexible in its use in more recent years, as the Hungarian labour market has become tighter; for example, women at home on leave can now break into their leave once a year and return to work. This benefit has been extremely popular, and well over 80 per cent of those eligible use it, at least for some period of time. (About 15 per cent of those eligible return to work at the end of their maternity leave, or sooner.) It is significant, however, that the less educated, less skilled, lower-wage-earning women use it longest, usually for the full period of entitlement, while highly educated and more skilled women use it for about one year, or until their child is about eighteen months old.

Czechoslovakia provides a similar benefit for second and subsequent children, for two years. The GDR and Austria provide cash benefits which under certain circumstances are available to mothers at home until a child is age one. The FRG is debating provision of a similar benefit, but probably on a means-tested basis, until a child is one, having recently extended its maternity leave to seven and a half months. Apart from these countries, no other provides a non-income-tested cash benefit, equal to a significant portion of wage, beyond the short-term social insurance benefit linked to post-childbirth leave.

A few countries do provide a long-term means-tested cash benefit for lone mothers. Many countries have experienced an extraordinary growth in the number of lone-parent familes – usually female-headed – during the last two decades. Indeed, lone parenthood – not just unwed motherhood, but also the result of more frequent separation and divorce – is an increasingly likely experience for many women in their childbearing years. Moreover, this status characterises a large percentage of poor families in several countries.

In the UK, the USA, Canada, Israel and the FRG, low-income lone mothers may be entitled to social assistance or supplementary benefits for as long as they have a minor child at home, or for a substantial portion of that time. Much current social assistance policy is based on the assumption that women do not – and should not – work; and that if a woman has no husband to support her, society will provide a substitute for the needed economic assistance. Clearly, this is an obsolete policy in those countries where most married women now work – including married women with young children – as well as most lone mothers. Given this trend, it is difficult to understand the rationale in countries continuing to subsidise low-income lone mothers to remain outside the labour force for a long time. Inevitably, these women will be thrust back into the labour market when their children are older. When that happens, the women are often destitute, with no labour market skills, left outside the mainstream of a society in which most adults work. The real issue should be how to supplement the income of a low-wage single earner in a family, rather than to offer support at home beyond a brief period of time.

Several countries do provide universal and/or selective benefits which supplement rather than substitute for earned income, and make it possible for two-parent families to manage on only one wage. These benefits are usually designed to be attractive to families in which the second wage earner is low-skilled and can earn, at best, only a low wage. The Swedish housing allowance, which is received by half the families with children under seventeen, offers this option to many low-income families. The French family allowance system is, of course, a much better known example. A combination of the universal allowance provided for all second and subsequent children and the income-tested *complément familial*[10] provided to families with at least one child under three or three or more children (both tax-free benefits), may offer inducement or compensation to *low wage earning* women, with husbands earning average or higher wages, to remain out of the labour force. But, except for the short-term and income-tested lone-parent allowances, none of the French benefits now provides a real substitute for earned income, a point returned to in the next section.

Family Income Supplement (FIS), in Britain, offers a means-tested income supplement to working parents. Eligibility is very limited, however, and the benefit is of real value primarily to lone parents for whom the definition of full-time work is now reduced to twenty-four hours per week. As a consequence, some low-income single mothers can now work part-time and receive income supplementation, making it easier for them to cope with their responsibilities.

To summarise:

1 Almost all countries provide a social insurance benefit protecting families against the loss of income following childbirth and the temporary withdrawal of the mother from the labour force. The standard length of this protection is about six months with some discussion of its extending to one year, but no longer. Three countries permit parents to share at least some portion of this leave, and pressure for this principle is growing.

2 Among those countries without extensive out-of-home childcare services for very young children, only one provides a universal subsidy that is equal to a significant portion of a wage. Even this benefit, in Hungary, is available for a maximum period of thirty-one months until a child is age three. The impact of the benefit is mixed, as to both fertility effects and labour market effects. For example, the extent to which labour market behaviour can be modified to respond to short-term swings in the economy remains an open question; policies instituted for one reason may develop a constituency and dynamic of their own and be difficult to change, even when the original reason for developing the policy is no longer present. On the other hand, the benefit does assure early labour market socialisation and long-term attachment. But it probably also reinforces traditional gender roles, at home and in the labour market.

3 Some countries provide means-tested cash benefits representing the equivalent of low wage (or partial wage) substitutes for lone mothers for an extended period of time. The consequences here seem to be the creation of an under-class or at best a group of women who are deprived to begin with and are then further alienated from the mainstream of society. In effect, women with marginal labour market skills are encouraged to let whatever skills they might have atrophy. The result is the creation of a distinctly marginal group in the society, at high risk of poverty and an economic burden to the society as well.

4 Some countries provide a cluster of what has been called elsewhere 'family benefits' – universal and/or selective cash or in-kind benefits which may supplement low family income so that families may manage, at least for a while, with only one parent as wage earner, or in the case of a lone mother, with one wage earner working part-time.[11] Included among these are family and housing allowances.

5   Thus far, few of these long-term benefits are available to men.
One consequence may be to disadvantage women even further in
those societies in which income is contingent on earnings and earnings
reflect labour market history and continuity. For single mothers, this
also means disadvantage for children.

Subsidising choice

The fourth theoretical model I have identified is a policy in which
personal choice and parental preferences are the dominant values.
This is a very popular option on the level of discussion in countries yet
to develop a distinctive policy. There is often consensus about it in
many forums in the USA, the UK and France. Indeed, the French
official policy stance is that national policy should be precisely this: to
support parental choice. In theory, this would mean sufficient
provision of subsidised child-care services so that all who wished to
use them could obtain a place, and sufficient income support so that all
who wished to remain at home to care for a child could do so without
suffering financial penalty.

To what extent does this exist in France? To what extent is it a
feasible policy option anywhere? According to French experts, the
reality is that only high-income families have a real choice in deciding
whether a lone parent or one parent in a two-parent family can remain
at home rather than work. To make this an option for low-income
families too, the French should provide sufficient places in crèches so
that all children in families with incomes under a specified level can
attend. At the same time, they should provide a cash benefit equal to
an average net wage for a lone parent and perhaps half an average
wage for a two-parent, one-wage-earner family, to those among this
same low-income group of families who prefer to stay at home.

Clearly, neither is the case at present. Half the children under three
in France have working mothers. Of these, a little over 40 per cent are
in supervised, licensed care (18 per cent in the *école maternelle*, 4 per
cent in crèches, and the remainder in licensed family day care); 20
per cent are in informal, privately arranged family day care; and the
remaining 40 per cent are in a miscellany of care including in-home
care by domestic servants, relatives, neighbours or friends. The
waiting lists for crèche places are very long. The costs for privately
arranged family day care are very high. Obviously, there are not
enough subsidised, supervised places for the children of all those
women who are now working, let alone those who are not working but
might decide to, if good, reasonably priced and convenient child care
were available.

The problem is similar if one explores the adequacy of benefit
provision, even without considering whether some of those using child-
care might prefer benefits, or vice versa. The average female wage in

France is relatively low, about 65 per cent of male wages, and median female wages are about equal to the minimum wage (2,100 FF, July 1979). Yet no benefit approaches this in value. Thus the *complément familial*,[10] at 395 FF (July 1979), is equal to less than 25 per cent of the minimum wage. An income-tested housing allowance supplements this somewhat. A recent French study found that for *some* families, the difference between family income which includes one wage plus income-tested but tax-free benefits, and family income with two wages minus benefits, taxes and contributions, is relatively small (CERC, 1979). For such families there may be little pecuniary advantage for women to work. However, it is unclear how large a group this is.

When discussing private choice as a policy option, many people really mean supplementing income, on the assumption that the only constraint on choice is the economic pressure to work. A private-choice model would make it possible for parents to choose either role – and to do that requires increased provision of services as well as a substantial cash benefit. Not only is this extremely expensive, but it is impossible to make any firm projections of take-up. Preferences have a dynamic all their own; they often change as reality and social context change. Thus the availability of more child-care services might stimulate more women to use them, or the expansion in benefit provision might have counter-effects. These cannot be determined at the outset.

Another problem with this model is its potential for leading to increased income inequalities among families. There is a distinct propensity for those with similar education to marry one another; and education is highly correlated with occupational status, and, more important, income level. Providing an incentive (a low-cash benefit) for low-skilled and low-educated women to drop out of the labour force, while highly educated women continue to work and earn relatively high salaries, would inevitably result in still greater disparity between rich and poor, since those families in which income is high even with only one wage-earner would be more likely to have two wage-earners and, therefore, a higher income.

To summarise:

1 A policy in support of real choice requires extensive provision of both child-care services and an extensive cash benefit, with no way of knowing, in advance, what take-up will be of each. (Indeed I would argue that supporting choice means making it possible for parents to manage both roles if they wish.)

2 If the benefit were universal, it would be extraordinarily expensive. If income-tested, it would have all the disadvantages of selectivity, exacerbated further by segregating low-income families from other families, and women from men.

3   No country has, thus far, implemented such a policy, although the French have begun to explore supporting choice for some low-income married women.

4   Most countries, when the issue of choice is raised, mean cashing-out the service provision and giving a cash benefit that families can use either to purchase care in the market or to supplement income. This has been partially incorporated in the US child-care tax credit, and partially in some of the discussion regarding a means-tested child-rearing grant in the FRG.[12] In neither case can this be viewed as real support of choice.

Restructuring work and family life

I began by exploring the implications of a country's declaring that the market and personal arrangements were the preferred societal response to increased tension between work and family life resulting from more women working outside the home. I described some of the consequences resulting from such an approach. I continued by describing a model in which the policy is to support out-of-home child-care services to make it possible for adults to work. However, as I pointed out, no country has full coverage for all children under two or three, and there is still a major problem in several countries for families with children aged three to six or older, when parents wish to work full-time, beyond the hours of the standard school day. Moreover, even where full-time child care is available, there may be a problem for some parents who are concerned about the length of time spent by their young children in a group, especially if the parental work day includes a long period of commuting.[13] There is also a disadvantage for women, if the family decision is for one parent to work part-time, since it is usually the woman who takes on such work. I then explored a policy strategy in which the parents of very young children are subsidised to remain at home. Although this policy is available to all families in only one country (and even there, only for women), it still warranted further exploration as to its potential feasibility elsewhere. In analysing this option, it seems clear that a full wage replacement for an extended period of time would be both unacceptably expensive and socially undesirable in that it would fix differences between low and high wage earners. Provision of a uniform benefit at a more economic level, even if it were universal, would attract only women, and usually the less educated ones, with obvious consequences. Moreover, subsidising women at home for any length of time would leave them disadvantaged in the labour market, just as prolonged dependency in marriage may create in later years the economically impotent 'displaced homemaker'. Finally, I have noted that the so-called choice model suffers from many of the same disadvantages of either the service or the benefit model, with some additional problems of its own as regards cost and the difficulty of projecting take-up.

What other alternative is there?

I turn here to the fifth policy model, restructuring work and family life to make it possible for adults to manage both roles simultaneously, without undue stress for any family member. One country, Sweden, has actively begun to discuss this as a principle for policy development. Sweden has moved only a small way in this direction, but its approach is worth describing as the only operating policy in which this principle represents a guiding value. It also provides a take-off point for suggesting the additional components needed to make this model truly workable.

Sweden provides an extensive parent insurance benefit, described earlier, which covers full wage replacement for either parent for a maximum of nine months following childbirth and permits three months of the benefit to be allocated over any time before the child's eighth birthday, either to extend vacations or to subsidise part-time work at a full-time wage. An amount equal to an adult's own sick leave, paid at the same rate, is provided, to permit an employed parent to care for an ill child at home, and there is also an entitlement to one day off per year per child to go to the child's school. Swedish parents now also have a right to take unpaid leave from work until their child is eighteen months old, and to work part-time (i.e. six hours a day) until a child is aged eight. Sweden is making extensive efforts to expand its child-care services (day nursery provision, for example, is due to double between 1975 and 1982, from 74,000 to 179,000 places). Unlike those of most other countries, these services are included in one pre-school programme for children aged six months to seven years (Swedish Institute, 1980).

All of this is provided in a society in which work and employment are central values, and where female wages are closer to male wages than in any other European country (now about 90 per cent of average male wages in industry) (Swedish Institute, 1980). Most women, however, still work part-time because child-care services remain in insufficient quantity for all those who need and/or want them.[14] Women – and lone mothers especially – still dominate the low income group.

A policy mix: the benefit–service package

I stated at the outset that although five theoretical models could be identified, in the real world countries tend to develop a policy mix, what has been described elsewhere as a 'benefit–service package' (Kamerman and Kahn, 1980). As women move increasingly into the labour market, all countries experiencing this development respond in some way – to make it easier for women to work, or easier for them to remain at home.[15] Since the phenomenon of women working has its own dynamic, only partly controllable by public policy, and each policy once implemented generates its dynamic too, countries find that *no one strategy* will satisfy all values. As a consequence, each country develops its own benefit–service package in which either the benefit or the service side may be given primacy, but the components vary over time and the balance shifts.

Thus, the GDR, which has needed women in the labour force in the past and continues to need them, has constantly stressed out-of-home child-care services above all else. Yet, faced with a declining population and birthrate, it developed a significant benefit package beginning in the early 1970s, to make it possible for women to manage family responsibilities in addition to work. In addition to extended maternity leave, women are also entitled to paid 'personal days' each month to take care of home responsibilities. Traditional views of gender roles remain, however, and the benefit package covers women only, in a society where women still carry the dual burden of home and work and still earn only about 60 per cent of male wages.

Hungary instituted its child-care grant to encourage low-skilled women to withdraw from the labour market for a few years, at a time when there was an over-supply of such labour. Concern about demographic patterns and fertility led to modifications of the grant (and other benefits) in pro-natalist ways. Now, with a much tighter labour market and a need for women to work, it is hard to change a policy which is extremely popular and fully integrated into the society. Despite its popularity, well-educated women want to work, and need child-care services. Thus, Hungary is making the child-care leave more flexible now. Furthermore, Hungary is also expanding its child-care programmes. At the same time, there is growing discussion of the inclusion of men as beneficiaries of both the wage-related post-childbirth leave and the child-care grant.

The French policy, which by definition involves both benefits and services, is still debated as concern grows about the cost of child-care services on the one hand, and the decline in fertility on the other. Support for the *école maternelle* is, however, overwhelming, and clearly this programme will expand to serve more two-year-olds, regardless of cost. The French policy debate is unusual in that here the context includes a long history of extensive popular support for pre-school education and relatively little concern with labour market policy. Thus, although out-of-home care is more readily available here than in any other Western country, it is taken for granted by many. In part, because labour market issues have always been less salient in the debate, there is little attention to other aspects of the work–family interface.

In other countries, such as the FRG, not only does the dominant ideology stress traditional gender roles, but the current economic situation reinforces the pattern. Women belong at home; what is more, given the growing concern with unemployment, it is better for the society if they remain there. If the employment situation should change, the FRG could return to a policy of importing more foreign labour than encouraging women to work. To some this seems shortsighted and costly. Despite this ideology, women continue to enter the labour force in growing numbers in the FRG. Whether expanded benefits can provide an incentive to counteract this trend remains to be seen. An alternative is that as more women enter the labour force, the FRG policy will be modified in other ways. The debate now deals with experimental family day care (but for the poor) and child-care grants (again for the poor, and experimentally in one state only for lone mothers).

Finally, in Sweden, labour market policy has been paramount. Women were needed in the labour force, and they needed support to enter. The Swedes deliberately decided to encourage women rather than foreign workers into the labour market. Among other reasons, foreign workers with families require a large expenditure for additional services: housing, health and education services. Encouraging women to enter the labour market may mean an increased expenditure on child-care programmes and certain benefits, but this is much less costly than the alternative. Moreover, many are convinced that such provision is essential for improving the quality of life generally in the society, as is achievement of a supplementary goal: equality for men and women.[16] One consequence is that Sweden has been one of the first countries to define the family – or social – policy debate in terms of the work and family relationship rather than as a sex-role issue.

Towards a closer relationship between work and family: a broader policy strategy

Clearly, my particular concern is with reducing the tension between work and family life and making it easier for all adults to manage both domains. Work remains a central role for all adults – not just men. Societies need children if there are to be future generations, and they need them to be well cared for if they are to function as productive and creative adults and nurturing parents to subsequent generations. Children are a source of personal joy to parents, too; and, it has become increasingly clear, children need care and attention from fathers as well as mothers.

As more women with young children enter the labour market, it becomes impossible to ignore the tension between work and family life for all. This then becomes an issue for the whole society. I repeat: my basic assumption is that women are in the labour force to stay and that despite any increase in temporary unemployment their labour force participation rates will continue to increase over the next decade. Growth rates may be less rapid in those countries where most women are already working, but there is no evidence that this trend will be reversed. Moreover, the non-pecuniary satisfactions are such that women, like men, will view work as part of their individual identities.[17]

One problem will be to make it possible for women to achieve wage and occupational equality with men. Such a goal entails addressing labour market issues as well as assuring women that they will not be penalised by having to carry both work and family responsibilities while men concentrate fully on work.

A more important problem is to make it possible for men as well as women to have satisfactory family lives, with adequate time and energy for parental and marital activities and responsibilities. Children need the attention and interest of both parents. Adults need the opportunity to participate in the two worlds of work and family, if they are to lead full lives.

Some countries will define the problem as a 'woman's problem' or a 'woman and child-care problem', designing solutions that take acount of the needs of women and children only.[18] Such a response will alleviate a portion of the immediate problem but will not address the more fundamental tension between work and family life. Nor can the needs of women, children and society be satisfied if men are not part of the solution.

The debate in many countries suggests some recognition of this. What was discussed in the 1960s as a problem resulting from the changing role of women in society and was debated in the 1970s as the problem of the changing roles of men *and* women, now, as we enter the 1980s, has been redefined. There is growing awareness that the fundamental issue is not just the changes in gender roles, but the nature of the relationship between work and family life in a society in which all adults are likely to work, yet children are wanted and the society needs them, and, indeed, needs them to be well cared for if the society is to survive.

Managing work and family life simultaneously is an overwhelming problem for families with young children – for the adults as well as for their children. To make this possible without harmful consequences for the family or the society at large requires a multi-faceted policy, involving public provision, employment adaptation, and individual flexibility. Family members have already revealed their willingness and capacity to be flexible. We need now to develop the other components. The ideal public policy benefit–service package reflecting the values which I have here expressed would need to include at its core:

1 A social insurance benefit covering wage replacement for either parent for one year after childbirth, to be shared between them, to ensure for children the opportunity to have the care and attention of both parents when it is most important and to permit parents to provide such care without economic penalty.

2   Full job protection including seniority and pension rights during this period.

3   An entitlement to paid sick leave for employed parents of young children to care for an ill child at home, on the same basis that they receive a wage replacement benefit when they themselves are ill.

4   Reasonably priced, conveniently located, good-quality subsidised group or pre-school programmes for children under compulsory school age, as part of a country's education system or independently administered. The consensus seems clear regarding such programmes for two-year-olds and older. Although there is no consensus as to the preferred programme type for younger children, it seems hard to argue for a separate, special programme for 1–2-year-olds, given the range of preferences parents express and the position various experts take. I would argue for adequate space in group care for the children of parents preferring such care, as well as continued support for licensed, supervised family day care, not only as interim provision but also for those who prefer this type of care and those with children who need the more intensive, potentially therapeutic environment of a specially trained family day-care mother.

Such a benefit–service package is still only a part of an overall policy directed at supporting work and family roles. Both a shorter work day and more flexible work schedules are obviously central here, too. For those who are convinced that technology will replace much existing work, a shorter work day for all is an obvious solution. Perhaps more important is the fact that there has been little change since the Second World War in the length of the work day and week in industrialised countries as workers have opted for increases in earnings rather than shorter hours. When the current inflation–recession–unemployment crisis is passed, it may be time to consider the alternative of a six-hour day. Certainly, if one important value continues to be male and female *equity* in both family and work, part-time work for certain jobs is not an answer as long as women are the ones most likely to take such jobs.

Finally, I would emphasise that the policy framework I am proposing assumes that employment opportunities and labour market policy are a cornerstone of social policy in industrialised countries.[19] Even where unemployment occurs, some attention must be paid to the implicit assumption that only male unemployment is a problem. What is more important, however, is that in those societies in which work is the primary adult role and a central ethic, support must be provided so that all adults can manage work and family life. Unless this is possible the society will suffer a significant loss in productivity in the labour market and in the economy, but perhaps more important, ultimately, in the quantity and quality of future generations.

5

Statutory Maternity Leave in the United Kingdom: A Case Study

Nickie Fonda

12 November 1975 marked a significant date in the relationship between work and the family in Britain. On that date, the Royal Assent was given to the Employment Protection Act which, for the first time, embodied a right for women to choose to combine work and parenthood by returning to their jobs after childbirth. This chapter reviews what is publicly known about how these provisions were incorporated into the Act, discusses what is known about employers' experience to date in implementing and operating these provisions and concludes with a discussion of some of the lessons to be drawn and of some likely (and not so likely) future developments.

Background

Until the mid-1970s it could be said that British government policy related to work and the family coherently embodied, and reinforced, the assumption that there should be a division of labour between the sexes: the man who is capable of work has a duty to provide the primary support for his family, while the woman's place is in the home, to care for the household and family. Only when the needs of the economy are such that 'women's work' is seen as necessary has this belief been modified, and then only for so long as the needs have lasted.

Social security and income tax legislation show this perspective clearly (Land, 1978), as does the provision of State child-care facilities. During the Second World War the number of day nurseries increased rapidly, from 194 in 1941 to 1,450 in 1944 – but the end of the war brought an immediate volte-face. Day-nursery provision was rapidly run down again, with the number of places halved between 1945 and 1954. As the Ministry of Health (1945) stated in a circular to local authorities at the end of the war: 'The ministers concerned . . . are of the opinion that, under normal peacetime conditions, the right policy to pursue would be positively to discourage mothers of children under two from going out to work . . . .'

The rapid and significant increase in married women's labour force participation after the war did not lead to a modification of this view. In 1968, the Department of Health reiterated that public-sector day nurseries were for children 'in special need', not for those with two working parents (Department of Health, 1968).

Not surprisingly, very few local authorities have taken initiatives to provide for pre-school children of working parents, except in so far as they supervise the growing market-place of private-sector provision: child minders and private day nurseries. Although there was a substantial expansion of nursery education and playgroups in the early seventies, it was not with the needs of working parents in mind, as most of this provision is part-time and nearly all is closed during the school holidays and limited to children over three.

Only once since the war has the Government modified its stance, and then only in the mid-1960s, when it responded to the then-current shortage of nurses and teachers by *permitting* local authorities to provide nursery school and day nursery places for the children of women in these professions, despite a general embargo on other new nursery facilities.

This reluctance to provide for the needs of working parents has not been limited to those with pre-school-age children. Although local authorities are empowered to provide 'out-of-school-hours' services for school-age children under the terms of a number of Acts, including the 1944 Education Act, provision of services has been patchy. Even though by 1975 at least three-quarters of authorities ran schemes of one kind or another, many had major limitations that considerably reduced their value to working parents (e.g. schemes open for only part of the week or school holiday) (Simpson, 1978).

On other fronts, however, forces at work in the early 1970s were putting pressures on traditional assumptions. Married women's employment rates were rising rapidly in a generally tight labour market, in a climate in which social justice was high on the list of political priorities, and the removal of discrimination against women on grounds of sex was becoming a political issue. An Anti-Discrimination Bill had been introduced into Parliament every year since 1967, and in 1972 the House of Lords had established a Select Committee on the Bill, chaired by Lady Seear, which uncovered and highlighted many of the formal barriers still faced by women. The House of Commons subsequently established its own Committee to examine the subject, the Conservative Government responded in 1973 by issuing a Green Paper entitled *Equal Opportunities for Men and Women* (Department of Employment et al, 1973) (which, incidentally, made no mention of maternity leave or child-care facilities) and the Labour Government elected early in 1974 expressed its willingness to take action.

In its manifesto for the October 1974 election, Labour claimed that in government it would 'seek to give real equality to women'. It went on to note that 'changes in our society over recent years have emphasised the importance of providing practical equal opportunities for women rather than making polite noises about equality' and noted that the 'Labour Government's decisions provide a new deal for women'. Among the decisions listed were the introduction of child benefit allowance, extension of nursery education and day-care facilities, legislation against sex discrimination and for equality of treatment in social security provision – and the provision for maternity leave. Looking at the full list today, it would appear that 'practical equal opportunities' meant reducing some of the barriers which limited women's opportunity to choose what role they would play. Missing from this perspective, however, was any awareness that the nature of employment conditions (e.g. hours of work) or the choices in practice open to men could affect the extent to which women had 'real equality'. Just how limited this 'new deal' for women would be – even in its own terms – would become clear later.

Britain's entry to the European Economic Community in 1973 provided further impetus to change. The Treaty of Rome protected women's rights in a number of ways and, in addition, it was widely recognised that one aim of the Community was harmonisation of social legislation up to 'best' practice. Among the original six EEC members, job protection for women giving birth was firmly established. Twelve to fourteen weeks' paid maternity leave was the norm, with some countries giving women further rights to reinstatement in employment for a period of up to a year.

Parliamentary progress

Against this backcloth, the Employment Protection Bill was introduced into Parliament in the spring of 1975 to fulfil part of the Labour Government's commitment to its 'Social Contract' with the Trades Union Congress.

The TUC's Women's Advisory Committee had become involved with maternity leave issues early in the 1970s as an outcome of its concern with the health and safety of women at work, and the TUC's original Charter for Working Women, drawn up in 1974 included a right to maternity leave as one of its aims. It is therefore not totally surprising that the TUC had included three rights for women giving birth among its proposals to the Government in the summer of 1974: a right to thirty weeks' maternity leave, a right to pay during the leave period, and a right for women to have their jobs kept open for them for a total of a year. These rights were proposed for women with one year's service with their employer.

On the whole, these proposals were in line with the current 'best practice' in the EEC, although the suggested period of paid leave – thirty weeks – went beyond European best practice; even Italy, the country with the most generous arrangements, only offered twenty weeks' pay. Significantly, it appears that the TUC was also adopting the European convention of distinguishing between a 'right to leave' and a 'right to reinstatement'. A 'right to leave' enables women to maintain their status as employees, despite being absent from work giving birth (as if, for example, they were on sick leave or study leave). This means, for instance, that the leave period counts as employment for the purpose of entitlements based on length of service, and that a woman on leave may also be eligible for other employee benefits. Moreover, the 'leave' concept does not require a pregnant woman to make any 'declaration of intent' to return to work; she simply takes her leave entitlement at the appropriate time. The importance of the 'right to leave' is that it protects both the job *and* the status of any employed woman who is entitled to this right during the period of childbirth. By contrast, under a 'right to reinstatement', employers acknowledge that a woman has worked for them before and must therefore be reinstated in her previous job, but do not acknowledge her as having employed status during the time she is away from work; all or most entitlements arising from this period are therefore foregone.

While the 'leave' concept was applied generally in the EEC at the time of the Employment Protection Bill's introduction, some countries, as already noted, also provided a 'right of reinstatement', covering a period of optional, unpaid absence from work, following the expiry of the initial and paid leave period.

When the Consultative Document on the Bill appeared in the late autumn of 1974 (Department of Employment, 1974), a proposed right to maternity leave was indeed included, but it had been significantly altered from the TUC's original proposals. Now women were to be entitled to nine months' leave, of which four weeks would be paid, and women would be entitled to reinstatement in the same or a similar job. The amount of weekly maternity pay, to be paid by the employer, would be the difference between the current level of national insurance maternity allowance[1] and a full week's pay, as defined for redundancy purposes. Pregnant women with at least one year's continuous service with their employer would be entitled to this right.

Although the rights to leave and reinstatement which appeared in the original TUC proposals were still present, the proposals have been tightened in a number of ways. For example, women were not to be entitled to return to their former jobs, only to 'the same or a similar' position. Only those with one year's *continuous* service would have access to the entitlement – a legal expression which excludes individuals working less than a certain number of hours per week. Women who were paying the 'married woman's option' in national insurance contributions, and who were thus not eligible for maternity allowance, were not to be entitled to have their pay made up. Finally, the reduction in paid leave from thirty weeks to four meant that the provisions no longer met the standard of the 1952 ILO Convention on

Maternity Rights, which specifies a minimum of twelve weeks' pay.

The decision to place on employers of women the obligation for maternity pay undoubtedly contributed to the significant reduction in the number of weeks' pay stipulated, as Government ministers stated later in the House of Commons that the cost to employers of these proposals had been estimated to be in the region of £14 million per annum. Ministers also stated at the time that the Government saw parallels with the German model in this respect, where employers 'topped up' social insurance benefits (Hansard, 5 August 1975). Why it should have chosen this mechanism, when many other European countries paid for maternity leave completely from social insurance funds, has never been made entirely clear, although Harold Walker, Minister of State for Employment, did say in the Commons on 5 August that this provision was part of 'an employer's social obligation to his employees', and some hint was given in the House of Lords that this approach had the advantage that a costly bureaucracy would not be needed to administer it (Hansard, 7 August 1975).

By the time the Bill was introduced into Parliament in April 1975, there had been further significant changes. Gone almost entirely was the original concept of leave: the employer was not to be obliged to maintain women on a contract of employment while they were away from work giving birth (although employers were not barred from such an arrangement). What remained was a right to reinstatement: a woman who declared an intention to return to work after childbirth would have the right to return to her occupation with her employer (later changed to 'the job on which she had been employed under her original contract of employment'), up to twenty-nine weeks after giving birth. Entitlement to this right was to be given to women with at least two years' continuous service with their employer and who had worked until eleven weeks before the expected date of birth. Women who declared their intention to return to work were to be entitled to full pay for the first six weeks of their absence from work, less maternity allowance and earnings-related supplement. As Albert Booth, Under Secretary of State for Employment, said in the Committee examining the Bill, these provisions were 'the vey minimum that we should be doing in this country at this time' (Hansard, 24 June 1975).

The entire Bill gave many signs of hasty drafting, and these provisions were no exception. Most of the maternity clauses were re-drafted during the Committee stage, and one further change was introduced: women receiving maternity pay were to be entitled to 90 per cent of earnings for six weeks, less flat-rate maternity allowance. Women's additional entitlement to earnings-related supplement would then bring their total income back to its original level. This alteration was apparently necessary because planned changes in the method of calculating earnings-related supplement would make it difficult for employers to work out women's entitlement.

Government ministers were never called upon to explain why they had dropped the European concept of leave, but they were asked to account for some of the other maternity provisions. Thus, we know that the need to work until eleven weeks before the expected date of birth is related to the fact that women are eligible for maternity allowance from that date. As the Government wanted a reinstatement period of nine months, this left about twenty-nine weeks after the birth, which, as Albert Booth said in Committee on 24 June, 'would give the employee a reasonable time to recover from childbirth and it is also generally accepted that the sixth month after childbirth is the time in which one can wean the baby'. The original entitlement to four weeks' pay after one year's service had been changed to six weeks' pay ater two years because 'the period of maternity pay was heavily criticised on the ground that it was totally inadequate. Yet the only way in which we could increase the period without increasing the already heavy cost to employers was by extending the qualifying period of two years' (Hansard, 5 August 1975). As it stood, the Bill's maternity pay provision was now expected to cost employers an extra £14.4 million per annum, while to reduce the qualifying period to one year and maintain six weeks' pay would cost £17.5 million.

Within Parliament, during the Bill's passage, aspects of these provisions were challenged both by the Conservative Opposition and by women Labour MPs. On the whole, the Conservatives welcomed the provisions, 'which begin to bring our law in line with the best practice within the European Community and elsewhere' (Hansard, 24 June 1975). They did, however, feel that a Code of Practice would have been a more appropriate mechanism for introducing these rights, as 'traditionally they are matters for voluntary arrangement and it would have been best to leave them for voluntary decision' (Hansard, 28 April 1975).

What concerned the Opposition about this part of the Bill, however, was the uncertainty, disruption and cost for employers (particularly small employers), and the resulting loss in job opportunities for young women, which the provisions would bring. To cope with this, they proposed reducing the post-natal entitlement to return to work from twenty-nine weeks to sixteen, and proposed that women give four weeks' notice to their employer of the actual date when they would return to work (the Bill required only one week's notice). These amendments were unsuccessful and Conservatives did not pursue them. More successful was their proposal to separate the right to maternity pay from the need to declare an intention to return to work. The Government agreed that there could be a tendency for women to make a 'false declaration' in order to gain pay if the two rights were linked, and as 'the Government . . . attach importance to the declaration being a reliable one' (Hansard, 24 June 1975), the Bill was amended. Henceforth women who met the statute's criteria would be entitled to maternity pay, whether or not they intended to return to work.

The one point over which the Conservatives exercised tenacious persistence was the method of financing the scheme. Initially they argued that 'maternity benefit should be met by the State and not by the employer or the employee' (Hansard, 28 April 1975). Then, in Committee, they pressed for benefit to be financed through the insurance stamp and, during the Report stage in the House of Commons, maintained that 'the best way to do that is through the employer's insurance contribution . . . It should be a levy imposed on every employer, according to the number of employees'. As the Government showed no signs of movement on this point, the Opposition pressed for exemption of small employers (those employing less than five employees) from an obligation to give maternity pay or to offer reinstatement, which the Government was not willing to concede.

Pressure on the Government to give way and change the method of funding continued to mount from a number of directions, however. An article in *The Sunday Times* (16 August 1975) came out in favour of state funding, Conservatives in the House of Lords raised the matter when the Bill was introduced there, and Baroness Vickers called for the establishment of a Maternity Pay Fund, similar to the Redundancy Pay Fund, to which all employers would contribute (Hansard, 7 August 1975). She also stated that a significant number of women's organisations had united behind this point and were lobbying for the change. At last, the Government conceded. On 14 October, amendments empowering the establishment of a Maternity Pay Fund, to which employers would contribute 0.05 per cent of their annual wage and salary bill, were introduced into the House of Lords and approved.

Labour women MPs[2] were less successful in their attempts. No women sat on the Committee considering the Bill, and the women mounted their challenge on 5 August, at the time of the Bill's Report and Third Reading. They sought to reduce the length of service requirement to one year, to increase the period of pay from six weeks to eighteen weeks, to extend the right to return to work to fifty-two weeks, and to allow a woman to postpone her return to work where 'no nursery or child-minding facilities are available for her child'.

In each case the women MPs argued on the grounds of the benefits of their amendments for women, and in each case they failed. With regard to the first two amendments, Harold Walker said, 'I am compelled to fall back on the argument . . . about the cost and the present circumstances'. On the third amendment, he said, 'if the extension is agreed . . . [employers] will face considerable problems . . . and [this] might result in employers tending more and more to discriminate against women of child-bearing age'. As to the final amendment, he argued, 'if too many grounds for extension are allowed, there will be a great deal of uncertainty among employers . . . this is not only outside the scope of the Bill but outside the responsibility of me or the Secretary of State [for Employment]'.

For good measure, he also noted that 'the circumstances envisaged . . . are not beyond her control in the same way or to the same degree' as the medical circumstances listed in the Bill. Thus these proposals largely failed to gain support because the Government took the side of the employers, and the Opposition was reluctant to back any extension to women's rights while women's employers were expected to shoulder the whole burden of cost. As James Prior said in relation to the first proposed amendment, 'we were not prepared to vote for a short period of qualification so long as the burden was placed on the employers, but if the burden were placed fairly on all employers there would be a general agreement' (Hansard, 5 August 1975). Interestingly, this statement indicates that women might have achieved a better deal with regard to pay and shorter qualifying periods if the Government had been willing to consider the Maternity Pay Fund earlier in the Bill's passage through Parliament.

The Employment Protection Bill, surely one of the longest Bills in history with its 115 clauses and numerous schedules, was rushed through the legislative process with tremendous speed. The Bill's maternity provisions were basically dealt with in two sittings on one day during the Committee stage, and clearly there was little time to reflect on its provisions at any length. This combined with the parties' concern for employers' interests and anxieties, no doubt explains to a great extent why so much that appeared, or did not appear, in the Bill was taken for granted. Thus the question was never asked as to why the concept of an entitlement to *leave* had disappeared, or why women would have to sign a declaration of intent to return to work, rather than simply taking their period of leave. Nor was the concept, implicit in the Bill, that pregnancy and childbirth are a 'temporary disability' (an American legal phrase), like an illness or a broken bone, ever questioned. Such an assumption ignores the fact that, for most women, the act of giving birth is only the start of a long-term change in their responsibilities and concerns, so that while physical recovery from childbirth may be quite rapid, women are not in the same situation after giving birth as before.

By accepting the 'temporary disability' model, however, there was no need to consider alternative employment arrangements for mothers, e.g. part-time work, or to take into account any needs of adoptive parents, although Baroness Vickers reminded the House of Lords that Sweden offered such a right (Hansard, 7 August 1975). Furthermore, although Conservatives twice mentioned the concept of 'paternity leave' – once in the Swedish context, and once in referring to proposals by the Association of University Teachers – no attempts were apparently made to extend the Bill's provisions to include fathers. On the other hand, neither were the provisions ever challenged in the Commons on the grounds that mothers of young children should be at home (the House of Lords appeared to be more divided) – it was accepted by all parties that women had a right, however limited, to regard maternity as a short interruption to working life.

Getting leave

Just how limited this right is can be ascertained by looking at the criteria laid down in the Act which pregnant women must meet if they want to return to their former employment, or want to keep their options open:

1 Contractual status Women must be employed under a contract of employment. Thus women who are self-employed (as many mothers are – see Chapter 2) would be excluded. Although many of these women could no doubt arrange their own 'maternity leave' (because they notionally 'work for themselves'), many could also lose access to their work because their clients might take their business elsewhere.

2 Length of service with the employer Women must have had at least two years' continuous employment with their employer at the eleventh week before the baby is expected. Thus, many women will not have a sufficient length of service to be eligible for their statutory rights. In 1975 it was stated in the House of Commons (Hansard, 5 August 1975) that, of women over eighteen employed full-time with their employer, 23.6 per cent in manual work and 25.1 per cent in non-manual work had been with their employers for less than a year. An even higher proportion would have less than two years' service, with the numbers highest among women who were already mothers (see Chapter 2).

3 Hours of work Women must have worked sixteen hours per week or more during the two-year qualifying period, or they must work at least eight hours per week, if they have been employed by their employer for five years or more. Thus, as many women have a very short working week, particularly those who are already mothers, another class of employee is excluded from statutory rights.

4 Date of leaving work Women must have worked up to eleven weeks before the baby is due. If they have resigned earlier in the pregnancy, for whatever reason, they lose entitlement, although certain other provisions of the Act protect women who have been dismissed by their employer prior to the eleventh week because pregnancy has made them incapable of doing their job.

5 Notice of reason for leaving Pregnant women are expected to notify their employer, in writing if so requested, that they are leaving work because of pregnancy or confinement. This notification is to be made at least three weeks before the date of leaving, or as soon thereafter as 'reasonably practicable'.

6 Notice of intention to return to work Women are expected to notify their employer, in writing if so requested, that they are intending to return to work after childbirth. As with the notice of reason for leaving, this notification is to be made at least three weeks before departure, or as soon thereafter as 'reasonably practicable'. In ordinary circumstances women who only notify their employer *after the birth* that they wish to return to work would not be eligible to exercise their statutory right.

7 Notice of date of return to work Women are expected to notify their employer of the date on which they expect to return to work. This notification is to be made at least one week before the expected date of return.

8 Date of return to work Women must return to work within twenty-nine weeks after giving birth, unless there are medical reasons why they cannot do so. Under such circumstances, they can postpone their return to work for up to a further four weeks. Thus, any woman who felt she could not leave her very young baby, or who could not arrange for acceptable substitute care, would be unable to fulfil this obligation.

To complicate matters further, these provisions of the Act came into force with relatively little publicity. Although the right to return to work was among the first of the Act's provisions to be implemented, on 1 June 1976, and the right to maternity pay came into force on 6 April 1977, the national press paid little attention to these developments and concentrated instead of the politically more controversial aspects of the law. Even women's magazine were relatively slow off the mark, perhaps because their long lead-times for publication meant that they were caught out when the Government announced its intention in April 1976 to introduce the right to reinstatement in June. Neither had the Department of Employment produced a 'layman's' guide for women or their employers, despite the comment by Albert Booth in Committee that 'if we were to rely on every employee who would have a right under the Bill to study [its] provisions . . . the take-up rate might be very poor indeed' (Hansard, 24 June 1975). (The first official guidance appeared in 1977, but the Department has never issued a guide designed primarily to draw the attention of women to their rights.)

As a result, it would appear that this part of the Act landed on a largely unsuspecting populace. My own discussions with personnel specialists and social workers in the middle of 1976 indicated that many of these professionals knew little or nothing about the relevant provisions of the law, and experience of the operation of the Maternity

TABLE 16 PAYMENTS MADE FROM MATERNITY FUND, MAY
1977–JANUARY 1979

PAYMENTS MADE DURING MONTH

	Number	Total Amount (£)
1977 May	13	2,425
June	2,062	418,984
July	4,390	868,606
August	5,393	1,058,622
September	6,488	1,325,373
October	6,744	1,391,454
November	7,702	1,730,058
December	6,539	1,449,777
1978 January	6,973	1,502,566
February	8,066	1,752,777
March	8,804	1,909,143
April	6,873	1,617,952
May	7,573	1,745,357
June	9,187	2,033,089
July	7,067	1,574,051
August	8,290	2,039,468
September	7,597	1,903,468
October	10,158	2,315,706
November	9,771	2,458,870
December	7,001	1,727,916
1979 January	9,703	2,326,504

Pay Fund since 1977 indicates that neither women nor their
employers were very knowledgeable in the early days. As Table 16
shows, payments took some months to build up to a stable level and
even in 1978 the number of women being given maternity pay was
running at only about 100,000 per annum, well below the annual
figure of 220,000 predicted at the time of the Bill's passage (Hansard,
14 October 1975). (At the beginning of 1979 the Fund had a £1
million surplus.)

That ignorance did not disappear quickly in many quarters is also
quite evident. In 1978 the Department of Employment sponsored a
survey of 301 small firms in five areas of England and Wales, in which
interviews with the owners or chief executives of these organisations
revealed that only 11 per cent knew that women had to work for their
employer for two years before becoming eligible for reinstatement
after childbirth, only 31 per cent knew that *any* statutory maternity
pay could be reclaimed and only 6 per cent knew that *all* statutory
maternity pay was reclaimable. In fact, only 2 per cent had experience
of giving statutory maternity pay (Dept of Employment, 1979e).
Further evidence comes from a study in 1978 of women in the Sussex

area who had taken maternity leave since the Act came into force. Interviewees said they were usually 'one jump ahead' of their managers when it came to knowledge of their rights (Adamson, 1979).

Most recently, Industrial Relations Services (IRS) (publishers of numerous specialist industrial relations journals) found in a random survey of 261 of their subscribers, undertaken at the end of 1979, that even some of *their* readers were unfamiliar with details of the law. At one firm it was believed, for example, that women had to declare an intention to return to work in order to claim maternity pay, while at another organisation the respondent assumed that a woman had a right to change her mind even if she had made a written declaration on leaving that she did *not* intend to return (Industrial Relations Review and Report, 1980).

What women's knowlege now is of the law's contents we do not know. But W. W. Daniel, at the Policy Studies Institute, and V. Rowlands, at Nene College, are both currently engaged on studies which should soon give us some clues.[3]

Employers' experience

Prior to the Act's implementation, a number of employers in the UK had been offering some form of maternity leave or right to return to work to at least some of their female employees. Between 1971 and 1975 surveys conducted by the Institute of Personnel Management (1971 and 1974), the Office of Population Censuses and Surveys (Hunt, 1975), Incomes Data Services (IDS) (1973) and the Alfred Marks Bureau (1975) all found between 15 and 20 per cent of employers operating schemes of some description. Many of these were among the country's largest employers of women – e.g. the Civil Service, the National Health Service, local authorities, the clearing banks, major retailers such as Marks & Spencer and the John Lewis Partnership – and it is possible that more than 15–20 per cent of employed women worked in organisations where provision for returning to work after childbirth already existed.

The public sector appeared to be better covered than the private sector, and to have operated its schemes for a longer period (Incomes Data Services, 1973), and the public-sector schemes tended to be more generous and more formalised than those in the private sector, although there were some exceptions. There was wide variation in the terms of such schemes, and virtually no employer's practices met the standards of the law on all counts, particularly in relation to the length of time women were allowed to be away from work. In some respects, however, these schemes were frequently more generous than the law. For example, many employers offered a right to return to work to women with one year's service, often irrespective of the hours per week which they worked, and many employers – particularly those in the public sector – offered some pay during the entire period away from work. Most employers also treated women who were absent as having the status of employees on special leave, although most employers did not give leave automatically – women had to request it (the Civil Service was a notable exception).

In the summer of 1975, I interviewed personnel officers who administered existing schemes in six public-sector and nine private-sector organisations and found that these organisations had experienced few, if any, major difficulties. This finding coincided with evidence given by Albert Booth in the House of Commons earlier that year that 'none of the [employers who operate such schemes] has suggested that the problems they have faced have been such that they would wish to return to the earlier situation' (Hansard, 28 April 1975).

Yet by 1976 the prospect of implementing the Act's maternity provisions was creating anxiety not only in organisations which had no policy, but also in some where a form of reinstatement was already available. The provisions created anxiety among personnel specialists on a number of points:

1 Women would return to work and therefore would block promotion opportunities for others which had traditionally been created when pregnant women left employment.

2 Women would not return to work, although they would say they intended to do so, and work would therefore be disrupted, recruitment problems would be created, and administrative burdens increased.

3 Women would return to work, but only for a short period, until they discovered they could not cope with both their work and family roles.

4 Keeping a woman's job open for up to nine months, or finding a suitable vacancy when she returned, would be very difficult.

5 Integrating the Act's provisions with other employment law and with the employer's existing policies and practices would be a complex, resource-consuming, frustrating business.

6 Employers would in future be reluctant to employ young women who might exercise their statutory right.

7 Pregnant women would be receiving better treatment than employees who had not left work to have a baby and those who were entitled to other forms of leave.

What this list shows is not only that personnel specialists were uncertain about how untried arrangement would work in practice and uncertain about what needed to be done. It also indicates, as Hunt (1975) had found previously, that these managers were not among the country's most fervent supporters of equality of opportunity for women. Yet, as discussed earlier in this chapter, little official support was available to assist employers to implement the legislation, or to facilitate a change in attitude.

None the less, once the Act came into force, most of the shouting died away quickly. By July 1977 Incomes Data Services were able to say 'the crises have not happened' (Incomes Data Services, 1977), while another DE-sponsored study, in 1978, on the effect of employment protection legislation on 301 firms in the manufacturing industry found that the maternity provisions were rarely mentioned as affecting management (Daniel, 1978). What has in fact happened is still somewhat difficult to piece together because, although we now have two studies by IDS (Incomes Data Services, 1977, 1979) and an Industrial Relations Services survey (Industrial Relations Review and Report, 1980) to draw on, plus bits and pieces of other published and personal information, no properly-structured, large-scale, in-depth study of the experience of employers or their women employees has yet been completed. The work currently being carried out by Daniel and by Rowlands will, one hopes, fill this gap.

In the meantime, what evidence is available would suggest the following tentative conclusions.

1   *Employers' experience of women exercising their statutory rights has varied widely.* The 1979 IRS survey of a random sample of 261 organisations in the private and public sector, employing together about 4 per cent of the nation's female workforce, found that 94 per cent of these employers had had experience of operating either the maternity pay or reinstatement rights in the period from April 1977 to December 1978. Yet only 55 per cent had experience of re-employing women after leave. Of the others, 28 per cent had experience of women declaring an intention to return to work. Overall, in the survey, 60 per cent of women taking maternity pay declared an intention to return to work, while just under one in four of these women, i.e. 15 per cent of those taking maternity pay, did in fact do so.[4] As the women who returned to work were congregated in just over half the organisations in the survey, the implication is that some employers have experienced high rates of return.

These findings are consistent with the information given to Incomes Data Services in 1977 and 1979 by a number of individual employers: in some cases up to 90 per cent of women who left to have babies returned to work, while in others no women either returned or declared an intention to return. However, both the IRS survey and the IDS studies were heavily biased towards large employers, and this may account for their inconsistency with the findings of the DE small firms study quoted above, where only 4 per cent of employers had experience of offering maternity leave, or of keeping a woman's job open for the statutory forty-week period (Dept of Employment, 1979e).

One factor, apart from size, which has clearly been associated with the wide variation in rates of return is the employer's geographical location. The 1977 IDS study reported that in 1976 United Biscuits had found '45 per cent of employees in London wanting to return and only 1 per cent in Teesside'. Also in 1976, Freemans (Mail Order) found that just under 40 per cent of its workforce in Lambeth who had become pregnant returned to work, yet only 6 per cent in Peterborough had done so. This is not a simple north–south split: British American Tobacco told the Industrial Relations Services survey that the return rate at its Liverpool factory was 71 per cent (40 out of 56 women) of those taking maternity leave, while at their London head office no women who had taken maternity leave had returned to work. Other factors are clearly operating here. One may speculate that the nature of the local labour market, the ethnic and marital composition of the workforce, commuting times, hours of work, the availability of child care and other variables are associated with this experience. Without further information, however, additional conclusions are not possible.

Two other influences have been found to be associated with high proportions of women declaring an intention to return to work, even though they do not need to do so in order to obtain statutory maternity pay. The first operates when management actively encourage women to keep their options open by declaring an intention to return. There is no evidence that this behaviour significantly influences the proportion of women actually returning to work in the short term, although no doubt it affects the outcome in some individual cases, as when a baby is stillborn. The second operates when the employer offers payment beyond the statutory period to women who say they intend to come back to work. Where women are under an obligation to hand back this pay to their employer if they do not return, this practice may have an impact on rates of return. Personnel officers in several local authorities, where additional pay must be given back to the employer if the woman does not return to work for at least three months, have reported high rates of return – at least for three months. These personnel officers have also noted their impression that many of these women resign after the three-month qualifying period. Whether this is so, and whether in general women who do return to work have higher turnover rates than the female working population at large, is unknown.

2 *In most circumstances, employers have experienced few significant difficulties in covering for the jobs of women who have declared an intention to return to work.* The two IDS studies and the IRS survey enquired extensively into employers' arrangements for ensuring that women employees had an appropriate job to which to return. All three studies found employers taking one or more of four possible options: hiring temporary replacements; hiring permanent replacements and hoping either that labour turnover would create another vacancy or that the women would not in fact return;

temporarily upgrading existing staff; re-allocating work amongst existing staff. The IRS survey found the first option to be the most common – 77 per cent of respondents hired temporary replacements in some or all circumstances.

In summarising its findings, the IRS survey reported the following experience:

> Some employers told us that clerical jobs have been fairly easy to cover since temporary staff can be employed during the period of absence of pregnant women. Since many clerical jobs only involve routine administrative tasks, outside staff have been able to take over during this period.
>
> Where production or unskilled jobs are concerned, or in industries with high staff turnover, covering for employees on maternity leave has caused no apparent problem . . .
>
> Companies appear to have coped particularly well with employees in managerial or specialist positions . . . by temporarily up-grading existing employees to those positions . . .
>
> [In one company] the post of secretary . . . was covered by reorganising the office and re-allocating the . . . work to other secretaries. This system worked so well that when the woman on leave decided not to return this new arrangement was retained . . .

Indeed, the only cases where circumstances had apparently proved to be particularly difficult were in small units, e.g. a branch office or small branch bank, where labour turnover is not high enough to guarantee a ready vacancy on return, and where no staff are available for temporary up-grading. Yet some small units apparently can cope – the IRS survey quotes two cases in which building society branches dealt with the work of managers on maternity leave by a combination of temporary up-grading and the hiring of temporary staff.

None the less, some employers would like greater flexibility in the range of jobs which they can offer women on their return: when asked if they would like to see any changes in the existing law, 13 per cent of the respondents in the IRS survey suggested that a woman's right should extend only to a 'suitable vacancy'.

Where employers have apparently been experiencing difficulties on some scale is not so much in covering for jobs as in knowing whether women will actually return, and when they will do so. As was noted above, 28 per cent of organisations in the IRS survey had held jobs open for women who did not return to work. Furthermore, 44 per cent said female employees took the full forty-week period on average, while 31 per cent said women generally returned within twenty and thirty weeks and 25 per cent put average absence at twenty weeks or less. This has led to some uncertainty as to how long temporary arrangements will need to last and may create difficulties with temporary staff – for example, one IRS respondent noted that 'many good temporary staff had left because of the uncertainty of a permanent position'. Thirty per cent of IRS respondents said they would like to see a statutory time limit at which an employer is entitled to know whether or not a woman intends to return, and 16 per cent wanted a binding commitment to return prior to absence.

3   *The majority of employers treat women who declare an intention to return to work as being on leave during their absence, but arrangements regarding contractual rights during the leave period vary considerably.* The 1977 IDS study of maternity schemes in practice in fifty-seven organisations in the public and private sectors concluded that 'most have decided on full continuity for most purposes'. However, the study found that practice with regard to certain specific benefits and entitlements was as follows. *Pensions:* 'In most contributory schemes most women stop paying contributions at the end of their maternity pay and, on return, have the option of making up the contributions'. *Service-related entitlements*: '[there are] numerous examples of those who freeze and those who allow accrual of annual leave'. *Wages, salaries and bonuses*: 'Most of the personnel managers contacted applied general pay increases to the employee on return . . . treatment of bonuses varied and some felt it would depend on each type of bonus'.

Further insight comes from the 1979 IRS survey, where 88 per cent of organisations treated a woman's contract of employment as 'suspended' until she returned to work – as though she were on unpaid leave. Only 12 per cent terminated the contract and reissued it if the woman returned. Thirty-two per cent of employers counted the period of maternity leave for pension purposes and continued to pay the pension contributions, and 72 per cent of employers responding to the question on death in service benefits indicated that women on maternity leave would be covered. Fifty-five per cent said that repayment of company loans or cheap mortgages would continue during maternity leave, although those organisations in the survey which operated cheap mortgages expected the employee on leave to pay the public mortgage rate. Only 11 per cent of employers made payments of a company bonus to women on maternity leave (in all cases she forfeited her right to any bonus), only 8 per cent would allow a woman to keep a company car, but 70 per cent permitted women to use staff shops and sports facilities and to enjoy company discounts and continued free BUPA coverage.

As this whole area appeared to cause a great deal of confusion when the Act came into force, and was fraught with pitfalls, it is likely that this variation in practice has arisen either because employers have taken whichever steps seemed easiest and most consistent with existing policy at the time, or because of union pressure on certain matters. Certainly, as a general rule, it would have been far easier for organisations which operate a range of benefits for their employees to regard giving birth as 'on leave' rather than to become involved in stopping and re-starting all entitlements when a woman is reinstated.

At this point we have virtually reached the end of the conclusions about employers' experience which can be drawn from existing evidence, except to note that, as with voluntary schemes before the Act, employers appear to feel that maternity provisions are working well in practice – or so 83 per cent of respondents to the IRS survey claimed. 'In the main,' the survey concluded, 'those employers who said . . . the provisions were not working well had not had any experience of the maternity leave provisions.' It could be that these employers are concerned because their female employees are *not* declaring an intention to return to work, but a more likely explanation is that most employers with experience have not found it to be as difficult as they feared, and a few have probably gained benefits from reduced costs through lower labour turnover and the retention of experienced staff – though this is undocumented as yet. Also still undocumented are two other management concerns mentioned earlier in this section – the impact on promotion opportunities of women returning from maternity leave, and the impact of the statutory rights on young women's employment. Although young women's unemployment rates have risen rapidly over the past few years (and are now nationally on a par with young men's), we have no evidence to suggest that this significant change is due more to the existence of the maternity provisions than to the general availability, and changing structure, of employment, or to the greater attractiveness of older women as employees because of their stability and maturity. In fact, the DE-sponsored small firms study found that only 8 per cent of the firms were employing fewer women than before the Act came into force, and none mentioned the maternity provisions as a reason (Dept of Employment, 1979e).

One final conclusion we can draw, however, is that employers' experience of maternity leave has not made them noticeably more willing to enable their employees to combine work and parenthood. If such a change in attitude had taken place, we would expect, for example, to find employers introducing entitlement to pay or leave which went beyond that laid down by law. Yet only 18 per cent of the IRS survey respondents had done so, and nearly 50 per cent of these were in the public sector, where more generous provision generally existed before 1976. Nor have employers seen the need to provide child-care facilities – only 5 of the 261 organisations in the IRS survey did so. Nor has a right to paternity leave (over and above annual holiday entitlement) become established – only 3 per cent of the IRS survey respondents offered paid paternity leave, normally of between two and seven days. Nor, apparently, have employers seen a need to facilitate a mother's return to work by allowing her to work reduced hours for a period following her return – the report of the IRS survey mentions only two employers which do so. Thus, it appears that although employers are willing and able to abide by the law, they have stuck closely to its letter and narrow intent except where, as in the case of the status of a woman's contract of employment, less work was involved in being more generous. The legislation has not encouraged a wide-ranging reassessment of policy.

Some general conclusions

By enacting the maternity provisions of the Employment Protection Act 1975, the Government of the day was breaking significantly with tradition by obliging employers for the first time since the Second World War to offer their female employees a choice about combining work and family roles. As such an Act was totally without precedent in the UK, it is perhaps not surprising that the Government, and male MPs of all parties, felt able only to produce 'the very minimum' of entitlement. Certainly the polititians had accurately reflected the anxieties managers expressed at the time the Act came into force, yet managers who have had to operate the law have apparently found the reality by no means as awful as they expected – they have indeed coped, and apparently coped very well. What they have not done, by and large, however, is to go beyond their statutory obligations, and in that sense the law has not provided a springboard for the extension of choice to women, or to men. It would appear that this legislation, by itself, has been insufficient to change employers' perceptions of their interests as regards the combination of work and family roles.

The law has apparently had more of an impact on some women as, in many organisations, women are exercising their right to combine work and parenthood by returning to employment after childbirth. There is even some evidence that, over time, an increasing number of women employed in certain organisations are doing so. Barclays Bank noted that the number of women returning to work after maternity leave went up over five-fold between 1974 and 1978, from 28 to 140 women, and United Biscuits reported in 1977 that it had seen the proportion of its female workforce who returned to work rise from 20 per cent in 1974 to 38–40 per cent in 1976. It may be, as many observers of the scene would no doubt hope, that this rise is largely accounted for by women who have lost their babies, or who are unmarried, and does not reflect any change in expectations on the part of the 'normal' mother in a two-parent family. Certainly, Barclays Bank's experience indicates that it is young mothers, i.e. those under 21 (and presumably those most likely to be unmarried), who have the highest rate of return from maternity leave – of these women who left for maternity leave between June 1976 and May 1977, almost 60 per cent returned to work (33 out of 56), while less than 10 per cent of women aged 21–30 did so (26 out of 228).

It would be most unlikely, however, for all of this rise to be accounted for by an epidemic of still births and perinatal mortality, and by an explosion in the rate of illegitimate births to employees in some organisations. Nor would the very high rates of return reported by some employers (Incomes Data Services, 1977) be accounted for solely by these factors. What is more likely is that it is already accepted in some social groups that mothers with young children will work, and is becoming increasingly acceptable in others. Thus, for example, we would currently expect to find high rates of return among certain groups of working-class mothers in the north-west, some parts of the Midlands and the Inner London area, among women from certain ethnic minorities, and among professional women living and working in London. We would further expect to find the rates of return rising over time where management is supportive, and where a few women 'pioneers' have shown that combining work and family roles is possible. The full impact of the legislation has probably not yet been felt in many areas, as major changes are likely to take time. Although these hypotheses have yet to be tested in a systematic way, and although there are undoubtedly other psychological and structural variables involved, what we can say is that many women who would otherwise have been without any security of employment have benefited from the Act's reinstatement provisions, and many more women would have gained these benefits if access to these rights had not been so restricted.

Even with the provisions as they are, Government could have done considerably more than it has to assist employers to implement the legislation, and to assist women to use their rights. We have mentioned above the lack of publicity given to this part of the Act, and the apparent consequences for women and their employers, and we have indicated that a part of managers' anxieties, even when they knew what the law said, probably stemmed from uncertainty and lack of knowledge about how to carry out the letter of the law. Admittedly, no great assistance was given by the Department of Employment on any of the Act's provisions, but without support and guidance, no matter what the legislative provisions, the parties involved are left to feel their way, to fall back on easy solutions and to rely largely on private initiatives for assistance (the management conference industry did very well out of the Employment Protection Act). The DE could, in theory, have arranged quickly for the publication of material for employers, which went beyond a re-statement of the Act's clauses by suggesting policy implications and giving examples of how employers who already operated maternity leave schemes had handled the situation. It could also have done a better job of telling women about their rights, by producing a guide designed for them, by making it attractive and easy to read and, most importantly, by widely publicising the Act's provisions and the guide's existence. Furthermore, the Government could have seen the maternity provisions as an opportunity to link the work of the Department of Health and Social Security, the Department of Education and Science and the Department of Employment, to help create the child-care facilities which would actually allow women who want to return to work to do so. This did not happen either. As a lesson about employment legislation the message is clear: if the Government expects employers to change their practices with minimum upheaval, and individuals to make use of their rights, it must invest some resources, and take some initiatives, to facilitate this occurrence, over and above adding new law to the statute books. When the new law in some ways marks a radical departure from tradition, this action would seem particularly important.

Both the Equal Opportunities Commission and the Conservative Government elected in 1979 have now pronounced on the working of the statutory maternity provisions (Equal Opportunities Commission, 1979b; Department of Employment 1979b). The EOC has concluded that 'the present provisions do not allow genuine choices for the majority of women', but it has also expressed concern that 'it is particularly difficult for small employers to meet [the reinstatement] obligation' and recommended 'wide discussion of possible ways in which employers might be able to confirm whether or not an employee still wishes to return to work after the birth of her baby'. To provide for genuine choices for more women, the EOC has suggested that:

1 The Act should be extended to all women workers, irrespective of the number of hours worked per week.

2 Women should become eligible for maternity pay after two years' employment – not necessarily with the same employer – and ultimately the service requirement for maternity pay from the employer should be reduced to six months.

3 Maternity payment should be at normal rates of pay, not at 90 per cent, for those women not entitled to an earnings-related supplement to the State maternity allowance.

4 Provision for a phased extension of maternity pay from six weeks to a longer period is desirable and could be combined with passing central responsibility for running the scheme to the Department of Employment, with the employer acting as agent.

5 The amount of leave available to those who meet the two-year service requirement should be extended, possibly in proportion to women's length of service, or arrangements for an initial return to work on a part-time basis should be introduced.

6   A period of partly paid and partly unpaid leave should ultimately be made available to either parent, after an initial period of leave on full pay for the mother, and in addition there should be a statutory period of paternity leave with full pay at the time of the baby's birth, to enable the father to give domestic support.

7   Women should ideally have complete continuity of service during the period of maternity leave.

Despite saying that 'to reduce the present [two-year] service qualification for leave entitlement would exacerbate [employers'] difficulties', the EOC also goes on to recommend that this qualification should be reviewed 'to consider reducing this initially to twelve months' employment with the same employer'. Although the EOC offers no recommendations to overcome the difficulties supposedly being experienced by small employers, it does suggest a requirement for women to communicate in writing with their employers some four to six weeks after the birth of their child to confirm whether it is still their intention to return to work within the 29-week limit.

While the EOC's proposals would certainly in principle increase the amount of choice available to women if implemented, its approach appears to be politically rather naive. The only particular experience of employers which it quotes is negative, and it argues for changes in the Employment Protection Act without a basis of facts and statistics, or a broad knowledge of employers' and women's experience and perspective. This is particularly evident in its suggestion that women notify their employer four to six weeks after giving birth – just at a time when women are probably least able to cope, both physically and mentally. Furthermore, the EOC does not seem to have thought out a politically realistic strategy for the changes it would like to see, nor has it apparently decided to take any initiatives itself in collecting and pulicising information (actually it has taken initiatives in this area[5], although this is not apparent from its official statement) or in engineering debates on the issues it raises.

Not surprisingly, therefore, the Conservatives appear to have largely ignored the EOC's proposals and have reverted to some of the arguments and proposals they made when the Bill was going through Parliament. According to the Government, 'practical experience in the operation of the legislation has shown the need . . . to change certain provisions which bear over-harshly on employers, discouraging recruitment, especially in small businesses, and to make certain adjustments to take account of problems which have emerged . . . .'
The Government's proposals for dealing with this situation included exemption from the reinstatement provisions of the Act for firms employing fewer than twenty people, an extension of a woman's notice of the date of her return from one week to four, and relaxation of her right to return to her 'original job' to a right to suitable alternative

employment. On one point only did the Government follow the EOC – it proposed that women be required to confirm within six weeks of their confinement whether they still intended to return to work.

At the time of writing, however, the Conservatives' original proposals have been somewhat modified in their Employment Bill. As currently proposed:

1   Employers with five or fewer employees need not reinstate an employee, or offer suitable alternative employment, if it is not 'reasonably practicable' to do so.

2   Employers with six or more employees need only offer suitable alternative employment if it is not 'reasonably practicable' to offer a woman reinstatement to the job she was doing under her original contract of employment.

3   Employers are permitted to request from employees written confirmation that they intend to return to work, not earlier than 7 weeks after the beginning of the expected week of confinement. If an employee does not respond within two weeks she will lose her entitlement to return.

4   Women must give three weeks' written notice of their intended date of return to work.

5   Women must notify their expected week, or date, of confinement when notifying their employer that they expect to leave work to have a baby.

Consequently, the Conservative's Bill as it currently stands is unlikely to affect women's legal rights significantly, despite the Government's apparent concern for employer's difficulties. Conscientious employers are probably already keeping in touch with women on leave, as commentators have been recommending for some time (Fonda, 1976), and the only new obligation on women is that they respond – and quickly – to their employers' solicitations. The scope for alternative employment is already broad in many cases because of the wording of women's employment contracts and, in any case, the burden of proof will be on the employer to show that it was not 'reasonably practicable' to allow a woman to return to her 'original job'. Furthermore, the Bill specifies that all but the smallest employers must have a suitable alternative vacancy available, if they cannot offer the woman back her former employment. It may actually be that individual women gain some added benefit from this change, if it encourages employers to offer work to women that is more attractive to them for some reason, e.g. part-time or nearer their home.

As for small employers, although as a whole they employ a large number of women (1.1 million in 1975), what evidence is available indicates that they have relatively little experience of operating the Act's existing provisions, and little knowledge of the current statute, and that these provisions have not affected their employment of women, as we have seen above. On what basis the Government can claim that small employers are being affected by the legislation is not clear. Certainly none of the small employers in the IRS survey wanted to be exempt from the legislation – only large employers thought they should be.

What neither the proposals of the EOC nor those of the Government tackle is the problem of lack of knowledge on the part of employers (although both express concern about this issue) and further changes in the law are only likely to exacerbate the situation without some government intervention. It is quite possible, for example, that if employers hear vaguely about the Conservatives' changes in the law, many will assume that they no longer have any obligation to reinstate women returning from childbirth, or that they do not have to be concerned if they do not off a woman her 'original job' back. Women may be equally confused if their employer tells them that this is so, and may assume that the employer is correct and foreo their entitlement. In addition, women may not be aware – if their employer does not tell them (and at the time of writing there would be no obligation for him to do so) – that they must confirm their intention to return to work within two weeks of hearing from the employer, or lose their entitlement.

In thinking about future developments, therefore, it would seem both highly desirable and politically feasible to suggest: (a) widespread publicity about women's legal entitlements; (b) dissemination of the experience of employers who have handled the maternity provisions effectively; (c) obliging, or at least encouraging, employers to notify their women employees of their rights.

All these aims could be achieved by issuing an official code of practice, which would have a certain legal status, as, for example, the Code of Industrial Relations Practice, issued early in the 1970s, does. Even if an official code were not forthcoming, a body like the Equal Opportunities Commission could always produce unofficial guidance, although it would not have the same impact or status. Beyond this, employers' apparent general satisfaction with the operation of the provisions probably means that they would be willing to extend them to women with less than two years' continuous service, provided they were obliged, or even encouraged, to take such action. A government concerned to increase the amount of choice open to parents could also begin to make plans to introduce a limited right to paternity leave of some kind. If it were merely raised as an issue under consideration, many of the larger and more sophisticated employers would probably begin to experiment more widely with this entitlement. Ultimately, by a series of incremental steps of this nature, the outcomes sought by the EOC – which *in vacuo* seem almost ideal – might be achieved, provided they were coupled with an increase in child-care provision.

However, although these steps seem reasonable in the current situation, and indeed necessary, in the current climate of government opinion they seem remote. As highlighted elsewhere in this book, the Conservative Government seems firmly of the opinion that father is the breadwinner, and that mother should be the dependent raiser of children. They apparently have no desire to further encourage women with young children to enter or remain in the labour market at a time when there is a general over-supply of labour. It seems unlikely that they will be sympathetic to any proposals which could offer greater choice to parents in combining work and parenthood. As a consequence, women and their employers will struggle on, and any freedom to choose will probably remain as it is – very limited – for the foreseeable future.

6

The Stance of Britain's Major Parties and Interest Groups

Anna Coote and Patricia Hewitt

Introduction

It is the experience of most families that where there are children to be looked after and no child-care facilities outside the home, one parent must stay at home, either working part-time or giving up work altogether; the parent who can command the greatest income is usually the one to stay at work; and in most families, that is the man. Therefore, if work and child care are to be considered in the context of 'equal opportunities', relevant areas of policy must include:

  a) education, training and job opportunities;
  b) pay, taxation and welfare ('the social wage');
  c) contraception and abortion;
  d) parental leave and accommodation of work hours to the needs of children;
  e) facilities for child care outside the home.

For the purposes of this chapter, we have confined ourselves to parties and interest groups which are able to have a direct impact on these policies: the Conservative and Labour parties, the Trades Union Congress (TUC), the Confederation of British Industry (CBI) and the Equal Opportunities Commission. It would have been impossible to include 'the women's movement' because it is not a coherent organisation with an agreed set of priorities, although certain basic demands have been formulated by successive national conferences of the women's liberation movement.[1] Of course, the women's movement has wielded a crucial influence over the last decade; to give just one example, the Sex Discrimination Act might never have been passed without its tireless campaigning. But the women's movement consists of a plethora of small groups and organisations, devoted to a great variety of feminist aims, not always directly concerned with government policy. Many groups have purposely distanced themselves from conventional politics and have tried instead to build their own alternatives. Only a few, such as the Women's Rights Unit of the National Council for Civil Liberties, Women in Media, the Equal Pay and Opportunities Campaign (EPOC), Rights of Women (ROW), and the Women's Financial and Legal Independence Group, have concentrated on trying to get legislative change. While each of these has slightly different priorities, they all have similar policies on work, the family and equal opportunities – which accord more or less with our own. However, they are (unfortunately!) a step or two further removed from government decision-making than the organisations we have selected for study here.

The five groups we have chosen do not have coherent and consistent policies in all the areas which we consider to be relevant. Rather than point out the gaps in the policies of each of the groups which we examine in this chapter, we have focused on the policies which they *do* have concerning women, work and the family. The absence of a consistent overview in these organisations' policies will, we hope, become eminently clear.

It is necessary to bear in mind the context in which these policies have been developed. Economic decline and rising unemployment have placed women in a more vulnerable position than they would have been in a period of economic growth. Where workers are laid off, part-timers – the vast majority of whom are women – are often the first to go. The fact that women tend to be less well organised in unions than men also makes them more exposed to the danger of redundancy. While the *idea* that women should have equal opportunity has gathered wide support during the 1970s, the practical measures needed to bring it about cannot be delivered as easily now as they might have been (had the political will been there) before, say, the oil crisis of 1973. If nurseries are to be built, if school text-books are to be replaced, if special training courses are to be provided, a great deal more commitment is now required to select these as priorities.

Conservative policy

At their 1977 Annual Conference, the Conservative Party began a campaign to put themselves over as, in Margaret Thatcher's words, 'the Party of the family'. In the Conference debate on 'The Family and Conservative Policy', Patrick Jenkin, then Opposition spokesman on Health and Social Services, constructed the philosophical pedestal on to which the family was to be placed:

> The family . . . has been the foundation for virtually every free society known to history. It possesses strength and resilience, not least in adversity. Loyalty to the family ranks highest of all, higher even than loyalty to the state. It is no accident . . . that dictatorships, whether of the Left or of the Right, seek first to devalue and then to destroy the family . . . .

In Conservative eyes, therefore, the family represents 'a counter-balance to the ambitions of an over-powerful State' and the 'embodiment of fundamental Conservative principles of freedom, responsibility and continuity' (Houston and Mockler, 1978). Central to the Conservative view on the family is that public services may sap the major strengths and virtues of the institution, undermining and weakening it.

If follows from this general view, that positive measures by government to ease the position of working mothers – or fathers – and to further the pursuit of equality of opportunity, are unlikely to be sympathetically received. In a speech made to the 1979 National Children's Bureau Conference at Bath, Patrick Jenkin, speaking now as Secretary of State for Social Services, made the Government's position on child care for working parents very clear. The official press-release of the speech summed up its tone and line: 'Vital Role of Responsible Parents should not be under-valued; increasing State intervention should be resisted'. Towards the end, Jenkin moved on to working mothers:

> Some mothers have to go out to work either to make an essential contribution to family finances but perhaps also for their own fulfilment. There is a need therefore for day care facilities of a satisfactory standard so as to ensure that children are properly looked after while their mothers are away. I accept that where parents [sic] wish to work or have to work there should be facilities for their children. I do not accept that these facilities should be provided free by the State. The State does have a responsibility to provide care for children whose family circumstances, such as poor health, bad social conditions and so on mean that parents are unable to cope . . . . For most families however these services are not appropriate. If they are made available at public expense too readily, then they can all too easily be seen as the expression of a philosophy which preaches that parents can do what they like and it is the duty of the State to look after the children.

This hostile view towards increased State-run or State-financed child care also coloured the Conservative response to the TUC policy on under-fives (of which more later). Nursery centres, advocated in the TUC's Report, made Lynda Chalker (Patrick Jenkin's Junior Minister) think of Russian nurseries (a term of disapproval in Conservative circles), while Patrick Jenkin was filled 'with dismay' because the TUC 'want child-minders to become a full-time, salaried and pensioned job paid by local authorities . . . . I cannot conceive of any change which would do more to turn a highly personal service into yet another arm of bureaucracy'. His preferred form of pre-school provision is playgroups, designed specifically for women without paid jobs and high on voluntary effort, but low public expenditure.

A second, related strand in Conservative thinking about the family, is a coolness, moving to downright hostility on occasions, towards mothers who do go out to work. Back at the 1977 Conservative Conference, Patrick Jenkin noted that family life was changing as more married women took jobs. But, he implied, this was not a healthy development. 'I am told that there is now a word for "latchkey kid" in every European language . . . there is now an elaborate machinery to ensure [that women have] equal opportunity, equal pay and equal rights: but I think we ought to stop and ask – where does this leave the family?' Patrick Jenkin made his own view even clearer during a televised discussion about working mothers when observing with theological certainty, that 'if the Good Lord had intended us to have equal rights to go out to work, he wouldn't have created men and women'.

More generally, though, the Conservative approach stresses that if mothers wish to work, it is their responsibility alone to make provision for children, while also emphasising the virtues of those mothers who stay at home. In his 1977 Conference speech, Patrick Jenkin proposed greater tax incentives for mothers who stay at home to look after their children. Not only would this save public expenditure (on child-care provision) but would re-assert the domestic role of women. 'The pressures on young wives to go out to work devalue motherhood itself . . . . Parenthood is a very skilled task indeed and it must be our aim to restore it to the place of honour it deserves.' Jenkin returned to this theme in his 1979 speech at Bath, while at the same time acknowledging that many women can be made miserable by having to stay at home with their children.

> Mothers who stay at home and who care for their children full-time instead of taking paid employment are somehow made to feel guilty that they are wasting their lives. Nothing could be further from the truth. I am convinced that a mother is by far the best person to look after her own young children. She knows them best, she cares for them, and her love, guidance and care are absolutely crucial to their wellbeing. Of course parents [sic] need help and support in tackling this work and they need outlets to relieve the loneliness, isolation and boredom which can too easily wear down a mother tied to her home by the demands of young children.

Given this general perspective, it is not surprising that the 1979 Conservative Party Manifesto had no proposals for giving women greater equality at work. Instead, the Employment Protection Act was to be amended where it 'damages smaller businesses – and larger ones too – and actually prevents the creation of jobs': (steps taken by the Conservative Administration to pursue this election pledge are discussed in Chapter 5). The Manifesto did include a section on *'Helping the Family'*, notable mainly for the strange mixture of proposals lumped under this heading (including, for instance, the Arts and the Environment) and for their emphasis on reduced public expenditure and increased private provision. There are pledges to encourage home ownership and the sale of council houses; to revive the private rented sector; to preserve grammar schools; to simlify and decentralise the Health Service and cut back bureaucracy; to boost the private health sector; to introduce tax credits; to restore the will to work by cutting income tax and acting 'more vigorously against fraud and abuse' among the unemployed; to phase out the earnings rule for pensioners; and to 'provide a coherent system of cash benefits to meet the cost of disability . . . as swiftly as the strength of the economy allows'.

Furthermore, the Manifesto made no reference to tax incentives for mothers to stay at home and it is not yet clear what will come of this earlier proposal. Sir Geoffrey Howe, speaking in the 1978 Finance Bill debate when he was Shadow Chancellor, referred to growing pressure for an end to sex discrimination in the tax system and suggested that this might be achieved by allowing each partner in a marriage to have an equal tax allowance which could be transferred to the other partner's income where only one partner was in employment. The cost and complexities of such a scheme (involving a woman, for instance, in getting back her tax allowance from her husband every time she moved into the labour market) may deter the Government, although ministers have spoken of a 'partially transferable' tax allowance, under which part of the tax allowance (conveniently set above a limit close to the average married woman's part-time earnings) could be transferred to the other partner.

The Conservative attitude to work, the family and equal opportunities has shown consistency over recent years, reflecting a clear set of views and values widely held in the party. The actions of the Conservative Government in its first year give no hint that any change in attitude is likely or even a possibility. With the prospect of four more years of Conservative rule, the chance of seeing any social or economic changes likely to increase equal opportunities at work or at home between male and female parents, is receding swiftly into the distance.

Labour Policy

In its years of government, Labour appeared to do quite a lot to promote equal opportunity at work. It passed the Equal Pay and Sex Discrimination Acts and set up the Equal Opportunities Commission. It introduced statutory maternity leave, with six weeks' pay and the right to return to work up to 29 weeks after the baby's birth; and it protected women from unfair dismissal due to pregnancy. Some effort was made, via the Manpower Services Commission, to encourage married women to return to work after they had raised their families and to make training available to women for jobs normally done by men. Free family planning advice was introduced. And there was a slight increase in the number of nursery education and day-care places for children under school age: the proportion of 3–4 year-olds

in nursery education rose from 28 per cent in 1974–5 to an estimated
36 per cent in 1977–8, while day nursery places rose by approximately
20 per cent.

In terms of helping the family, the Government's replacement of
child tax allowance with child benefit (in 1979, £4 per week per child,
paid in cash to the mother) must qualify as the most progressive step
since the advent of family allowance.

In 1978 James Callaghan, the Prime Minister, made a big effort to put
Labour into competition with the Conservatives in the pro-family stakes.
In his speech to the National Conference of Labour Women in May
1978, he recognised, as Patrick Jenkin had done, that the rising number
of employed women was having a profound effect on family life.

> Now these changes are already having an impact on the family and
> in years to come I believe they will have an even bigger impact with
> more mothers going out to work, more girls getting higher
> educational qualifications. What effect is it going to have?

His answers to the question and his proposed solutions to the
problem were more ambivalent than those of Mrs Thatcher and Mr
Jenkin. By the time he made that speech his party had too many
commitments to the idea of equal opportunity to pursue a straight-
forward 'back-to-the-kitchen-sink' line. Instead, Mr Callaghan had to
start (at least) with a constructive approach to helping working mothers:

> I think it is time we organised ourselves much better than we have
> done so far so that the burden on the working mother is more
> bearable than it has been . . . .

At the same time, he perceived the absence of women from the
home as a danger to the conventional social fabric. He referred to 'the
growth of vandalism and hooliganism' and the consequent need to
preserve 'the beneficial influence of the family as a whole . . . in this
changing situation'. And he made the same connection as Mr Jenkin
had made between strengthening the family and caring for the old and
the sick:

> The nature and strength of the family and our attitude towards it
> will influence our attitude to care for the old and the weaker
> members of our society . . . .

In essence, Mr Callaghan's prescription for curing the ailing family
differed from the Conservatives' in one respect only. Women were not
to be discouraged from working. Instead, their employment was to be
adapted to enable them to perform their work in the home more
efficiently:

> We have got to pay much more attention than we have done in the

past as to how industry organises women's role at work, so that her influence as the centre of the family, and the woman usually is the centre of the family, that that influence is not weakened . . . . It is important that we should study and if necessary be ready to change in industry the patterns of work – much more than we have done so far – the overriding social concern, in my view, is to preserve and enhance the influence of the family as a whole.

For Labour, then, the family was to be strengthened by such measures as wider application of 'flexitime' and more part-time jobs for women. Nowhere was there any suggestion that the role of men in the family should change, nor any recognition of the fact that the care of very young children occupies only a small part of a mother's adult life.

Committed to public spending cuts, the Labour Government was able to deliver very few of the positive changes it promised. True, it could boast a small increase in the number of nursery places, though most of these were for children over three, but the fact remained that the vast majority of women with children under school-leaving age could not enjoy equal opportunity at work unless they could afford to pay a substantial amount for private child care. If more of them were able to get part-time jobs, or work longer hours on one day of the week in order to spend more time shopping for food on another, that did not amount to equal opportunity at work.

By the general election of 1979 it had also become clear that the 'equality laws' which had been passed in 1975 were making very little impact. From 1977 to 1978 the gap between men's and women's pay actually widened: as the Trade Union Research Unit of Ruskin College, Oxford, pointed out in February 1979, women's gross hourly earnings rose from 63.1 per cent of men's in 1970 to 72.1 in 1975, 75.1 per cent in 1976 and 75.5 per cent in 1977, but then slipped back to 72.2 per cent in 1978.

Clearly, legal prohibition of sex discrimination at work was not going to be enough to achieve equal opportunity. Positive measures were needed, not only more nursery places but also special training and recruitment schemes for women, to shift entrenched patterns of discrimination and to begin to change the status quo. The Labour Government paid lip service to this, but made no effort to introduce positive action programmes of any kind.

Furthermore, the Labour Government's policies on social security did not demonstrate any consistent commitment to equality of treatment. An important advance was the introduction of the Social Security Pensions Act in 1975, which will protect the pension rights of a woman or man who remains at home to care for children or a dependent adult relative. But the principles behind this scheme did not extend to the Labour Government's treatment of other benefits. Family Income Supplement, for instance, continued to be restricted to male breadwinners in two-parent families, thus debarring thousands of low-paid women. The non-contributory housewives' invalidity benefit included a discriminatory test of ability to do housework for married women who were already too disabled to take up paid employment – and the Government insisted on reversing, during the parliamentary recess, a decision of the National Insurance Commissioners which would have reduced the impact of this test.

Even more depressingly, the Government's attitude to the proposed Common Market Directive[2] on equal treatment in social security provision reflected the attitude expressed by one DHSS minister that society's general expectation that the husband should provide for his wife should be reinforced by social security law. DHSS ministers proposed, for instance, that if the Directive were to cover dependants' benefit for the sick and unemployed (which currently exclude married women unless the husband is incapable of self-support), then the rights of married men should be *reduced* rather than be extended in their present form to married women.

Nor did the Labour Government produce proposals for a fundamental reform of discriminatory tax laws. (Tax discrimination, far from being an academic matter, results in a married woman who has achieved equal pay with a married man taking home at least £3.75 a week less at standard rates of tax.) Administrative reforms were introduced by Joel Barnett, then Chief Secretary to the Treasury, in August 1978, but the long-awaited Green Paper on tax reform was buried by the general election.

Labour was unwilling to put its money where its mouth was, and as a result life for the great majority of women remained unchanged between 1974 and 1979.

The TUC and the trade unions

On paper, the TUC's policy on equal opportunity and the family is impressive. It has had a Charter of Aims for Working Women since 1963 and this was updated in 1975 and 1977 so that it now has fourteen clauses covering education; job and training opportunities when starting work; marital status; the elimination of all pay discrimination against women workers; promotion; occupational pensions; sick pay; health and safety at work; family planning and abortion; maternity rights; helping women resume paid employment; child care; part time work; and women as members of the community (see Appendix 1).

In 1978 the TUC endorsed a Charter on Facilities for the Under-Fives. In its introductory statement, the General Council remained uncommitted on the fundamental question of whether mothers of young children *should* go out to work:

> There is ambivalence in Government circles as to whether it is
> desirable for the mothers of young children to work outside the
> home. The General Council note that there is no agreement as to
> whether the emotional development of children is jeopardised
> when parents work . . . .

Instead, the General Council focussed attention on the very real need
for child care:

> What we do know is that very serious damage to children can and
> does occur when no proper education and care facilities are made
> available to cater for children whose parents may be working . . . .

The charter refers to 'parents' rather than just to 'mothers' but it does
not tackle the question of fathers' responsibilities at all. The TUC
takes the view that the child-care 'problem' can be solved by 'A
comprehensive and universal service of care and education for
children from 0 to 5 . . . made available by public authorities'. When
viewed in isolation, the demands of the Under-Fives Charter (see
Appendix 2) are remarkably progressive. While recognising that the
kind of comprehensive, universal under-fives service it seeks will 'take
some time to achieve', it nevertheless declares that 'such a service
must become a major priority for this country, since anything less will
not meet the needs of children and of their parents'. Such a service
would depend, of course, on public spending of a level never
contemplated by the last government, let alone the present.

The 1979 TUC Congress passed resolutions strongly defending
women's right to 'free contraceptive and abortion services on request',
and opposing the wholesale abolition of the protective laws (which
prevent employers forcing women to do shiftwork and long hours of
overtime), as recommended by the Equal Opportunities Commission.
However, the TUC has not yet taken the logical step from recognising
this inequality to knowing how (and being willing) to eradicate it. An
underlying assumption of TUC policy, as with Labour policy, is that
work must be adapted to women's home life, rather than that domestic
arrangements might be adapted to meet the needs of parents – both
mothers and fathers – who go out to work.

The TUC Congress passed several resolutions between 1976 and
1978, aimed at enforcing the spirit of the Equal Pay and Sex
Discrimination Acts. In 1978, for example, a resolution from the
(then) National Union of Bank Employees called on the General
Council 'to organise and lead a campaign which will enable us to
progress towards equality as rapidly as possible'. And in 1977 a
resolution from TASS, the white-collar engineering union, called for
amendments to the Equal Pay and Employment Protection Acts 'to

ensure that the courts do not nullify progressive legislation' and to enable women to claim statutory maternity rights after being in employment continuously for two years (not, as at present, after working for the same employer for two years).

Inevitably, the power of the TUC to influence government policy has diminished since May 1979. But even before then, it showed few signs of willingness to make the demand for women's equality a real priority in its dealings with employers or with government. Similarly, individual unions have not used their strength to enforce the laws and to negotiate better opportunities for women at the workplace – although there have been some exceptions, such as the equal pay battles won by the white-collar unions TASS and APEX.

In the recent London School of Economic Equal Pay Project, which monitored twenty-six employers between 1974 and 1977 to see what effect the equal opportunities legislation was having, employers were shown to have gone to some lengths to minimise their obligations under the Equal Pay Act – from segregating men's and women's jobs, to altering factors in job evaluation schemes to favour work done by men. In this they were influenced by their fears of reactions from male workers and by lack of positive pressures from unions:

> In almost every case, management conceded to the men's demands in order to avoid possible disruption and conflict . . . . In several cases, unions actively colluded with management to minimise [their obligations] or allowed management to carry out such actions without protest (Snell, 1979).

The LSE researchers concluded that active involvement by trade unions at the workplace could have a tremendous impact on pay and opportunities for women – by monitoring management practices, identifying inequalities and pressing for change – and that this could have more effect than actually amending the laws. What is more, 'the project findings make it clear that women's greater involvement in unions and pay determination is essential if women are to safeguard their interests at work'.

In fact, women have been joining unions in increasingly large numbers, but the level of their active participation in trade union affairs has remained low. Why? Plenty of explanations have been offered: women cannot get to union meetings because of their domestic commitments; they are less experienced than men in union affairs and so hang back, letting men take the lead; they need to be encouraged by positive measures to be more active . . . and so on. But these deal only with practicalities and the question remains: why do men (who have the power to change the unions, while women are excluded from power) fail to act? It cannot just be lethargy, since they are often found to be busy resisting change.

Unions still operate according to the principles on which they were founded – to protect their members' interests – and the strongest groups within the trade union movement are normally the most successful at protecting their own interests. Acts of altruism, which involve self-denial without prospect of future gain, have never been a primary function and seldom enter into collective bargaining. As trade unionists, men have always had more muscle than women, and most of them suspect that they have nothing to gain and possibly much to lose from promoting equal pay and opportunity for women. They feel this more strongly than ever when the job market is contracting and when money is short. Arguments about men's lives being improved eventually by sex equality tend to be complex and abstract, and not to carry much weight with male workers. In the immediate sense, then, there is a conflict of interest between men and women in the trade union movement.

Men wish to preserve for themselves the role of the 'family breadwinner', which implies not only that their work is more important than that of the women they share their homes with, but also that their capacity to earn a wage is more important than anything else. Men dominate the decision-making process in every union and, as Beatrix Campbell and Valerie Charlton recently pointed out (Campbell and Charlton, 1978), their strategy in collective bargaining 'historically has not expressed any responsibility as active *fathers*, because they have none'.

> The ramifications of this go beyond the failure historically to equalise women's earnings. They affect the male dominated trade union movement's inclination to spread its struggles against capital beyond the wage.

Women represent nearly one-third of the membership of TUC affiliated unions and there are some strong indications that if they were able to exert influence in proportion to their numbers, they would radically change the priorities of collective bargaining. What is more, they know what steps are necessary to increase their own participation – and thereby their influence. The trouble is, they do not have the power to ensure that those steps are taken.

The TUC Women Workers Conference, held annually, is an excellent forum for discussing ideas and problems and for formulating policy, as well as for giving female trade unionists experience in speaking and for breaking down any sense of isolation they might feel. Since the mid-1970s, when the ideas of the women's liberation movement began to filter through to the trade unions, this women's conference has become increasingly lively and has begun to formulate quite radical policies. In 1977 – and again in 1979 – it demanded seven additional places for women on the TUC General Council, and for the number of women elected to the Women's Advisory Committee to be doubled (at present the majority are appointed directly from the General Council, which means they are inevitably male and less than wholeheartedly committed to equality). In 1977, the women's conference set the wheels in motion for the Under-Fives Charter. In 1979, it called for a programme of positive discrimination at work as an essential step towards realising equal opportunity, and for a six-week extension to the current maternity leave entitlement 'to be taken by either the mother or the father as they determine'. In the debate on the latter resolution, it was clear that delegates thought it more important to demand *parental* leave to be taken by either parent, than just *paternity* leave to run concurrently with the mother's leave for a few weeks at the time of birth (although this was always considered necessary). They wanted to establish that, in two-parent families, a father was not just an optional extra on the domestic scene, but had equal responsibilities as an active parent. Another resolution to the 1979 conference called on the TUC General Council 'to campaign for a shorter working week for all wage workers to offset the effects of unemployment and to campaign among male trade unionists to use the extra time available to spread the burden of housework and child care'.

These demands make it clear that women trade unionists are no longer in any doubt about the need for men to understand that both men and women have equal responsibilities at home, and that this is an essential prerequisite for genuine equality at work. But in 1979 the Women Workers Conference went further still by endorsing a draft Charter of Trade Union Aims, which sets out positive measures for increasing women's involvement in trade union affairs. Among other things, it provides for special training for women trade unionists and for special seats to be reserved for them on union committees, where they are under-represented. A brief description of this Charter was presented to the 1979 TUC Congress and went through on the nod, but what will become of it in the next few years is by no means clear. At the time of writing there were no signs of male trade unionists rushing off to their shopfloor and office committees to put it into practice.

The Women's Conference is purely advisory and the only way to get their policies taken up with any force by the TUC is to have them re-submitted as resolutions to Congress, so that they can be fully debated and voted upon there. Each union can bring only two resolutions to Congress, and since men dominate union executives, they usually find 'more important' matters to raise. True, the TUC embraced the Under-Fives Charter, but that called upon the *government* to do something. Provisions for the under-fives are seldom the subject of collective bargaining, let alone a priority in negotiations. Likewise, the TUC is willing to pass motions calling for amendments to the Equal Pay Act, but at a shopfloor level the most that can be hoped for is action against the most blatant forms of inequality.

In short, there is a deadlock. Male trade unionists collude with employers to maintain unequal pay and opportunities because they suppose that progress made by women will threaten their interests as 'family wage earners'. Women wield insufficient power to overcome men's resistance and the male-dominated trade union movement is in no hurry to take the positive steps that would enable them to do so. One hope of a breakthrough – though not a particularly happy one – may lie in the drastic changes which will be brought to industrial life by new technology. Rising unemployment and shorter working hours may force male workers to reassess their relationship to their home life, to their children and to leisure. The 1979 Congress reaffirmed TUC policy in favour of a shorter working week and a reduction in overtime:

> So far the campaign for 35 hours has made little headway, as the demand has usually been jettisoned in return for wage gains. But as the threat to jobs intensifies it may take a higher priority, and may even be succeeded by demands for a further reduction in hours, for longer holidays and for work sharing. If not, we shall find ourselves with an elite of full time 'breadwinners' and a vast – and predominantly female – army of unemployed.

It is not within the scope of this chapter to examine the policies of every individual trade union, but it is worth looking briefly at what some of them have been up to, so that we can see what are the possibilities and limitations of union activity. Their records vary enormously, and white-collar unions seem to have achieved rather more than others. An interesting comparison can be made between the National and Local Government Officers' Association and the Transport and General Workers' Union. The size of their female membership is similar (337,778 and 329,534 respectively) yet these figures represent very different proportions of total membership (46 and 15 per cent respectively). NALGO has an Equal Opportunities Committee made up of three members of its National Executive Council and a representative from each of the union's districts. This produces a regular bulletin, with news of campaigns on various aspects of equality and of progress made by different branches of the union. It has published a step-by-step negotiating guide on how to set up a workplace nursery and a maternity rights negotiating kit with a model claim which includes six weeks' paternity leave and eighteen weeks' maternity leave, both on full pay, plus forty-five weeks' parental leave on full pay, to be taken by either the father or the

mother. It also includes time off on full pay for parents to attend ante-
natal and child health clinics and for all members to look after sick
dependants. So far these claims are little more than an ideal, to be
worked towards over the coming years, but NALGO is committed to
negotiating for improved provisions for parents, both at a national and
local level. In November 1979, NALGO's Equal Opportunities
Committee launched a campaign against the public expenditure cuts
introduced by the new Conservative Government, with particular
reference to their impact on women. The Camden branch of NALGO
has managed to negotiate with Camden Council a formal 'equal
opportunities policy' which is probably the nearest thing we have in
Britain to an affirmative action programme and which is promoted as a
model for other branches. The union is making special efforts to
encourage activity by women in the districts and branches – many of
which have their own equal opportunities committees.

The TGWU, on the other hand, has done far less to promote equal
opportunity and the special needs of its women members have been
virtually ignored by its policy-making bodies. It holds a women's
conference every year, but this exerts no noticeable influence and very
little effort has been made to increase the level of women's participation
in the affairs of the union. At the TGWU's biannual delegate
conference in July 1979, a resolution was passed calling for women's
committees to be set up at national and regional level, but by the end of
the year there were no signs of anything being done to implement the
decision.

The generally better record of white-collar unions is further
exemplified by the clerical workers' union, APEX (The Association
of Professional, Executive, Clerical and Computer Staffs), which in
1977 and 1978 conducted detailed surveys of the participation of
women at all levels of union activity. The picture was not particularly
encouraging. In a union where 53 per cent of the members are women,
only one out of the fifteen Executive Council members in 1978 was a
woman. (Interestingly, in 1965 there were six women Executive
Council members, partly because, for historical reasons, two seats
were then reserved for women. The National Union of Public
Employees (NUPE), another union with a majority of women
members, has now introduced 'women-only' Executive seats in order
to ensure better representation of women.) As part of its campaign to
encourage women's participation, APEX has established women's
rights sub-committees at national and area levels. Between 1973 and
1975, APEX was particularly active on equal pay, supporting a
number of strikes on this issue. Attention now seems to have shifted to
other conditions, such as maternity and paternity leave, and to the
introduction of positive discrimination in the union's education
programme, organising courses solely for women to train and

encourage them to become staff representatives and apply for other positions. Finally, APEX has published a fairly detailed guide on equal opportunities policies, including, for instnce, a proposal that questions on marriage and children should not be asked until after the appointment is made, and recommending special induction courses for women returning to employment in later life.

This is not to imply, however, that the manual workers' unions have done nothing. For example, the General and Municipal Workers' Union (over one-third of whose members are women), in addition to having a full-time officer responsible for sex discrimination questions, organises annual equal-rights conferences at national and regional level, and has given detailed guidance to negotiators on maternity leave and equal-pay agreements. The Tailor and Garment Workers' Union, with one of the highest proportions of female membership (over 90 per cent), has geared its activities and policies to women's needs and takes positive steps to ensure that delegations include a high proportion of women, with, for instance, nine out of the sixteen delegates to the TUC Annual Congress being women, as are nine of its forty-five full-time officials (unlike most unions which have none).

Confederation of British Industry

The CBI has firmly committed itself to the principle of equal opportunity and the elimination of discrimination, and encourages companies to implement 'constructive' equal opportunities policies. To do otherwise, as their director-general points out, 'would not only be unfair to the individuals concerned, but also socially and economically short-sighted'. Although the CBI recommends that employers adopt written equal opportunity policies, it has refrained from issuing any model statement, simply offering advice to individual employers.

The CBI guidance on equal opportunity policies, however, does not go beyond urging compliance with the law. The only exception is a brief reference to the need for special facilities for certain categories of employees, such as language training (for ethnic minority workers). Nowhere in its brief, two-page guidance is there any reference to the 'positive discrimination' sections of the Sex Discrimination Act, which permit positive steps to be taken to train and encourage women (and men) to qualify and apply for jobs in which they are now under-represented. Nor, despite the claim that the guidance has been based on 'members' practical experience of operating such policies in their own companies' is there any detailed example of the actual requirements or effects of such a policy.

The CBI has for many years favoured the removal of the protective legislation governing the hours of work of women manual workers. Indeed, a proposal to repeal the protective laws was made in the 1970–4 Conservative Government's Green Paper on equal opport-

unities legislation. The CBI view has now been adopted by the Equal
Opportunities Commission (although with the dissent of two of the
TUC members on that body), and its implications are examined in
detail below.

Equal Opportunities Commission

As part of its statutory duties, the Equal Opportunities Commission
was given the task of reviewing the protective legislation which affects
women workers employed on manual jobs in factories. Its report is an
important indication of the Commission's general attitude towards its
work and, in particular, its narrow interpretation of its duty to work
towards the elimination of sex discrimination.

The EOC recommends that the bulk of protective legislation should
be repealed, on the grounds that it acts as a barrier to equality of
opportunity. But the EOC report fails to deal satisfactorily with a
central difficulty. If the protective legislation is abolished, women
employees faced with a choice between working longer or less
convenient hours, and being dismissed, will have no effective protection
whatsoever against unfair dismissal. Both the TUC and the NCCL
(National Council for Civil Liberties, 1979) take the view that
protective measures should, wherever possible, be extended to men,
rather than taken away from women. But the support of the CBI for
their abolition, together with the attitude taken by the 1970–4
Conservative Government, makes it likely that the EOC recommendations will be implemented.

On child care, however, the EOC's policy coincides in many
respects with that of the TUC (Equal Opportunities Commission,
1978). It even goes beyond the Under-Fives Charter by stating
explicitly that child care is a matter of concern for both parents:

> The Commission would like to see the implementation of policies
> which maximise choices for both sexes and which make it feasible,
> for parents who wish to do so, to combine work and family, their
> domestic and their public lives. This applies not just to mothers, but
> to fathers who want to contribute more to the care of their children
> than is currently possible.

As with the TUC's policy on child care, the EOC's recommendations
cannot be carried out without substantial expenditure – and so will
remain wishful thinking while there is a government in power
committed to public spending cuts.

The EOC has a reasonably progressive policy on maternity rights –
although it does not go far enough (Equal Opportunities Commission,
1979b). It recommends, among other things, that the state maternity
grant be increased to £100; that the period of qualification for paid
leave should be reduced to six months, or 'at least to allow those

women with two years in employment to claim irrespective of whether the employment was with the same employer'; and that payments should be made from the Department of Employment's Maternity Pay Fund directly to the employee, rather than via the employer. It does not recommend that the period of paid leave should be extended, and it implies that there is a case for exempting small employers from their duty to hold jobs open (which fits in neatly with the Conservatives' plan to exempt them from the provisions of the Employment Protection Act). On paternity leave, it says:

> The aim should be to work towards a situation where a period of leave on full pay would be available on a statutory basis for the mother, followed by a longer period of partly paid and partly unpaid leave available to either parent .... It would be helpful to have a statutory period of paternity leave with full pay, to be taken within a certain time of the baby's birth to enable the father to give domestic support . . . immediately after the confinement.

With a failure of nerve that has become all too typical, the EOC does not include any reference to fathers in its final recommendations.

The EOC has recognised the need to reform the tax system, which currently discriminates against married women, but has been unable to come forward with any firm proposals, beyond saying that the married man's tax allowance in its present form should be abolished (Equal Opportunities Commission, 1979c). The question of what should be done with the money saved by the Treasury thereby remains unanswered.

As far as equal opportunity at work is concerned, the EOC has tended to concentrate on law enforcement – helping individuals take cases to tribunals; producing leaflets and booklets explaining how the laws work; and carrying out a limited amount of research. It has been widely criticised for not using its powers properly, for prevaricating and for erring too much on the side of the employers. One of its first major exercises in the employment field was a study of 500 large employing organisations to discover their policy and practice. When the results were published it turned out that the EOC had simply asked the employers what they were doing – and did not bother to ask employees for their version.

If it is accepted that equal opportunity and equal pay cannot be achieved just by taking individual cases to tribunals (and the evidence so far confirms that view), there are other, more effective, courses of action which the EOC could take. It could carry out more formal investigations into firms and other organisations where it suspects that there is unlawful discrimination; it could take action against 'discriminatory practices' (e.g. recruitment policies of firms which have traditionally excluded women and which make no effort to encourage them now); it could seek out more cases of indirect discrimination and fight them through the tribunals; and it could promote positive discrimination. To date it has launched no more than half a dozen formal investigations and has tended to conduct them as conciliatory, rather than investigatory, exercises. It has done little on discriminatory practices and has given financial backing to only one notable case of indirect discrimination at work (the case of Belinda Price, whose victory at the Employment Appeal Tribunal forced the Civil Service to raise its age limit for Executive Officer jobs).

One of the main problems of the EOC is that it was designed, and its Commissioners selected, in such a way as to provide the maximum of balance and the minimum of determined campaigning for change. Its Commissioners are chosen to represent various interest groups (three for the TUC, three for the CBI, one for Education, one for Scotland, one for Wales, etc.), rather than by virtue of their ability to promote equal opprtunity. Since it is funded by the government, it is not in a strong position to criticise the policies of government. Hence the EOC has no muscle, or cannot flex what little it has. Its policies are likely to have very little impact, except where they coincide with the wishes of the government of the day.

Conclusion

It is instructive to compare the often *ad hoc* policy formulation of key British interest groups with that of the Swedish Labour Market Board. Its programme explicitly opposes 'the view that women ought to be economically supported by marriage as this view is a direct obstacle to the economic independence of women . . . . The husband's traditional obligation to support his wife must be modified to constitute a responsibility, shared with her, for the support of the children', and links the need to open up work opportunities for women with its goals of improvements in the working environment and conditions of work, improved social planning and meeting individuals' needs to work (Swedish Labour Market Board, 1977). The Swedes have had only limited success in transforming this policy into practice, but at least they seem to be trying. For example, as we have already seen in Chapter 4, there is statutory parental leave available to either the mother or the father, and the Swedish federation of white-collar unions has been actively campaigning to persuade fathers to take up their option.

In Britain there is some talk but little action. We have yet to make the leap from a negative stance *against* discrimination (which can achieve very little) to a positive commitment to transform the status quo. What is strikingly absent from the policies of the major parties and interest groups in the UK is any real grasp of the scale of the changes that are required – and that (as we indicated at the beginning of this chapter) is very substantial indeed. There still seems to be a widespread belief that women have been lucky to get the concessions made to them thus far, but now there are more important matters to get on with, such as protecting men's jobs and earnings. Any further complaints from women are likely to be regarded as an unreasonable excess.

APPENDIX 1
THE AIMS OF THE TUC CHARTER FOR WOMEN AT WORK

1. Education

The Sex Discrimination Act says that there must be no discrimination against girls in education but positive action needs to be taken. There is still an undue emphasis on traditional sex-roles in school curricula. Fewer girls than boys stay on at school beyond the minimum school leaving age or go on to unviersity. So most women still start their working lives at a disadvantage because they have lower educational qualifications than men.

UNIONS WANT real equality of opportunity for girls with boys right through the educational system.

2. Starting Work

Although the Sex Discrimination Act says that almost every job must be open equally to women as to men, not many young women are able to enter jobs which will be interesting throughout their working lives. And except in hairdressing, few girls get a chance to become apprenticed to a skilled craft – or day release from work for further education.

UNIONS WANT complete equality of job opportunity for women with men; apprenticeships for girls on the same terms as they are available to boys; and day release for further education for all young workers – girls as well as boys.

3. Marital Status

The Sex Discrimination Act prevents married women being discriminated against. But it is still possible for employers to discriminate against unmarried women – such as unmarried mothers – or women who have been divorced.

UNIONS SAY there must be no discrimination whatsoever against any woman worker on grounds of her marital status.

4. Pay

The Equal Pay Act is helping but there are still many

employers looking for ways to avoid giving all their women workers
the rate of pay which men would have if they did the job. Equal pay is
more likely to apply where trade union organisation is strong.
UNIONS CALL for the proper rate for the job for all workers, male
and female, and an end to all pay discriminations against women
workers.

5. Promotion

There must be no discrimination against women in promotion says the
Sex Discrimination Act. Yet most women are still in low-grade and
low-paid jobs. Less than six in every 100 women at work are
supervisors or managers compared with 16 in every 100 men. And
women rarely reach such high levels in management as men.
UNIONS WANT women to have equal promotion opportunities
with men.

6. Occupational Pensions

Legislation is now being discussed to give women equal rights with
men in occupational pension schemes but unions know that some
sections of employees, which are predominantly female, may still
remain outside such schemes.
UNIONS SAY that the coverage of occupational schemes should be
the same for men and women and that they should contribute on the
same basis with equal pension rights.

7. Sick Pay

In law employers must now treat their women employees no
differently from the men in respect of sick pay entitlement. But unions
know that not all workers get sick pay from their employers and it is
still more likely to be women who are in jobs where they do not receive
pay when they are ill.
UNIONS WANT sick pay to cover all workers and will not accept
any discrimination against women.

8. Health and Safety at Work

Because women become mothers special care must be taken of their
health and welfare at work as well as elsewhere.
UNIONS OPPOSE any moves to allow women to work on jobs
which might endanger their health or that of an unborn baby.

9, Family Planning and Abortion

Free contraceptive advice and abortion facilities are now available
through the National Health Service. Unions recognise that the
decision whether or not to use such facilities is completely a matter for
the individual.

UNIONS SUPPORT the extension of such services and OPPOSE any moves to restrict women's access to any family planning or abortion services.

10. Maternity

As a result of union pressure the Employment Protection Act gives a woman with over two years' continuous service in a firm the right to six weeks' paid maternity leave and the right to return, if she wishes, to her job within seven months of the birth of her baby. This is a useful first step but
UNIONS WANT improved maternity provisions.

11. Returning to Work

Many women who leave work when they have their children want to resume paid employment at some time in the future. But little is done to help them to find a job which they would like to do.
UNIONS WANT advice centres in local employment offices and job centres to assist women to return to work; refresher courses for women who want to take up the same kind of job again; and training for women who want to learn new skills and enter new fields of employment.

12. Part-time Work

Two in every three working women are married and many of them have dependent children. And many women – single as well as married – look after elderly or infirm relatives. Often these women cannot work full-time because there are not sufficient support services, so about one third of all working women are part-time workers.
UNIONS SAY that part-time workers should receive pay and conditions at least pro rata to the full-time workers with whom they work.

13. Care of Children

There are still far too few places where mothers can safely leave their young children while they are at work, or where care will be taken of older children during the school holidays.
UNIONS SAY local authorities should be obliged to provide day nurseries, open throughout the day (and throughout the year) to assist working mothers; nursery school education for children below school age; and interesting activities for school children after school and during holidays.

14. Members of the Community

It is now illegal to discriminate against women when making

agreements for the supply of goods, facilities and services including hire purchase, tenancies, and mortgages. But discrimination against women continues in many areas, including social security and taxation.

UNIONS SAY women are equal members of the community with men and all discriminations against them must be abolished. Men and women should organise and work actively within the trade union Movement to achieve this and all the aims within this Charter.

APPENDIX 2

The main requirements of the TUC, as set out in the Charter for the Under-Fives

(i)   A comprehensive and universal service of care and education for children from 0 to 5 must be made available by public authorities. A national programme for pre-school services must be drawn up by the Government jointly with the unions.

(ii) Pre-school services must be available on demand to all those wishing to make use of them, which will require a major expansion of all pre-school services on the basis recommended in this report.

(iii) Pre-school services must be made available free of charge to parents.

(iv) A statutory duty to provide pre-school services must be placed on local authorities.

(v)   A service for the under-fives must be based on the principle that there can be no distinction between the education and welfare needs of young children.

(vi) All pre-school facilities must have flexible hours to meet the needs of working parents; and for schoolchildren a service of extended day and school holiday schemes should be made available.

(vii) The national plan for extended pre-school services should be based on an extension of nursery centres, combining care, education, health and welfare facilities for under-fives. Centres should co-ordinate all under-fives facilities in their areas. Child-minders and playgroups should be 'attached' to nursery centres, which should provide them with training and back-up services.

(viii)Existing facilities should be improved to provide a more comp-rehensive service – i.e. day nurseries should employ teachers as additional staff; nursery schools and classes should provide an 'extended day' and also facilities in school holidays.

(ix) Childminders should be employed by local authorities; attached to nursery centres and day nurseries; and provided with back-up services. New legislation on childminding should be introduced laying down minimum national standards. Local authorities should have a statutory duty to administer and enforce such legislation.

(x) Where workplace nurseries are provided, this should be on a basis which ensures joint union/parent/employer control and full local authority involvement, plus collectively agreed sufficient safeguards to protect the legitimate interests of the workforce.

(xi) Consultations should take place between the Department of Education and Science (DES), Department of Health and Social Security (DHSS), the relevant unions and the Council for National Academic Awards (CNAA) and the Local Government Training Board and the Nursery Nurses Education Board (NNEB) on an improved training and career structure for nursery officers. Discussions on integrated training and service conditions for teachers and nursery staffs should also be encouraged.

(xii) Discussions on ways of achieving far closer integration of the Government Departments responsible for under-fives services should take place. Local authorities should also integrate their services. A single development plan with joint funding should be provided.

(Trades Union Congress, 1978)

7

The Impact of Work on the Family

Rhona and Robert Rapoport

Work and the family interact in many ways. Work affects the family and family life affects the work of its members; trouble or alienation at work can bring irritability at home, just as discord at home can reduce productivity at work. Not only do the influences flow in both directions, but they may be beneficial or deleterious. Usually they are some mixture of both, and all patterns of work–family relationship includes strains and gains. Families and work groups organise themselves in various ways, and family members develop their own particular patterns of involvement in both places, producing what for most people is the core of their life-style. Both change as people progress through their lives. Similarly, the social and economic context of family and work life is constantly changing.

It is therefore simplistic to speak about the impact of work on parents or children as though there were a straight-forward or unidirectional effect. Yet many analyses have taken this form, seeking to isolate single variables to which overriding causal effect can be attributed. Working mothers and absentee fathers have been prime targets of such analysis. Many recent studies of the impact of work on the family have been concerned with maternal employment, and early studies in particular focused on potentially harmful effects, seeking a relationship between the variable of mother's employment and various negative outcomes for children, marriage or some other aspect of family life. Working mothers continue to be the target of such over-simplified approaches and thinking. An example is an article by a professor of psychiatry in the London *Times* in 1977, entitled 'Getting to the Root Cause of Delinquency':

> . . . The fact that anti-social behaviour by juveniles increases year by year indicates that the causes are not properly appreciated . . . . Juvenile anti-social behaviour – vandalism, break-ins, mugging, violence, hooliganism – were rare thirty years ago. Scientific logic leads to the questions: what environmental factors affecting the development of personality have changed over the past thirty years? One such factor is the parent–child relationship, as the result of the increasing number of mothers who take up full-time employment.

Professor Krebs goes on to say that parents who work often spoil their child out of guilt and fail to provide the necessary discipline. This is on top of not being there to give the warmth and comfort that a growing child needs.

As well as being simplistic, singling out one variable from a complex of social changes and assigning causal effects to it, this kind of analysis has two other defects. First, it is one-sided, neither putting the case *against* mothers staying at home nor the case for positive yields from mothers working. Secondly, even to the extent that it is a valid formulation, its impact is time-biased, implying that because certain effects have been observed to occur, they are an intrinsic part of the natural order. Early post-war cohorts of working mothers suffered more guilt than mothers in the late 1970s. There has been a marked reduction in the degree of social disapproval for married women working and this has reduced the strains associated with feeling 'deviant'. Though this factor has not been eliminated altogether, and there are other sources of strain, the change in this variable illustrates how important it is to conduct an impact analysis within the context of a dynamic, rather than a static conception of the social context. We return to this point later, and look then more closely at some of the important changes that have occurred in recent years in the social context and which bear on the relationship between work and family.

It is not surprising, in view of what has just been said, to find that when careful study replaces stereotyping there is no simple, causal link between a particular type of occupational status and particular types of family outcome. It is now quite clear, for instance, from the wide range of studies reviewed by Lois Hoffman (1974, 1979) in America, and Doria Pilling and Mia Kellmer-Pringle (1978) in the United Kingdom, that there is no direct or intrinsic relationship between mothers working and negative outcomes for other family members, or indeed for themselves. Generalisations cannot be made, unless they take the limited form of 'depending on . . .'.

An adequate analysis of the impact of work on the family must cover both strains and gains, and the wide variation that exists in the balance between them in different families. The outcomes are so varied because they are the product of processes that are themselves very complex, involving the interplay of several important sets of variables. Occupational circumstances, family structure and patterns of relating to work, formal and informal support systems and other resources available to families, levels of family stress and problems, and group, family and individual values and expectations all play a part. Matters are further complicated because the outcomes resulting from such complex processes may in turn feed back to influence ensuing processes. Strains, for instance, may give rise to new support systems or to alterations of family structure. Gains have similarly complex effects on values and expectations.

We suggest that two types of impact need to be distinguished. They entail two distinct though related ways in which the impact of work on family life can be said characteristically to occur:

1   *structural impact*, where the effects observed are a product of patterns of relating to work that are relatively stable over longer periods;

2   *event impact*, where the effects observed are consequences of critical events in the world of work, usually of shorter-term duration, such as uprooting and relocation, temporary unemployment and job change; conversely, in both instances, family structure and events can have considerable impact on work.

In the rest of this chapter we look in more detail at the variables involved in the process by which work impacts on the family. We then look at two examples of structural interaction, the conventional and dual-work patterns of work/family organisation. We then discuss, also illustratively, the specific sort of impact caused by critical events, and conclude by considering some of the implications for research, employment and social policy. But first we return to an earlier point, about the importance of avoiding an analysis that is time-biased and which ignores the social context and its potential for change.

The social context

An impact analysis must take into account both the wide sweep of historical change and the specific context of a particular age-group in recent social trend processes (see Kanter, 1977a, b; Kamerman, 1976; Elder, 1974). At least six elements of recent social change have had a conspicuous effect on occupational and family circumstances and the relationship between these two areas:

a) technological changes;
b) the changing nature of the family as a social institution;
c) changes in contraceptive practices and reproductive patterns;
d) changes in women's education;
e) changes in attitudes about sex roles;
f) changes in women's participation in the labour force.

Although some of these changes have already been described in Chapter 2, and especially (c), (d) and (f), other aspects of them may usefully be elaborated here.

Technological changes have provided some of the most obvious examples of change in work and family life. Their impact on industry is obvious and has been described in many accounts elsewhere. The impact on the family, due to easing of domestic work and home amenities has also been very powerful but is perhaps less widely appreciated. Buckminster Fuller has observed that the application of machinery to household tasks has placed the equivalent of armies of slaves at the disposal of ordinary families. Luxuries of royalty and aristocracies in past times are now available to ordinary households, in developed countries, and this has happened over a brief historical time span. Quentin Bell (1972) vividly describes how the domestic tasks confronted by working wife Virginia Woolf differed from those confronted by today's working wife:

> . . . in the evening you can make a light with which to read . . . by pressing a switch. The room is warmed by central heating, you turn a tap and hot water pours into your bath or into your sink, you pull a plug and cold water gushes into your lavatory. You may do your own cooking and your own housework, but you are probably assisted by dozens of mechanical devices, tins and tin-openers, frozen foods, refrigerators and plastic containers. Heaven knows how many thousand horses give their power every day at the touch of your fingers. No very serious effort is demanded of you when ovens have to be heated, foods ground and mixed, floors swept, rooms lighted and fires made.
>
> Now, when Virginia Woolf went to Asham she found none of these commodities. To get there at all she had to walk or bicycle for several miles or to go to the expense of a taxi or a fly. To make a light she had candles which dropped grease on the carpet, or lamps which smoked and had to be refilled with oil and trimmed every morning; heat was supplied by wood or coal . . . the coal had to be carried about in scuttles, grates had to be cleaned, fires laid, and if they were not competently managed they would fill the room with smoke or die miserably. In the country you got hot water by boiling it over a stove. Cold water had to be pumped up into a tank every day and Asham was furnished only with an earth closet. There were no refrigerators or frozen foods, a tin-opener was a kind of heavy dagger with which you attacked the tin hoping to win a jagged victory. All the processes of cooking and cleaning were incredibly laborious, messy and slow. There are still plenty of people who live in conditions of this kind or worse – far worse – but obviously in these circumstances someone must be perpetually at work if any kind of comfort or cleanliness is to be maintained.

Virginia Woolf and some of her Bloomsbury friends, who were against the use of servants which were available to many middle-class families of the day, felt themselves to be on the horns of a dilemma. The dilemma remains to some extent, though there are few 'servants' today even for those who have much money and few ideological scruples. Some families have responded to the new technology by raising their standards, filling available time with new kinds of domestic work. Others have used the time freed from drudgery to take on activities outside the home, among them paid work.

The changing nature of the family Young and Willmott (1973) have argued that the miniaturisation of machines and their application in the home has contributed not only to the reorganisation of domestic time-budgets, but to a changed conception of home and family life. The home is increasingly a centre for leisure activities – many men return home after work, instead of going to clubs or local pubs. Here they join their wives and children in home-based leisure activities – from television to DIY repairs and a range of hobbies.

One consequence of this trend toward home and family life occupying a more central place in peoples' lives (countering the long trend toward 'stripping' the family of its functions) is that family factors are becoming more powerful as causal variables. As Kanter has put it, the family is 'fighting back'. People explicitly take or reject jobs, alter work schedules, adopt attitudes towards career advance- ment because of their family involvements – as well as vice versa. Employers seek to entice workers to new towns by providing family amenities; wives as well as husbands are brought to view new job environments – and in some cases, prospective employers seek to find an appropriate job for the spouse lest the wanted new employee decline an otherwise inviting opportunity (Berger, Foster and Wallston, 1978).

Young and Willmott also argue that the growth of the family as a unit of consumption is accompanied by an evolution of family structure in the direction of greater symmetry. They see men's and women's roles as coming more to resemble one another, each having an important occupational *and* domestic component.

Changes in reproductive patterns Technological advances in medical and allied fields have produced a situation where contraception can now be practised widely and reliably. It is within the capacity of every individual and family to plan their pattern of reproduction. Not all families do, and the rejection or neglect of use of available contraceptive resources may be the results of many factors in given situations. Nevertheless, trends have been toward having smaller families, and 'compressing' child-bearing into a narrower band of the life course, and for many people choosing not to have children at all. The net effect of these social trends has been for both men and women to have longer time spans during their lives for activities in which children are less central.

Changes in women's education The convergence of men's and women's educational experience has led to an increase in levels of aspiration and expectation for members of both sexes. This has contributed to a new orientation to work and family life, reinforced by the shift in available time already described. One consequence has been that family life is not now seen as an adequate channel for lifelong personal fulfilment for many women.

The increase in women's interest in developing skills deployable in the labour force has made it possible for their husbands to consider career patterns which allow for giving work less centrality, particularly in late mid-life. There is a shift toward the pursuit of educational goals as a lifelong process for both men and women, and for this to be reflected both in the development of similar personal interests in men and women and in the participation of both on a more equal footing in the workplace, though this is, obviously, a process which is far from being fully realised.

Changes in attitude toward sex roles Toward the end of the last century there was a dominant view about sex roles – male-centred and paternalistic. There was also a counterpoint orientation which contained the seeds of the more egalitarian approach to follow. The conventional paternalistic orientation, emphasising the merits of contrasting and segregated roles, was prevalent in all walks of life. It was lyrically expressed by Alfred Lord Tennyson, Queen Victoria's poet laureate, who wrote:

Man for the field and woman for the hearth:
Man for the sword and for the needle she:
Man with the head and woman with the heart:
Man to command and woman to obey:
All else confusion

The counterpoint, expressed in the liberal philosophy of John Stuart Mill and Harriet Taylor Mill (1869) emphasised the overlap of interests and the importance of sharing and equality if a sense of social justice was to be achieved: 'laying the foundation of domestic existence upon a relationship contrary to the first principles of social justice must, from the very nature of man, have a perverting influence'. The Mills did not mean that women should be encouraged to pursue careers on the same basis as men, only that they should be viewed as equals, allowing each to work out a destiny freely. The logic of their position has, however, inevitably extended itself to include equality of occupational as well as other opportunities in life.

The shifts in balance of views present in our society has been remarkable. It is startling to realise that a short time ago the architects of the major social policies governing our society today were assuming that women would never want to go out to work in large numbers: Beveridge's assumptions, for example, have already been quoted in Chapter 1. Even in the late 1960s, when we began our study of *Women in Top Jobs*, an eminent psychiatrist told us that while he agreed that there would always be a small number of highly motivated women who would *need* to work, it would never apply to the majority whose natural instincts made them more home-centred. And, to dramatise the way in which public attitudes have changed, it was Margaret Thatcher herself who said that she did not think there could be a woman prime minister in Britain in her lifetime.

Clearly there are several dimensions to be considered under this general heading. First, men and women have conceptions of themselves different from those held previously, and there is a greater tendency to recognise similarities in their capacities. Men need not see themselves only as aggressive, competitive, 'instrumental' to use the Parsonian sociological jargon; and women need not see themselves as only dependent, supportive, 'affectional'. Men can *feel* and women can *work* effectively and both sexes are seen more widely to have both these traits.

In terms of actual behaviour, sex-role changes are less marked. Women's achievements in the occupational system and men's sharing of domestic duties and responsibilities fall short of expressed ideals. There are disjunctions between attitudes and practices, ideals and realities. Partly this is due to the fact that the presence of an ideal in our society does not mean that everyone shares it equally; there is still considerable diversity, both of attitude and behaviour. But it is also partly due to difficulties in implementing ideas that require structural changes, even for those who hold the ideals most strongly.

But despite the limits it is important to recognise that the beginnings of change have been occurring. Most time-budget studies conducted early in the process of change in women's participation in the workforce showed that there was no corresponding shift of men's participation in domestic work (Szalai, 1972; Haavio-Mannila, 1972; Walker and Woods, 1976). But in a re-study of American family patterns in the late 1970s, Katherine Walker found some indicators of change. Though there was little or no change in the time spent by men on most domestic tasks, there was a significant increase in the area of child care. While levels of male involvement in domestic tasks remain generally low, such increases as there have been are likely to have an impact on future levels of participation, making it increasingly acceptable for others to follow.

Changes in women's participation in the labour force Women's participation in the labour force has changed conspicuously, but once again attitude changes have often been in advance of behavioural changes. Women now state more openly similar motivations for working to men's, including 'social' and 'career' motivations. But there is the oft-noted shortfall in the level of attainment of qualified women, despite facilitative legislation. Various reasons are suggested for this: discriminatory practices, women's own 'fear of success' (Horner, 1971), and the constraints of the competing attractions and distractions of family life. The PEP study of women graduates provided some insight into the last of these patterns. Single graduates of both sexes indicated a fairly high level of aspiration eight years after leaving university, 45 per cent of men and 37 per cent of women wanting to 'get to the top' or 'hold a high position'. Of married graduates, 74 per cent of married men with no children and 69 per cent of married men with children indicated this set of high aspirations, as compared with 24 per cent of married women with no children and 14 per cent of married women with children. This does not seem to be entirely a matter of the less ambitious women choosing marriage and childbearing rather than a career. The married women with lower levels of aspiration reported having had comparable levels to their unmarried counterparts earlier in their careers (Fogarty *et al.*, 1971).

We now turn to an examination of some of the main components involved in the process which determines the impact of work on the family, starting first with work and the variations that exist in occupational circumstances.

The worlds of work

Occupations vary in the demands they make and the conditions under which they are performed as well as in their rewards and social status. There are many kinds of occupation and many ways of classifying them and their characteristics: no way is able fully to express the range of differences that occur. The most widely used classification of occupational type in Britain is that of the Registrar-General, while in America it is the classification used by the Bureau of the Census. Both are based on levels of qualification and skill required. In a very general way, these classification systems are correlated with levels of pay, conditions of employment and job satisfaction; the higher the social class of occupation, the higher the remuneration, the better the conditions and the greater the job satisfaction. The classification is widely used as an index of social class. This, in turn, is related to physical and mental wellbeing and to a range of social and cultural elements – attitudes, values, habitual forms of behaviour and so on. We shall return to these, considering them separately as they do not flow entirely or automatically from work itself and are therefore best considered as factors mediating the effect of occupation and family structure.

The associations that exist between social class and occupational characteristics are rough ones. Many occupations, as classified by the Registrar-General, cover a considerable span: people classified as 'managers', for example, run all the way from proprietors of small shops to directors of large multinational corporations. So size of organisation is an important variable, one of the factors likely to affect the sense of personal involvement in the job and sense of control over decisions affecting one's work life. This in turn relates to the degree of flexibility that may be available to make arrangements for altering work schedules.

There are of course many other variables, cross-cutting the Registrar-General's occupational system and which define important aspects of the individual's work circumstances and experience. To take just a few as examples, some jobs are performed by people on their own account and some for others, either public or private sector employers. Jobs may be varied and changing or monotonous and boring; they may engage the mind and the body in varying ways. Some jobs are considered suitable for young people and others for older people, some for men and others for women; some jobs have high prestige while others are despised.

Occupations can also be described and classified in more complex ways. Miller and Swanson (1958) distinguish between 'entrepreneurial' jobs (in small organisations, with low capitalisation, high risk and much personal decision-making) and 'bureaucratic' jobs (in large organisations, with many layers of authority and more corporate forms of decision-making). Workers in 'entrepreneurial' jobs emphasise in their family life the importance of independence, self-control and an active approach to manipulating the course of experience, while 'bureaucratic' workers' families place more emphasis on accommodation, looking to others for guidelines and so on. Jobs also vary in how demanding they are. The more demanding occupations, described as 'greedy' by Lewis Coser (1956), include both those which elicit a high degree of commitment on moral grounds (e.g. the clergy) and those in which material rewards are high (e.g. senior managers in industry). Sofer (1970) showed that managers on their way up are so absorbed in the process of trying to get themselves into the desired positions at the desired time that shortfalls are acutely experienced as failures. Rosebeth Kanter has further elaborated the dynamics of managerial mobility in large American organisations and interpreted the intense pressures towards conformity as reflecting the need to perceive others as reliable in a situation of high uncertainty and low visibility of work products.

This special situation of occupations which are highly absorbing not only places members of those occupations under stress; it affects their families in ways not dissimilar to those of absentee parents such as seamen, lorry-drivers and commercial travellers, whose absence from the family produces characteristic strains (Gronseth, 1957; Odegaard, 1936). Parents in 'greedy' occupations may be seen to be doing their jobs 'for the family', but they cannot give themselves to their family relationships in the same way as people who are in less demanding jobs. Studies of upwardly mobile managers (Rapoport, 1970; British Institute of Management, 1973) have shown that a mid-career choice often has to be made by successful ones – between increased responsibility and remuneration on the one side, or more time for family and leisure interests on the other. When the choice is made for the former, there may have to be a trade-off with the family, either by providing more immediate tangible benefits (such as a second home or car, holidays abroad, private schools for the children) or by holding forth the prospect of deferred benefits such as an improved overall life-style and more comfortable retirement. Beric Wright (1972) has warned such managers, however, that unless they maintain a certain balance, they may never live to enjoy their retirement – and this may mean depriving their wives of the most-wanted benefit.

We do not here attempt an exhaustive classification of relevant occupational characteristics, but rather try to suggest the variety involved and illustrate some of the effects of different circumstances on family behaviour. Variety in work is matched by variety in family structure, a second key component in determining the impact of work on family members. We turn now to consider this part of the process in more detail.

Family worlds

It is still widely assumed that there is a single, standard, 'normal' kind of family that most people live in, and many policies are based on this assumption. When we hear commentators speak of 'the British family', or 'the modern Western family', we assume that they are talking about the family that lives in a separate household, father providing for it economically and mother looking after the home and their two or three children. Descriptions of the quality of life in such family households vary widely. The idealised conception depicts this family unit as the 'keystone of society', as well as the mainstay of individual well being. On the other extreme, it is heavily criticised as distorting the opportunity structure for children, implanting personal neuroses, biasing life chances and exploiting the labour of females. One psychiatrist (Cooper, 1970) has caricatured the intense patho-genic elements of the modern nuclear family by likening it to a 'psychological gas chamber'.

In fact, for a variety of reasons – including migrations and the presence of ethnic sub-cultures, the rising tendency and normalisation of women's work at all stages of the life cycle, increased life expectancy, the tendency for elderly people to live alone, the increase in divorce and its aftermath including remarriage and reconstitution of new family units – families are highly variegated, and nearly anything one can say about families is true of some. Conversely, as Michael Rutter has remarked, 'any generalisation about the family is bound to be wrong'.

There has always been diversity in family life, but no sources of data or systems of classification exist that are adequate to describe and encompass this diversity. Government statistics are organised mainly in terms of households and household types, a household being defined as 'one person living alone or a group of people who all live regularly in the same address and who are all catered for by the same person for at least one meal a day'. While households and families mostly coincide (i.e. most households consist of only one family unit), in some there are two or more families (e.g. a lone mother and child (Family A) living with the mother's parents (Family B)). 'Household types' therefore must usually serve as a proxy for 'family types' and from the 1976 General Household Survey the types shown in Table 17 are immediately discernible.

TABLE 17 HOUSEHOLD TYPES (percentages)

Married couple with children –	
Single breadwinner	20
Two earners	20
Married couple, no children	27
One-parent family household	8
One-person household –	
Over retirement age	15
Under retirement age	6
Two or more people, not a family	3
Two or more families	1
Total	100

Source: Central Statistical Office (1978), Tables 2.2 and 3.4

These figures reflect the significance of a number of recent social and demographic trends. Non-pensioner one-parent households have both been increasing in number, and now account for nearly one in seven of all households. Among two-parent families with children, those with two earners are as common now as those with a single breadwinner, which is itself a general indication of a movement to more varied patterns of relating to work. Other equally important trends are not reflected in the figures. They do not show, for instance, unmarried couples living together: between the late 1960s and 1975, the number of couples cohabiting before marriage more than tripled (Leete, 1979a). Nor do they show the increase in 'reconstituted households': it was estimated that 31 per cent of all 1976 marriages had one or both partners previously married, as compared with 18 and 20 per cent in 1951 and 1971. Then, there are those family households that contain foster or adopted children, and a smaller proportion containing unorthodox domestic arrangements of one kind or another. Finally, the potential for diversity in the way in which domestic and child-care tasks are organised and distributed within families is probably increasing, but data on this aspect of family life are scarce.

These sorts of variation, striking as they are, reflect only two types of family diversity, variations in structure (e.g. whether or not there are one or two parents, which members are economically active) and variations in life-course stage (e.g. of the 21 per cent of one-person households, 6 per cent are adults below retirement age and 15 per cent are older persons). They do not show more subtle phenomena, such as value orientations and motivations, nor other important and relevant aspects of family life, such as resources and non-work stresses. These other aspects are all likely to influence the effect of work on the family as important mediating factors. We consider them next.

Resources, stresses and values

The resource position of each family has an important bearing on its ability to cope, and in the way it copes, with life in general and with the demands of work in particular. A family's resources partly consist of the material and non-material capacities that the family has available to cope with the challenges it confronts. To some extent the material capacities of a given family are determined by income level – that is perhaps the first and most obvious kind of impact that work makes on family life. But some families' material resources are inherited and some earned, and some are provided in cash and some in kind (e.g. women's free domestic labour). So the matter is not simple.

Families also have non-tangible resources which are associated with the history of the particular family and its position in the local community. Families' personal social networks, variously constituted of kin, friends, professional relationships etc., may function as informal support systems in cushioning the impact of work on family life: we have already seen, for instance, in Chapter 2 how relatives and friends continue to play an important part in the care of children of working mothers. Elizabeth Bott (1957), in one of the classical studies of social networks in urban British life, distinguished between 'tight knit' networks (characteristic of the kind of stable working-class neighbourhood studied by Young and Willmott in Bethnal Green) and 'loose knit' networks, more characteristic of families living in more anonymous parts of cities and in certain 'dormitory' suburbs. Even in such suburbs, networks do exist and can play an important supportive role: Gaynor Cohen has described how British suburban wives of managers, who work long hours and travel a great deal, cope by forming self-help social groups, feeling less lonely and rejected by banding together with others in the same boat (Cohen, 1977).

As well as resources, families vary in the amount of stress they have to cope with. Epidemiological studies have shown that families high on the social-class scale are not only better off economically, but face fewer illnesses and less disruption in their lives generally (Leighton *et al.*, 1963). Conversely, those lower down the social scale are more prone to illness and disabilities, and to disorganisation. There are of course many exceptions to this general relationship between social class and degree of disorganisation and stress. A statement such as 'coronary heart disease is correlated with social class' is based on statistics which show that 88,000 men from professional and similar status occupations died of ischaemic heart disease in 1970–2, compared with 111,000 unskilled workers. To think of heart disease as primarily a problem of lower social classes risks disregarding the many sufferers in higher-status occupational groups.

The first area of potential variation to be covered in this section is the extensive and amorphous one of values and culture. There are considerable differences between the cultures of sub-groups, especially the importance attached to different values. These differences make themselves felt in expectations and opinions, and in preferred patterns of family behaviour and relationships. Most of the available studies of these aspects of the family use social class as the basis for comparisons. Studies of social class culture (as correlated with occupation) in all advanced industrial countries indicate some characteristic value orientations, affecting attitudes and behaviour in the areas of marital relationships and child-rearing. In simplified form we summarise in Table 18 the main patterns reported (cf. Bott, 1971; Goldthorpe *et al.*, 1969; Inkeles, 1960; Newson and Newson, 1970; Working Family Project, 1978; Kohn and Schooler, 1969).

TABLE 18 SOME SOCIAL CLASS DIFFERENCES IN MARITAL RELATIONS AND CHILD-REARING PRACTICES

	Middle Class	*Working Class*
Marital relations	More emphasis on sharing, equity, communication	More emphasis on 'the place' of men and women, less verbal communication
	More 'joint' division of labour	More 'segregated'
	more 'planful'; instrumental	less planful
Child-rearing practices	High value placed on internalisation of values; reasoning, self-direction, initiative	High value placed on obedience
	Emphasis on ambition	Emphasis on conforming with authority
	Discipline by reasoning and reward/love witholding	Discipline more physical

The general patterning of social class culture, or world-view as Kohn and Schooler (1969) call it, operates in the environment of families, whatever their particular family–work pattern. To some extent middle-class families share similar orientations to the marital relationship and to parenting by virtue of their class position. But this provides only one set of influences on parents and children, and families vary in the extent to which they accept or reject the orientations of the class cultures to which they are assigned. Stereotyping families by class variables alone can be mistaken. Recent surveys such as that of Yankelovich (1974) indicate a trend toward congruence of values between the social class groups, and John Goldthorpe and his colleagues (1980) indicate the emergence of substantial sub-groups with low 'classness'.

There are also sub-groupings other than social class which influence individual values and attitudes, and may indeed cut across that of social class. One of the most obvious has to do with *ethnicity*, but even within each ethnic category – Jewish, Irish-Catholic, West Indian, South Asian, etc. – there are contrasts. Some are more traditional-minded or orthodox, others are assimilationist. And within larger ethnic categories, such as South Asian, there is a range of cultural variation: Muslims, Sikhs, Hindus, Goans, and so on are at least as diverse among themselves as are different European nationalities. Yet they are often classed together, and many feel a sense of shared values (Ballard, 1981).

An even more subtle, less easily measurable basis of family diversity is 'family culture'. Each family, even of the 'standard conventional' variety, has a culture which is in some ways uniquely its own. Hess and Handel (1959) have reported on the 'psychosocial interiors' of families and indicated how families construct their own 'family worlds' reflecting the values and beliefs, personalities and patterns of relationship that have evolved within the specific family. This notion of family cultures is relevant to any proper understanding of the impact of work on families, because it helps us to explain why families respond differently to the same events – *as* families. But systematising such classifications and making them more widely usable has only begun.

Finally, differences in values, attitudes and preferences may exist at a purely *individual* level, cutting across family, class or other group influences. Among working mothers in all classes, for example, some work for economic reasons against their personal convictions of the proper role of women, while others do so because they want to and as an expression of their egalitarian convictions. Recent research suggests that such personal attitudes to work, and general job satisfaction, play an important part in determining the impact of work on mother, child and their relationship, much more so, indeed, than the fact of whether the mother works or not. Yarrow and her colleagues (1962), for instance, found that the greatest satisfaction in, and best standards of, mothering occurred when mothers were at home *and wanted to be*, followed by mothers who were at work and wanted to be, and were lowest in the two 'misfit' situations – the reluctant workers and captive wives. In her review of the literature, Hoffman concludes that mothers satisfied with working and with their jobs are warmer in their interactions with their children and place less demands on them to work in the house, while unsatisfied mothers are more removed emotionally and make excessive demands on their children, who respond aggressively, so starting a vicious circle.

We have touched on some of the factors likely to have a bearing on the structural and event impact that work has on families. The factors are numerous and varied, the interactions between them complex and not well understood and outcomes difficult to predict precisely or at any level of generality. In the next section, we concentrate on structural impact, considering some of the possible strains and gains that can flow from two of the patterns of relating to work that are available to families – *conventional families*, where the husband is the sole breadwinner and the wife is the full-time home-maker, and *dual-worker families,* where both parents work continuously outside the home while raising at least one child.

Structural interaction between work and family: conventional and dual-worker families

The conventional pattern

Families who operate the conventional pattern, where husband/father is the exclusive breadwinner and wife/mother is the full-time housewife, have characteristic satisfactions and strains associated with them (Bernard, 1972; Young and Willmott, 1973; Rapoport *et al.*, 1977; Campbell *et al.*, 1976; Oakley, 1980).

The immediate impact on parents and children of these families is that fathers, being away from home most of the day most days, are much less involved in child care than are their wives. As Michael Rutter (1972) has put it, parenting in conventional families has come to mean mothering. Young and Willmott found that London fathers spent 7.1 hours daily at work or travelling to work, and 1.4 hours on household tasks which included DIY, helping their wives with washing up and so on, as well as interacting with children.

While we found in a survey of a London Borough that a high proportion of women who accept the housewife role express satisfaction, intensive interviews with these women uncover a number of character-istic dissatisfactions. Some of these are attributable to the role as well as to other conditions of their lives such as housing, neighbourhood, and so on. The greatest strains are felt by wives who have small children. They are at a point in the family life course which Wilensky (1968) has characterised as the 'life cycle squeeze'. Their husbands are out working full-time, or more in many cases, in order to be able to pay for the costs of establishing a home and providing for young children; and the wives are left to cope on their own. Wives who come through this period without being able to develop meaningful personal interests show, according to a Tavistock national stress study, a high degree of psychosomatic symptoms by the time they reach thirty-five (Irving and Hilgendorf, cited in Rapoport *et al.*, 1977).

There seems to be two sources of housewife dissatisfaction in the early phase of family life and child-rearing: alienating characteristics of the housewife role which Ann Oakley (1974) has compared with a semi-skilled factory worker's job; and strains of near solo-parenting with little practical or emotional support from husbands. This is most acute in working-class families where, as Brown and Harris (1978) have recently demonstrated, the lack of a confidante is an important contributing factor to the onset of psychological depression. It has long been recognised that women generally suffer more than men from depression (Guttentag and Salasin, 1975), that communication difficulties contribute to depression (Weissman and Paykel, 1974) and that working-class wives feel less able to turn to their husbands to discuss problems than do middle-class wives.

The conventional pattern appears, on the whole, to be more satisfactory for husbands than for wives. But men have begun to question whether as fathers they may not be losing out on something important to them by their low participation in parenting. Biological analyses have now indicated that the human primate's hairlessness produces an animal which can enjoy tactile stimulation with children as well as with members of the opposite sex (Rypma, 1979). If given a chance to form a bonding relationship with their offspring, male monkeys, for example, will show similar protectiveness and involvement with the infants and similar signs of rage and grief when separated, as do females (Redican and Mitchell, 1972). This checks with findings in humans. Greenberg and Morris (1974) found in a study of thirty first fathers in three London maternity hospitals that they showed 'engrossment', bonding, absorption and preoccupation with the baby. The researchers interpreted this to mean that fathers have a potential for parental involvement that is not usually expressed in our culture but could be. Robert Fein (1974), in a similar study in the USA, indicates how fathers feel constrained from participating with their newborn children as much as they would like by the requirements of their jobs. Gronseth's (1978) study of work-sharing families in Norway, in which both fathers and mothers worked part-time so that they could share domestic tasks, indicates that many fathers derive particular pleasure from child-care experiences.

Katherine Walker (1979), in two domestic time-budget studies, a decade apart, of American families, found that child care was the only area of domestic tasks in which fathers significantly increased their participation in domestic life. Whereas fathers in two-child families spent half an hour daily on non-physical care of their children in the 1960s, similarly placed fathers averaged a full hour in the late 1970s. (They also increased their share in 'meal preparation' and 'dishwashing', but it was 'not very dramatic . . . husbands' time doubled from 0.1 hour per day to 0.2 hour for food preparation . . . an increase of six minutes per day for an activity in which the wife used 1.5 hours if she was not employed and 1.2 hours if she was.')

Some studies also indicate the strain on men who are the family's sole breadwinner. It is suggested that this may be at the root of men's special vulnerability to heart diseases and ulcers. One American study by Chen and Cobb (1960) showed a correlation between the number of children a father had and his proneness to ulcer. The study did not, however, control for the wife's occupation, so it can only be taken to be suggestive.

As for the impact on child-rearing and the development of the child, some view the peripherality of the father as having two undesirable effects on children: it allows for the possibility of an over-developed mother–child bond, and it deprives the child of some fathering. Pedersen (1976) notes than conventional fathering situations have, as a positive element, the intensification of father contacts with the child. They become more impressive partly because of their scarcity value; 'father says' carries more weight because he is not always around 'saying'. This is said to help the child's development because it offers a social psychological bridge to the infant's larger environment, and facilitates the development of autonomy and the capacity to sustain other relationships. On the other hand the peripherality of the father in conventional families also allows for the possibility of father's becoming a really remote figure for the child – either because he is away a good deal on his work, or because he is emotionally removed from involvement with child-rearing. Both are, in a sense, legitimated by the conventional definition of parental roles.

The range of disorders associated with father absence in any extreme degree is well documented in the literature and is now recognised as a psychological hazard that requires special attention. Conventional families with fathers in occupations such as seamen, long-distance lorry drivers, airline pilots, managers in multinational corporations and so on, experience specific forms of deprivation. Among lower-class families, where fathers may be particularly vulnerable to job instability, the need for adolescent males to assert their masculinity in breaking away from the intense attachment to mother may make them prone to delinquent activities. Higher up the social-class scale, father's absence may contribute to identity issues or confusion in the development of interests and attachments. For most conventional families, the degree of removal of the father from child-rearing is not so extreme. Nevertheless, some observers speak of the 'hidden wound' that the widespread deficiency in active fathering produces in children (Le Masters, 1957; Biller and Meredith, 1974; Pleck and Sawyer, 1974).

Dual-worker families

There have always been families in which both husbands and wives have worked regularly. Shopkeeping families like the baker's family described by Peter Laslett (1971) in *The World We Have Lost* persist to the present day; and shiftworking couples like those described by Michael Anderson (1973) for nineteenth-century Lancashire may actually be on the increase. There are many small businesses – pubs, inns, boarding schools, restaurants and the like – which rely on the team effort of a working couple.

But the modern pattern of dual-worker families, while somewhat similar to these long-standing patterns, is in many ways a new phenomenon. It arises through the increase in the number of married women choosing to work on a regular basis, and at the same time to have a family. As there are many motivations for the choice and many conditions under which it can operate, it is not surprising that there are various forms it can take. These affect the impact of the pattern on parents and children. We now have three generations of research on aspects of this pattern (Rapoport and Rapoport, 1978c); with all the variations there are some generic issues that occur, and some characteristic ways of resolving them (Gowler and Legge, 1981).

Peter Moss has indicated some of the *economic* issues associated with the pattern. The consequences, if not the intentions, of operating the pattern are very different for those at the lower end of the social-class scale than for those higher up. At the lower end, it has the effect of keeping families above the poverty line. Higher up the scale, it enables families to increase their standard of living, taking holidays abroad, making home extensions or buying second homes and so on. It also has the effect of providing security against rapid downward mobility in the event of unemployment or career reversals of a breadwinner.

Another general feature of the pattern, also mentioned above, is that though there is a substantial basis in social values, particularly middle-class values, to support the pattern as an expression of an egalitarian orientation, the observed behaviour of husbands leads to the conclusion that this is often lip-service. Generally speaking, husbands do not replace the time by which their wives reduce household work. Sometimes, as Ann Oakley (1974) has shown, part of the husband's replacement takes the form of skimming off more enjoyable elements like playing with the children, leaving the wife with a more unremitting portion of drudgery. One writer on 'dual-career' families (Mortimer, 1977) noted that husbands in such families are often not aware of the discrepancy between what they say and what they do.

Nor is work outside the home a panacea, even when freely chosen. Weissman and Paykel (1974) noted that employed wives who are mismatched with their jobs are prone to depression in a way not dissimilar to 'captive housewives'. If a married woman, for example, takes a job for which she is over-qualified in order to escape the loneliness and boredom of being a housewife, she may come to feel that she has jumped from the frying pan into the fire, as regards the degree of personal stress she has to endure. This highlights the importance of 'fit' between person and role as an important intervening variable.

Just as there is a sub-group of conventional housewives who are reluctant in their role and would prefer to be at work, there is a sub-group of reluctant working wives. A recent study (Moss and Plewis, 1979) suggests that these women are more prevalent in the lower income groups, and that most of them would not like to stop work altogether but would rather work a little less in order to achieve a better balance between what a recent Russian study with similar findings called their functions as 'toilers, mothers, child-rearers and home-makers' (reported in *New Society*, 30 August 1979, p. 450). Though this is a statistical tendency, reflecting the strains on women who have low income, ungratifying jobs and unsupportive husbands, it probably has wider validity.

However, for various reasons and in various ways, increasing proportions of families are adopting a dual-worker pattern. It is not, as some early commentators on research on dual-career families held, a freakish pattern tenable in peacetime only by a privileged minority. It is being chosen by increasing numbers of families because of its appeal to ordinary people – and its demonstrated feasibility. But, as with other patterns of work/family interrelationship, it has both gains and strains.

We are now able to define the issues with a fair degree of precision. Research on dual-worker families has now reached a stage where it is possible to say that many of the early 'doomwatcher' hypotheses are 'unproven', and many of the 'advocacy' hypotheses can now be placed in perspective for further investigation. To illustrate this, there are two 'doomwatcher' hypotheses which can be examined:

(a) that dual-worker marriages will produce marital conflict;
(b) that dual-worker marriages will produce a poor environment for parenthood, leading to neglected 'latchkey' children who

will swell the ranks of the delinquent, retarded and mentally disordered.

(a) Impact on parents Most of the reviews of literature that could help us to assess the hypothesis are inconclusive. Either they relate to overlapping but not identical populations (e.g. Hoffman and Nye's (1974) review of literature on working mothers; and Michael Rutter's (1972) review of literature on maternal deprivation); or they show no statistically significant relationship (which does not, of course, mean that there are never any negative consequences of the pattern). There are, however, some useful studies which contribute insight into the issues involved.

One American study by Orden and Bradburn (1968) of the National Opinion Research Center in Chicago suggests that marital happiness depends less on whether or not both partners work than on whether their choice was freely entered into. This work highlights the importance of the *meaning of work* (as well as the fact of working) as part of assessing work's impact on family life.

A study of British graduate couples by Lotte Bailyn (1971) indicates that while conventional families show a slightly higher proportion stating that their marriage is 'very happy', the proportions are not significantly less for working couples. Moreover, the latter are less likely to give stereotyped 'happiness' responses. But the sub-group which are markedly *low* on marital satisfaction are those in which the husband is extremely 'career-oriented' – i.e. seeks his major life satisfactions from his work and not at all from his family life (as distinct from men who place career first but also rate family as an important source of satisfaction). This circumstance occurs in conventional families, as well as dual-worker families.

Heather Ross and Isabel Sawhill (1975) of the Urban Research Institute in Washington note an association between the rising divorce rate and the rising rate of wives at work. They observe that the economic benefits of marriage are less decisive for wives who are independent earners, and that divorce has a different sub-cultural meaning among secular urban couples than in more conventional settings. The whole issue of the significance of divorce, and its occurrence at different points in the family and career cycles is involved here, but research to date provides more questions than answers.

On the other side of the coin is the body of literature from case studies of dual-worker families in which wives who hold satisfying jobs by choice express the view that they are more fulfilled; while husbands view them as more interesting marital partners. They emphasise the idea that both as spouses and parents, it is 'quality' rather than 'quantity' that counts, and that though the pattern is stressful they prefer it to the alternatives that they see for themselves, e.g. operating the conventional pattern and feeling bored and resentful.

They see the latter alternative as less likely to allow them to exert a good parental influence. They emphasise that they invest the time they have at home with a sense of value, and bring to the relationship interesting experiences from outside the home. Also the tendency in such situations is to try to involve their spouses more in domestic life, which is mentioned as having a beneficial effect.

(b) Impact on children Early indications from data gathered in a national cross-sectional study in the UK indicated a slight retardation of reading age in children of working mothers, particularly those who worked full-time from an early age of the child (Davie *et al.*, 1972). This is now being reassessed, and Mia Kellmer-Pringle (1974) puts the issue in perspective by indicating that 'it is not so much the mother's working outside the home which affects the child's development as the quality of substitute care'. Similarly, early reports that children left with child minders were at risk of retarded cognitive development are also being reassessed. There is indeed a risk when there is poor-quality child minding, but the association with the dual-worker family pattern *per se* is not tenable (Jackson and Jackson, 1979).

On the positive side, there are indications that the dual-worker pattern is associated with a lower degree of sex-role stereotyping (Hoffman and Nye, 1978), and with a higher degree of independence, particularly in female children (Sundby, 1980; Coopersmith, 1967 and a number of other researchers).

These are illustrative findings. Our theme throughout this chapter is that outcomes can only be understood in terms of the complex of factors operating in particular situations. At a microscopic level, the outcome depends on how particular family units respond to characteristic dilemmas associated with each work/family structure. We isolated five dilemmas in our early research on dual-career families (which seem to hold for working-class dual-worker families as well, though more research on this is called for):

1 *Role overloads* With both partners working and a diminished amount of time for household tasks, time off work has to be taken to catch up on domestic work. Women still bear the brunt of this, so that the common complaint is that they have 'no time for free time'. Some men deplore the diminution of being looked after. Joint leisure activities often suffer. A pressured domestic atmosphere may develop. It is important to note that the overload is a psychological as well as physical one.

2 *Identity dilemmas* Personal doubts may occur about whether this is the right thing to be doing, and whether one is being deficient in nurturing (a 'bad mother' or a 'selfish person').

3 *Role cycling dilemmas* involving decisions about whose job has priority. Typical situations are where one partner is offered a new job

or promotion involving a move and the other cannot locate a job immediately in the new area. Or, if a child is ill or needs transport, how is the task to be accomplished? If one is free and the other tied up, or both are free, the decision is easier. If both are tied up, the decision is more difficult.

4 *Social network dilemmas* Dealing with relatives, friends, colleagues, neighbours and others with whom one has relationships becomes more complicated when there are two timetables to coordinate and a high degree of overload to cope with.

5 *Discrepancies between personal and social norms* provides another kind of dilemma. One may feel that what one is doing is personally acceptable, but is perhaps considered wrong by others with whom one has relationships.

Studies of how these dilemmas are dealt with suggest that the availability of high income helps but does not assure positive outcomes, and that positive outcomes are possible at lower income levels as well as among more privileged families. The crucial element is the way in which couples deal with the problems raised. Having an array of helpers, such as grannies, au pairs, nannies, live-in or live-out domestics may be very useful, but there are social and psychological issues also involved. Parental neglect can obviously occur at high social-class levels as well as lower down the scale. But, in most dual-career couples that we have worked with, helpers are used primarily to free the working parents from routine household chores to concentrate on their children.

Research has indicated that though there are difficulties in altering sex-role patterns of handling housework and child care, the difficulties are neither necessary nor universal. In specific cases accounts are available not only of the resistance of husbands to change but of their willingness to change toward a more egalitarian role. Laura Lein and her colleagues of the Harvard Working Family Project (Working Family Project, 1978) found in a sample of mixed dual-worker families that several patterns in the division of domestic work work are feasible: the wife retaining most of the actual tasks and responsibilities just as if she were a conventional housewife; the husband sharing some of the tasks but the wife retaining overall responsibility; and the husband and wife sharing both the work and the responsibilities of housework and child care. The important point in retaining a sense of parental harmony in the family, according to the Harvard group, seems to have been less which pattern was adopted than whether the pattern adopted was felt to be freely chosen by the couple as reflecting their joint decision given the constraints in the situation. This is similar to the findings of Orden and Bradburn, and reflects an emphasis on 'equity' rather than 'equality' in any mechanistic sense (Rapoport and Rapoport, 1975).

Studies which take into account family life-course stage indicate other elements in the impact process. Dual-career families may begin with an explicit recognition of the importance of 'trade-offs' in the relationship. If a decision is made, for example, to maximise the husband's career advantage early in the family cycle, it may be felt that the wife should have a chance to maximise her opportunities at later points if there are conflicts of interest. Several studies indicate the difficulties that husbands have in acting on this conviction, particularly during their middle working years. The dual-career pattern is found empirically not to jeopardise the husband's career (as some early indications suggested might be a 'cost' of the pattern); but this is usually at the expense of the wife. Academic wives, though often suffering shortfalls in their own personal career advancement into senior posts, have been shown to produce more publications than a matched control group of professionals married to conventional husbands (Bryson *et al.*, 1976).

Valerie Oppenheimer (1974) suggests that in addition to the early 'squeeze' in the family cycle, where the husband/father is struggling to establish himself in his work or career just at a point when his family's needs for his presence at home are greatest, there is a second squeeze. This is when adolescent children are still at home and costing more than is covered by the increases in earnings that the husband/father has been able to manage. This squeeze, like the first one, is affected by a number of situational factors, including the overall work/family pattern that the family sustains.

Table 19 summarises the interactive character of work and family relationships in the two types of family just considered, and highlights the fact that there are gains and advantages, as well as risks,

TABLE 19 STRUCTURAL IMPACTS OF TWO WORK–FAMILY
          SITUATIONS

	CONVENTIONAL PATTERN		DUAL-WORKER PATTERN	
	Gains	*Risks*	*Gains*	*Risks*
PARENTS	Clear sex-linked division of labour; low conflict	Wife's boredom, depression, feelings of inequity	Higher standard of living; marital enrichment via growth of both parents	Marital strains and conflicts; tensions and overloads
CHILDREN	Clear sex-role models	Over-mothering, limitations of role modeling because of stereotyping	More independent, self-reliant; wider range of models because of less stereotyping	Neglect; Accidents; identity confusions

associated with each. The particular configuration of work–family interaction and the particular balance of gains and strains in any specific situation depend not only on the individuals and their capacity to cope with the situation, but on the stage they have reached in the family life-course and the local situation in which they live, including the availability of supportive resources. It also depends on their experience of, and response to, critical life events; a series of disruptive events at work or in the family can destroy even the most favourable work–family balance. We consider such events in more detail in the next section.

Event impact

Aside from the stable patterning of work–family relationships, critical events occurring at work may have a considerable impact on parents and children, and this is true even of valued events such as promotions. Promotions often entail increased responsibility, more travel, perhaps change of residence. These consequences affect both the marital relationship and the children's development. Children, for instance, may see less of their fathers, they may have to make new friends at school and find this very difficult, or they may even find themselves living in a country in which no one speaks their language. While such experiences can be 'broadening' and contribute to growth, Seidenberg (1975) believes on the basis of clinical experience that most families with school-age children find such moves extremely disruptive.

One of the most common of 'non-valued' events, and one that is bound to increase, is unemployment. Daniel and Stilgoe (1977) have shown that for most unemployed workers, the event causes only a temporary disturbance: like most divorced couples, the unemployed father soon finds another attachment. But for those who are not so fortunate, *chronic* unemployment can be devastating both for the individuals concerned and for their families. Following earlier studies of the impact of unemployment on family life in the Depression of the 1930s, Powell and Driscoll (1973) have studied the phenomenon of long-term unemployment and detailed the successive stages through which the unemployed worker goes: at first (after an initial quasi-holiday phase) there is a period of mobilisation of effort. When this is ineffective there tends to be considerable conflict, with the feeling sometimes expressed that the unemployed person is not really trying – that being in continuing unemployment is his/her fault. Finally, there is despair when efforts to find new jobs yield no results. Husbands and fathers tend to lose not only their self-esteem, but their authority in the family. Paradoxically, some studies in Britain report that wives of unemployed workers (particularly those higher in the social scale) reject the idea of taking a job if they are not already working because they do not wish to 'rub it in' (Gowler and Legge, 1980).

Most of the other main work events – accidents or injuries, trips away from home for extended periods of time, job changes requiring residential relocation, mid-course career change and occupational retirement – also entail impacts on parents and children. The general points that seem to emerge from available research are as follows:

1   *Critical work events*, whether valued or otherwise, are by definition disruptive and tend to have a disturbing impact on family life. They may require readjustment of domestic routines; they may entail loneliness; they may place the other parent in situations with which he/she feels unable to cope; they may involve loss of old support networks and the need to build new ones (e.g. in moving from one town to another).

2   *Family coping capacity* Families vary in the degree to which they are able to cope with the disturbing effects of such events. Among the elements which 'protect' them and help to make the outcomes more positive are: the ability of the partners to communicate with one another and to make decisions that take into account the needs of both; the capacity to make new relationships; the strength of personal identity and family ties that can override frustrations and allow for an adaptation of oneself and family in the new situation. Among the elements making specific parents and children more vulnerable in these events are lower degrees of communication and resourcefulness; less firm personal identity and affectionate regard for the others in the relationship; excessive involvement in persons and situations preceding the event with low flexibility to make adaptive change.

3   In both these sets of factors – the event and the family coping capacities – families are helped if they have financial resources and physical strength and energy; but it would be a mistake to assume that these are enough.

Finally, there are a whole range of family events likely to have an impact on work performance, and ranging in significance – some like pregnancy may be valued, others like illness of a family member will not be – and in duration. Like work events, all are likely to have disruptive consequences, beyond their immediate compass.

Summary and conclusions

Work has both positive and negative impacts on family members and vice versa. The process is interactive. Generalisations about the impact of one on the other must be qualified by an awareness of individual occupational and family circumstances and other factors. Assessments are best made using data which are highly specific to the circumstances under consideration.

Most research to date on the impact of work on family members has been inconclusive, contradictory or contingent on other intervening variables. There has been a tendency not to allow for or incorporate the complexity and diversity of the subject. In our view, a more productive approach would centre on a number of 'balance' issues. For instance, in families where the mother works she may show less quantitative interaction with her children, but more stimulating interaction when she is present.

There are a number of other issues, where results so far have been inconclusive, which require further research. For example, there seems to be a relationship between women being 'career-oriented' and their likelihood of divorcing. Divorce, in this context, is regarded as liberating by some, and as a failure in an important intimate relationship by others. As far as impact on children is concerned, a recent American study (Zill, 1978) suggests a continuum, using school problems as the dependent variable: the fewest problems were found in children from intact happy homes, with children from unhappy but intact homes next. Children from divorced homes showed the greatest number of problems in school. But this raises the whole issue of the 'intrinsic' v. 'situational' character of observed effects. There is a substantial body of professional opinion which holds that it is the poor management of divorce which produces this kind of effect rather than the divorce itself.

One new development, which is only begining to be studied systematically, is the whole complex of factors associated with father's work and family roles. The importance of father's participation in family life is receiving more explicit recognition – for himself, for his spouse and for his children. Aside from the family 'survival' elements of father's participation, which have been stressed in conventional role definitions, fathers are now recognised as important in providing other kinds of family support: to complement and enlarge the sense of family cohesiveness, and to contribute to the child's sense of competence (technical and interpersonal). In fathering, as in mothering, the importance of quality is increasingly stressed. A father who is there all the time, e.g. through being unemployed, is not necessarily useful as a shared-care resource. He may be depressed and self-deprecatory, and may exclude child care from his conception of a proper father's role. Much depends on how roles are defined and relationships worked out in the family.

Another phenomenon requiring much more focused study is work and the one-parent family. Much is known about the financial hardships and pressures suffered by these families. More needs to be known about the implications for parent and child(ren) of the lone parent opting to take employment rather than depend on other forms of support. For women, who constitute the greatest proportion of lone parents, many of the issues they face in becoming economically active are similar to those experienced by their married counterparts. But we need to know a lot more about how the strains of having to carry the domestic situation single-handed are managed, and about the consequences for the children in various circumstances.

Moving from research to social policy, there are three levels at which social policies can evolve to ameliorate risks associated with particular work/family patterns and enhance the potential gains:

1 *Macroscopic* This involves changes in the larger structure of society and employing organisations and could have widespread and beneficial effects: changes include such things as hours of work, scheduling of meeting times, flexibility of work times, benefits and allowances associated with family events (such as childbirth, illness, etc.).

2 *Familial* The enhancement of familial coping capacities through the provision of information is an important focus of policy concern. Research has a role here, and research reviews and analyses. An example is the recent American work by Joyce Portner (1979) of the Minnesota Council on Family Relations. Along with an excellent review of the findings of research on *The Impact of Work on the Family* Portner and Etkin provide a handbook for family group discussions, useful in working through resolutions to family problems and dilemmas in the light of other people's experiences.

3 *Professional* Guidelines for counsellors and consultants dealing with specific work/family issues (Shaevitz and Shaevitz, 1979; Sundby, 1980) are important here and action research has proved to be a fruitful channel for testing the validity of new policies. Specific problematic situations, such as executive travel, have been studied and acted upon in association with research of this kind (Renshaw, 1976).

According to situation, action in one or another of these levels may be applied. There is no reason why they should not be used simultaneously.

Ideally, one is searching, through social policy and other means, for resolutions that will benefit both work interests (i.e. employers, clients and others in the labour market) and family interests (i.e. fathers/ husbands, mothers/wives, the marital relationship, and the children). As the best way to achieve this resolution is a matter of conjecture in many instances, it is important at this stage to formulate the right questions and to suggest possible answers, which could be the subject of testing through research and action. The following points form foci for discussion (Seear 1981).

The structure of the working day How important is it that the day be structured in one way or another (e.g. 9.30 to 5.30)? How important is a certain order of work – e.g. meetings in the late afternoon? Could shiftwork be made more flexible and be more widely applied? Shiftwork has become associated with lower-skill jobs, part-time workers, low pay and poor prospects; need this be so?

The structure of 'conditions of employment', e.g. child-care leaves, pensions and insurance Could men more often have leave when they become fathers? Could women have similar pension benefits to men? What benefits accrue to the organisation as well as to the individual worker through improving these conditions? What are the costs and benefits of providing child care, e.g. crèches at the workplace of mothers and fathers?

The structure of careers Does there have to be a seniority sequence associated with age and length of service? There are indications that many organisations as well as many individuals would benefit by having a different kind of middle and late career structure and this might allow women late entry without so much stress.

Mobility and travel Are there alternative ways to provide a person with the kind of experience important in his/her career without moving him/her around so much in the familiar 'spiralist' pattern? Is travel necessary as frequently and as out of coordination with family events as it has been made to be in large organisations?

Through seeking to identify and answer such specific questions, real progress may be made towards reducing the tension that often occurs in the work–family relationship, and towards achieving a better balance between these two important domains.

8

The Future Prospect

Peter Moss and Nickie Fonda

Previous chapters have touched on a number of economic, technological, social and demographic changes likely to occur in the next ten to fifteen years which will affect the relationship between work and the family. Forecasts indicate that technological developments, especially the microprocessor, will have a widespread impact on the structure of employing organisations, the services they offer and the products they make, and on the skills and other requirements needed of the workforce. They may also lead to a net reduction in employment, though whether they do or not, unemployment will still rise to record post-war levels, the product of a low- or no-growth economy and an increasing labour force. Though this rise in unemployment will hit both sexes, the increase will be larger for men and the total number of men in employment will continue to fall. Lower demand for labour will also reduce the rate at which married women are drawn into the labour force, though there will still be a modest net growth in female employment, owing to an increase in jobs in the service sector. In the total labour force, male and female, the proportion of workers in non-manual occupations, service industries and part-time employment will continue to increase.

Within the family, compressed fertility and smaller family size will remain predominant patterns of child-bearing, despite an upturn in the birthrate. Divorce and remarriage will continue to increase.

> If current divorce rates persist, in excess of one quarter of [all couples] born in the early 1950s, who first married in the early and mid-1970s will have divorced by age 50 . . . [while] if remarriage were to remain at current levels it is estimated that approaching one in five men and women born around 1950 will have entered a second marriage by age 50. (Leete, 1979b)

About half the people divorcing in a given year remarry within five years (Leete and Anthony, 1979), though this trend in remarriage also brings with it another, a rise in the number of men and women divorcing for a second or subsequent time. The rate of increase here has been faster than for the 'first-time' divorces, partly because more people are remarried and therefore 'at risk', but partly because divorce rates among those marrying a second time are much higher than those for people married once only for equivalent durations of marriage (OPCS, 1979c). Taking all the changes into account, there will be increasing numbers of lone parents, the number of households headed by a lone parent aged forty-four or under being expected to rise from 400,000 in 1976 to 900,000 in 1991 (Central Statistical Office, 1979: Table 2.5). More and more parents, therefore, will experience marital breakdown, a period of lone parenthood, followed by the formation of a second family unit – and then, increasingly, a second marital breakdown.

More and more parents will also choose to reject marriage as a necessary or ideal requirement of parenthood. In recent years, increasing numbers of unmarried women have opted to keep and care for their children and many unmarried mothers live in *de facto* unions (currently around half of all illegitimate births are registered on the joint information of both parents – one indication of the growing number of couples cohabiting before or instead of marriage). These trends may well continue.

> With declining marriage rates at young ages, coupled with increased rates of cohabitation outside marriage, annual numbers of illegitimate births could even begin to grow, as has been the case in some other Western countries ... many such births would [however] probably be to couples living in stable unions. (Leete, 1978b)

The sort of changes outlined above are bound to affect the relationship between work and the family and the rate of progress, if any, towards greater equality of opportunity. More unemployment among men and more families headed by working lone mothers will mean more female breadwinners. The numbers will increase further if improved educational attainment, growing familiarity with and use of maternity leave and the gradual widening of employment opportunities for women lead to more mothers in higher-status jobs, earning as much, if not more than, their husbands. Such an increase may not be dramatic, but could still be significant, especially if viewed against the small number of families where the woman's earnings currently account for at least half of gross family income: in 1974, for instance, only 5 per cent of all working wives, or 3 per cent of all wives with husbands below pensionable age, made such a contribution, while for working mothers the proportion was even lower (Hamill, 1978).

Although the number of mothers in better-paid, higher-status jobs may increase in absolute terms, the continuing growth in part-time work is likely to worsen the job position of working mothers in general, pushing up the proportion in poorly paid, low-status work. The position could be further worsened if homeworking increases, one possible consequence of the widening application of micro-electronics which will increasingly make it possible for people in clerical, professional and managerial occupations to work from home at least part of the week. Greater freedom to work at home may increase not only the number of low-paid women workers but the number suffering isolation, cut off from the stimulation of workplace contacts and confined to one environment for the major part of the day. Against these possible drawbacks, there are also potential benefits from more homework:

> If more people are able to work at home, the isolation of spouses, children or elderly parents at home from those at work could be reduced and those in employment would be more accessible to deal with minor crises among children, friends and neighbours. The time saved in travelling might more than make up for the distractions involved in working from home. (Central Policy Review Staff, 1978b)

More opportunity to work from home, at least for part of the week, is one of the factors working in favour of men spending more time at home. Others include the possibility of longer annual holidays and a shorter basic working week – adding up to a shorter working year – as the result of technological change, collective bargaining and the effects of the secular and continuing trend from manual to non-manual jobs, which has increased the proportion of jobs in non-manual work from 31 per cent in 1961 to 48 per cent in 1976, with a further rise to 61 per cent projected for 1986 (Leicester, 1978a, b, c,). As noted earlier, in Chapter 2, non-manual jobs offer shorter basic hours, less paid overtime and longer holidays.

Pulling against these 'home-centred' forces, there is the continuing growth, within non-manual work, of managerial and professional jobs which, we have also noted, often demand longer work hours in total (taking travel and unpaid overtime into account) and a generally greater preoccupation with work. The net effect of these changes on the balance of men's time and involvement in work and the family is impossible to calculate: but, taking increased unemployment into account, it seems possible that men could on average spend rather more time at home, just as the modest increase in women's employment rates will mean that they spend rather less.

Though the possibility, even the probability, of change, and its general direction, may be apparent in many areas, the actual course of change, let alone its full impact on the relationship between work and the family and on equality of opportunity, is hard to predict with any degree of accuracy or confidence. The pace, extent and actual nature of future developments are often impossible to determine. Technological change, for instance, will obviously proceed as in the past, but how far, how fast and in what direction? How quickly will microprocessors be applied? What will be their effect on employment? Will they wipe out millions of jobs, as some predict, or generate new employment and new tasks for existing workers? And will new technologies emerge, as micro-electronics has done in the 1970s, with even more widespread social, demographic and economic implications? By the end of the century, could politicians be under pressure to sanction the widespread production of test-tube babies, a prospect considered a real possibility by some futurologists? (Morrell, 1977).

There are other imponderables, too. Attitudes, expectations and values are likely to change. Opinions about sex equality, sex roles, cohabitation and sexual relations outside marriage, child-rearing and the relative importance of work and family have all changed considerably in the last twenty years. This process is likely to continue during the next twenty, with substantial implications for the behaviour of men and women at work and at home. The rate and character of the changes are, however, harder to forecast.

Finally, the behaviour of employers, trade unions and government in initiating and responding to change remains an unknown quantity. In its approach to the microprocessor, the TUC emphasises the need to use the introduction of this technology to improve the conditions of the workforce:

> At every stage, technological changes should be linked with a reduction in the working week, working year and working lifetime. This should be seen not just in the context of sharing out less work to avoid increasing unemployment, but in the more positive light of job-creating targets for enterprises. These should be accompanied by measures which enable existing workers to take some of the benefits in the form of increased leisure whilst providing more jobs.
> Priority should be given to movement towards:
> the 35 hours week;
> a reduction in systematic overtime;
> longer holidays;
> better provision for time off and public and trade union duties;
> sabbatical leave; and
> early retirement for older workers. (Trades Union Congress, 1979)

Such an approach to the introduction of new technology could have a major impact on the relationship between work and the family – but is it likely to be adopted? Will the trades union movement in the 1980s give more priority to actions which have a potential for promoting equality of opportunity and better meeting the needs of working parents, supporting its good resolutions with firm and committed action? To what extent, if at all, will employers respond positively to demands to help employees combine work and family responsibilities more easily, or perhaps even adopt an innovatory role before pressure is brought to bear? And, finally, what role is the Government likely to play in work–family relations and equal opportunities, and how will it discharge this role?

The role of Government

Combining work and parenthood is a proper and feasible aspiration for men and women to have, but pursuing such a course at present is often made unnecessarily difficult, producing in turn unnecessary strains and disadvantages. Much of this difficulty could be removed or substantially reduced through more active Government intervention to mediate the relationship between work and the family, preferably with the active and willing co-operation of employers and unions. Government should take a more positive role, not just because this would increase the welfare of many, but because it has a responsibility in these matters. This responsibility arises from an official commitment to equal opportunities, which requires positive and wide-ranging action if it is to be properly met; and because working parents make an important contribution to the common good, both as workers and parents, in return for which Government has both a responsibility for and interest in helping working mothers and fathers to manage these two roles with as little strain and disadvantage as possible.

More active Government intervention might involve some or all of the following roles:

1 *Monitoring the situation*, through the collection of information about work and the family, to provide a comprehensive and regularly updated pool of data. This could answer the sorts of question posed in this book, which bear on the relationship between work and the family and on equal opportunities.

2. *Assessment and evaluation* of the likely impact on families and their individual members of (i) policy options and proposals and (ii) economic, employment and technological trends and developments (e.g. microprocessors and other technological changes, trends in working hours including shiftwork, the growth of unemployment); and of the likely impact on employment of changes in family formation, structure and organisation. The adoption of such a 'family perspective' in employment matters would involve the development and application of techniques enabling such analytic and predictive studies to be undertaken. Such assessments would provide a better basis for decision-making, a greater awareness of the nature and direction of change and its implications, and a preparedness for coping with change which has been totally lacking to date.

3 *Dissemination of information and stimulation of public discussion,* so as to raise public knowledge, awareness and debate on work–family trends and issues, and on possible policy options and their implications. The recent report by the Central Policy Review Staff

(1978a), *Services for Young Children with Working Mothers*, provided a starting-point, with its discussion of the child-care needs of women with pre-school and primary-school children. This initiative, which has so far drawn no Government response, needs to be followed up and its scope broadened to cover working parents, older children and employment issues and measures.

4 *The encouragement of innovation* and good practice by employers and local authorities and in families themselves, to help parents combine work and parenthood. Innovations in employment, child-care provision and family organisation need evaluating and supporting, with publicity and other backing (including financial support) given to successful innovations and good practice. In particular, Government could use its own position as a major employer to innovate and evaluate forms of employment practice designed to help parents. Such a lead role for Government has been proposed in a recent consultation document prepared by the Norwegian Government, which also illustrates the role of Government in stimulating public discussion and awareness:

> Parents must be assured more time together with their children and for activities concerned with the family's welfare.
> An important goal for the Government is to ensure that women and men have equal opportunity of choice and that women have a greater freedom to choose their own way of life. This involves an increased effort to secure women's right to work . . . . At the same time caring for children is time-consuming and it is therefore important to adapt working life to an increasing extent to the needs of parents – both mothers and fathers – of small children. [Among measures considered to be important in this respect, is] a reduction in working hours for parents of small children. During the period 1978–81, the Government expects to put forward a proposal regarding working hours for parents of small children. As work on the reform proceeds, the Government will carry out experiments with reduced working hours for parents of small children in selected State organisations and industries. (Family Affairs and Equal Status Dept, 1978)

5 *The provision of a basic benefit–service package* to help parents to manage work and family responsibilities simultaneously, without undue stress for children or parents. Such a package would include:

  (a) ensuring a sufficient supply of good-quality child-care, suited to the hours and other needs of working parents and their children. A number of methods of achieving this are available, depending on political and other considerations, including direct local authority provision; subsidies to voluntary and self-help groups; subsidies to or requirements on employers to make their own arrangements; and cash benefits, tax relief or other subsidies direct to parents to help pay for places in private provision.

(b) Legislating for a basic framework of employment measures, supported by earnings-related benefits to compensate parents for loss of income when taking these up. The two basic measures would be:

> (i) *a parental leave entitlement* of a given number of days per year (related to the number of children a parent has), to enable a working parent to undertake certain important parental and family duties without financial penalty These duties would include caring for a sick spouse or child, attending the birth of his child, settling a child at nursery or school, attending welfare clinics or other important appointments concerning his or her child's health, and visiting his or her child's nursery or school to talk with staff;
>
> (ii) *a post-natal leave entitlement* for a period immediately after the birth of a child, supplemented by an additional leave entitlement to be taken at any time in the child's early years, possibly up to the age of 8–10: the details of this supplementary leave are discussed further below.

For both types of leave, *each* parent would have his or her own individual entitlement, e.g. if the post-natal leave were, say, for six months, then each parent would have a six-month entitlement, to be used concurrently or consecutively with the other parent's: a lone parent would automatically have a double entitlement, making up to one year. Loss of earning would be compensated for by an earnings-related benefit.

Other, related measures in the package would include the development of job counselling, placement and re-training services specifically geared to the needs of parents wishing to resume work after an extended period of full-time child-care.

These five roles would make considerable demands of Government. In particular, they would require the development of effective and permanent interdepartmental coordination, to provide the joint approach to policy that most of the roles imply. Government bodies needing to be involved in such a joint approach include the Departments of Health and Security, Education and Science, Employment and Industry, the Treasury, the Civil Service Department, the Inland Revenue and the Central Statistical Office. Another major demand made on Government would be to find the funding – which would be substantial – for an adequate benefit–service package.

Four alternative sources of funding might initially be considered:
1 The cost of benefits paid during periods of leave might be wholly or partly met from increased *national insurance contributions*. In this

way, loss of earnings at certain stages of parenthood, and especially early parenthood, would be compensated for in the same way as losses due to illness, unemployment and old age, with the cost spread over the workforce and employers as a whole and over an individual's work life. In Sweden the cost of the earnings-related benefits paid during parental and post-natal leave (described in Chapter 4) form part of the national insurance system, with 85 per cent of costs coming from employers' contributions and the remaining 15 per cent direct from central government.

2 *The withdrawal of the married man's tax allowance*, and its replacement by an ordinary single person's tax allowance, would provide considerable additional revenue to cover part of the package. The married man's allowance is provided whether or not a man's wife is employed and whether or not there are any dependants in the family. It is a relic of earlier days when most wives were not at work and the husband was expected to be the only earner in the family. At present, the allowance is 55 per cent more than the single person's allowance, involving a loss of tax revenue of £2,500,000,000 a year (in 1979–80). Removal of the married man's tax allowance should be complemented by an increase in child benefit, to protect the financial position of families with children. Part of the revenue currently foregone on the allowance might be used to this end.

3 *Employers* could meet a share of the costs, by paying (a) a larger insurance contribution, or (b) a levy into funds specifically earmarked to provide for nursery expansion or leave benefits (e.g. along the lines of maternity or redundancy pay), or (c) all or part of an employee's earnings while he or she was on leave, or (d) all or part of employee's child-care costs.

4 *Parents* could be required to contribute more, mainly via fees for child-care services, with a means-testing element to safeguard lower-income families.

Final funding arrangements might include a package of any or all of these four sources, the final decision depending on political and economic considerations. Additional costs imposed on employers would, of course, be passed on to the population at large in the form of higher prices, and it would be necessary to assess this effect to arrive at a full appreciation of the distributional impact of each approach.

Some final issues

The present relationship between work, the family and equal opportunities causes many dilemmas and tensions; any attempt to alter the relationship will throw up new ones. We conclude by considering a few possibilities that particularly interest and concern us.

First, how far can parents be provided with real choice in combining work and parenthood, and in particular as to whether or not they work and whether they work full-time or part-time? A policy model based on 'choice' is discussed in Chapter 4 by Sheila Kamerman, who points out that it is a popular option *at the level of discussion* in countries 'yet to develop a distinctive policy'. Sheila Kamerman also touches on the problems associated with implementing a 'choice' option. These include the high cost if choice is to be real (e.g. with benefits paid at levels providing proper compensation for lost earnings); the possibility of a 'choice' option actually failing to provide real choice (e.g. via inadequate child-care provision, low benefit levels); and the potential for a 'choice' model simply to reinforce existing social and economic inequalities, with, for example, the 'stop work' option taken up mainly or wholly by low-skilled and low-educated women.

Despite these dangers, the possibility of introducing a substantial element of real choice for parents in how they combine work and family involvement has obvious attractions. Parents, like children, are individuals, with different characteristics, goals and needs. No single type of work–family relationship is likely to suit all parents equally well or, indeed, an individual parent equally well at different stages of parenthood. Real choice in this area is an integral part of the realisation of the concept of the 'protean family', described by the Rapoports as

> . . . the kind of family best suited to be a model for the future. The protean family is not a single type [of family] but an idea of variation and change in the family structure to suit on the one hand the makeup of individuals, and on the other the situation they confront – in their internal life, in their occupational and community life and in different phases of their life cycle . . . it is an enabling family assisting its members to adapt and to overcome the various structural bonds and constraints that impede them in their quest for personal satisfaction. (Rapoport and Rapoport, 1978b)

To provide real and complete choice to mothers and fathers in how they combine work and family throughout parenthood seems, in present and near-future circumstances, unrealistic, even if considered desirable. The cost of providing financial benefits, adequate to compensate for lost earnings, to non-employed or part-time employed parents would be prohibitive. Having accepted this, the provision of real choice at certain, limited stages of parenthood and an attempt to provide a greater degree of choice at others may still be worthwhile aims. The sort of benefit–service packages outlined above would enable the first part of this aim to be met, the combination of child-care provision, post-natal leave entitlement and earnings-related benefits providing a high degree of real choice for parents in a child's first year or so. The actual time would depend on the period of leave allowed for in the benefit: an entitlement, for instance, of six months per parent would give a potential maximum period of twelve months when one parent or the other could choose whether to be at home full-time or continue at work, but the entitlement could be set for a longer or shorter period.

With the expiry of post-natal leave, as the last child in the family passed the time limit of the entitlement, and faced by the impossibility of continuing to provide adequate compensation for loss of earnings through the remainder of parenthood, the main issue would shift to the feasibility and desirability of increasing choice through making part-time work opportunities readily available. The drawbacks of part-time work, as currently constituted, are real and their consequences have been described in detail in Chapter 2, in particular the high concentration of part-time workers at the lowest level of occupational status and earnings, with little or no prospects and few occupational benefits. It also seems inevitable that women will occupy most part-time jobs for some time to come.

Despite these drawbacks, and the threat part-time work can pose to equal opportunities, we believe that part-time work, and its potential place in a total package of measures to help employed parents, cannot be ignored or dismissed. In recent years, it has been the only area of employment growth, and is likely to continue to expand: it is, in short, unlikely to go away. It also probably fits the needs of many parents, at least at certain stages of parenthood, who find that full-time work requires too much of their time and energy, leaving them insufficient for their parenting.

One may hope that, in the future, hours of full-time work will decrease considerably, as they have over the last century. Most people may then work what are now considered part-time hours today, and the issue will be largely resolved. Until this occurs, some sort of compromise on part-time work seems called for, accepting the existing appeal of part-time employment but seeking to reduce the disadvantages associated with it and encouraging more fathers to take it up (the two steps are, of course, closely related). In particular, the availability of part-time work needs to be extended, to all industries and occupational levels. This might be achieved in part by giving parents the right to return to part-time employment either in their former position or its equivalent, on completion of post-natal leave. This follows the practice in Sweden, where parents are entitled to reduce their working time to six hours a day until their child is eight years old, though without compensation for lost earnings for the greater part of this period. Such an entitlement needs to be combined with a genuine willingness among employers to extend the number and range of part-time jobs and to consider part-timers as eligible for promotion. Here, the role of Government, in developing measures to encourage such employer attitudes and behaviour and in setting a good example in its own capacity of employer, would be important.

Compensation for all or a substantial part of lost earnings for parents employed part-time is likely to be too costly to contemplate as a general principle throughout parenthood. It might, however, be considered on a more limited basis. Once again the Swedish approach provides a useful model: following the end of the six-month post-natal-leave period, either parent in Sweden is entitled to a further period of paid leave to be taken at any time until their child is eight years old. This special parent's allowance is divided between mother and father in a two-parent family, coming to forty-five days per parent. This period may be taken as six weeks full-time leave or three months half-time leave or six months quarter-time leave (i.e. working a six-hour day); it can also be varied, so that part may, for example, be taken full-time and part on a quarter-time basis, and one parent can make over his or her benefit to the other without giving any special reason for doing so. Such a measure increases real parental choice within limits, giving maximum flexibility as to when and how to use leave. There is, of course, nothing special about the Swedish entitlement of forty-five days per parent: the entitlement could be fixed for any period, from a few weeks to a year ot two.

A final element in any part-time compromise must be a concerted effort by Government, unions and employers to remove the current disadvantages associated with part-time work, in terms of benefits, training, promotion prospects, etc.

It is easy in a book such as this, with its emphasis on parents, to give the impression that, in a two-parent family, the mother and father must have similar views, aims and interests. In practice this is not always so; more opportunities for women outside the home and changing views about sex roles and behaviour offer a potential not only for better and more fulfilling lives for both parents, but also greater conflict between them. Apart from steps to better prepare parents to confront and deal with such differences, a major part of the responsibility for reducing tension and conflict must lie with men. Changes are required in their attitudes and behaviour – but how can such changes be encouraged?

The most immediate possibilities lie in the attitudes and behaviour of influential individuals and institutions – schools, the media, health education, hospital and other health services, employers, trade union leaders, politicians, etc. Government could and should take a leadership role in encouraging men to participate more actively in parenting and family life, as happens already in Sweden – another example of how Government might act to encourage innovation. By emphasising the importance of the father's role in the family and the need for this role to include active involvement in pregnancy, birth and

domestic and child-care tasks, these various influences could do much
to encourage new expectations. But such encouragement, important
though it is, is unlikely to be enough by itself – other inducements are
needed.

Providing opportunities for fathers to be more involved with their
children is essential. Entitling *both* parents to periods of paid leave to
care for children and see to their interests, as the Swedes have done,
would not only contribute to a shift in expectation but would provide
the means for fathers to take a more active part in family life. The use
that men might make of such entitlements were they to be made
available in Britain is, of course, difficult, if not impossible, to judge.
All we have to go on is the Swedish experience, in the few years since
their employment measures were introduced. We summarise this
below, using official statistics prepared by the Swedish Ministry of
Health and Social Affairs (1979).

Just over 2 per cent of eligible fathers took part of their post-natal-
leave entitlement in its first year of operation in 1974. Three years
later, this figure had risen to 11 per cent with 'leave-taking' fathers
using, on average, 40 out of the 210 days available, while for 1978,
Sheila Kamerman quotes a further increase, to 14 per cent. Latest
available figures, for 1976, for the other type of leave introduced in
1974 – to enable parents to undertake various parental duties such as
the care of sick children – show that:

1 64 per cent of eligible fathers took leave of absence, averaging 7.5
days each, in connection with the birth of a child, to care for existing
children while the mother was in hospital and to look after mother and
baby when they came home;

2 Paid leave to care for sick children was taken in 40 per cent of
families with two working parents, with fathers accounting for some of
this leave in a third of these families. In families where fathers took
leave, they accounted for more than half of all days taken off. Overall,
while 'mothers assume most of the responsibility for the nursing of
sick children, regardless of the age of the child concerned and the
number of siblings in the family . . . if father makes use of the parental
insurance scheme, there is a good chance of the benefit days being
shared fairly evenly between the parents'.

The Swedish experience cannot be taken as a reliable guide to what
would happen if similar measures were introduced in another country:
each society is too idiosyncratic to make direct comparisons reliable.
The Swedish measures are also still very new. Having said that, there
are still some interesting and possibly relevant features in the record to
date. First, a significant, though still relatively small, number of
fathers have taken quick advantage of the new measures. Secondly,
the proportion of fathers taking post-natal leave has shown a steady
increase, after starting from a very low 'take-up' rate in its first year:

like most innovatory measures, the initial response is unlikely to be a good indicator of future use, and the full impact will only be apparent over fifteen to twenty years. A final point, again bearing on post-natal leave, is that

> the employment situation of the mother has a major bearing on the father's participation. The [higher the status of] the mother's occupation and the higher the earnings, the larger is the proportion of fathers taking full time leave. The number of fathers availing themselves of the scheme is two to three times as large in families where the mother [has a professional or managerial job] as in families where the mother belongs to the 'assistant staff' or 'unskilled' category. (Swedish Ministry of Health and Social Affairs, 1979)

This last point suggests that men's behaviour and attitudes are likely to be influenced by the job status and earning capacity of their wives, both because wives in 'good' jobs are likely to make greater demands of their husbands and because their husbands are more likely to see and accept the value and validity of their wives' employment aspirations. Job status and earnings are also, of course, likely to influence the attitudes and behaviour of women themselves: in Chapter 2, for instance, we saw that these factors affected the reasons given by mothers for working and their satisfaction with working, while in Hungary the child-care grant and associated leave for women with very young children, described in Chapter 4, is used *least* by highly educated and more skilled women. All this points to a chicken-and-egg situation, in which progress to equality of opportunity and the attitudes and home conditions to support it are interrelated and reinforce each other. Progress breeds further progress, so that improvements in women's employment position, once having reached a certain stage and momentum, might largely become self-perpetuating: that point is, however, obviously still a long way off.

If employment measures available to both parents were introduced in this country, and it is a very big 'if', are there pressures or even sanctions that could be brought to bear to encourage men to take up their share of such entitlements? And if so, should they be applied? The problem is made harder because we are dealing with individuals, with individual preferences, aptitudes and ambitions. In some cases, fathers don't want to play an active part in the upbringing of their children, except through providing the necessary income, and their wives are genuinely content to give up employment to concentrate on home and children. Suppose, in such a family, that a father was reluctant to take up his post-natal-leave entitlement. Should he automatically be able to transfer his entitlement of paid leave to his wife? Or should no transfer be permitted or perhaps only in very exceptional circumstances?

Easy transferability takes all pressure off the father, and essentially condones the general continuation of the status quo; it might, in some cases, lead to pressures being put on the wife to agree to take over her husband's leave, though not really wanting to. Non-transferability, on the other hand, lays a firm parental responsibility and clear expectations on the father, which might just tip the balance in some cases and persuade him to take the leave – and, just possibly, find it a rewarding and enhancing experience. If, however, the father still refuses to take leave, or where both partners are genuinely agreed that they don't want him to, then the mother is left at home without the advantage of the father's transferred benefit entitlement. Again, a couple may decide that one parent would like to take both parent's entitlement for one child, while the other takes the joint benefit for the next: a tough line on transferability would make such flexibility difficult to achieve. (An alternative to individual leave entitlements with transferability is for a period of leave to be available per family; where there are two parents, this may be divided between the parents or used entirely by one, as they decide. In Sweden, the post-natal leave operates on the latter principle and the special parent's allowance on the former, with one parent able to make over his or her benefit to the other 'without having to give any special reason for doing so.')

The issue of transferability between the sexes – and, of course, transfer could be from mothers to fathers as well – is just one example of the dilemmas of tactics and principle posed by any serious attempt to loosen the vice-like hold that work has on men, and to achieve a more equal balance between work and parenthood for both sexes. But should such an attempt succeed, partially at least, and a substantial proportion of men devote more time, energy and general commitment to their role as parents, a further dilemma could emerge. A wide gulf now exists between the position of employed mother and fathers, to the disadvantage of mothers. This gulf – which represents the general male–female differential in employment in its most extreme form – might evolve into a gulf between parents and non-parents. An increasing number of fathers might 'trade-off' the benefits of more and closer contact with children (through taking up, for instance, post-natal leave or part-time work) against lessened involvement in work, for a period at least, and consequently poorer employment prospects. The present situation, where those who actually look after and take responsibility for children rarely get to occupy the most senior and influential positions in society, would become even more pronounced, with the added difference that more childless women were on one side of the divide, while more men with children joined the majority of mothers on the other.

The alternative is to seek ways of managing work and family life which avoid the need for such 'trade-offs', enabling people instead to alternate periods of high work and high family involvement – and indeed periods of higher involvement in other areas, such as education – without necessarily damaging employment prospects. On the employer side, in particular, it places an onus on conceding that working parents have other demands and constraints made on their time and energy by children, that parenthood represents an important and necessary social function and that the circumstances and needs of working parents should be recognised and accommodated within employment. A successful strategy to improve the lot of working parents must rely heavily on the goodwill and support of employers and their willingness to examine how far existing employment habits and patterns could be changed, starting with the sort of questions posed by the Rapoports at the end of Chapter 7. What needs to be sought through such questioning is a compromise between a world of work which has little or no time for children or parenthood, and a world of family life which cannot accommodate, for many parents, a proper and equal place in the world of work.

What chance change?

In this chapter we have dwelt on whether Government could or should become more involved in the relationship between work and the family and play a more active part in the pursuit of equality of opportunity. Whether Government could or should, the most pressing and present question is whether Government *will* do these things, to which it must be answered that the prospects are not promising. The forces against any change are substantial and dominant while the forces likely to initiate and fuel change are weak and seem unlikely to grow stronger.

Four potential forces for change can be identified. First, labour shortages are great catalysts for action and innovation: the growth of the child-care services in the Second World War, when female labour was desperately needed for the war effort, is just one example. Over the next ten to fifteen years shortages may affect particular occupations or employers, possibly encouraging new attitudes and measures to cope specifically with them, but shortages will clearly not be a general phenomenon. Secondly, concern about low birthrates and population decline have spurred some countries to action, to facilitate women's employment and avoid the need for choosing between children and work. Such concern, however, has not been a consistent and important influence in British public affairs, and is unlikely to be so in the future: over-population, indeed, has been a more recurrent and influential concern.

Thirdly, changes by employers and governments may be more directly brought about by powerful political pressures applied by influential groups. But here again, the prospects are poor. The trade unions, as we have seen, are unwilling in general to attach priority or clout to the excellent positions they often take on paper, and more traditional concerns – pay, working conditions, the impact of technology, unemployment – are likely to assume even greater importance in times of recession. Outside the trade unions, the women's movement is, politically, of little weight, particularly when faced by a Conservative Government with a large majority, and when forced to fight, with its sympathisers, to try to protect the modest gains made in the 1970s. Neither political party has a strong body of opinion ready to press for action, the few supporters of action being quite outweighed by a more general uninterest or opposition. In particular the position of the Conservative Party towards intervention in employment and more positive action to hasten equal opportunities is cool if not downright hostile. The Prime Minister, herself a mother of two, in her own words 'did not need the Equal Opportunities Commission' – only the services of an English nanny; while her Secretary of State for Social Services, Patrick Jenkin, recently remarked that 'if the Good Lord had intended us to have equal rights to go out to work, he wouldn't have created men and women'. One of his junior ministers, Lynda Chalker, when an Opposition spokesman observed that paternity leave 'would disrupt industry . . . [and that] maybe in years to come, the country will look at the labour market and decide that, perhaps, it would be better for women with children to stay at home'.

Such views probably reflect a considerable body of political and public opinion that is disturbed by and antagonistic towards the economic, social and moral implications of change in family life and work–family relationships. It believes that if parents – or more specifically mothers – choose to work, then they must take responsibility for making all necessary child-care and other arrangements. Behind such views, often very near the surface, is the desire to return to the safety and order of a 'golden age' when mothers and fathers had, knew and were satisfied with their own distinctive roles in the family. Whether such a time ever existed remains open to question, as with all 'golden ages': the myth, however, remains powerful and emotive.

The only remotely likely prospect for change stems, ironically, from the prospect of large-scale unemployment, in a context of rapid technological change. Such a prospect provides opportunity and incentive for far-reaching changes, especially in employment practice. The sort of employment and benefit measures outlined in this chapter offer one means of tailoring a growing labour force to a static or even falling number of jobs, and to tackling the paradox of many parents and others being unemployed while other parents have too little time for home life or other interests and suffer unnecessary tension trying to combine work and family life. Will the opportunity be taken, or will recession provide an excuse for further neglect rather than a reason for taking long overdue action? One thing is sure: a creative response to the needs of working parents and growing unemployment, supported by positive employer and trade union attitudes and a readiness to question and innovate, could make the 1980s a hopeful and better decade for working parents and their children.

Notes

1 Introduction

1 The 1911 Census was the first to give separate employment figures for married women.

2 'Economically active' covers both people with a job *and* those unemployed but seeking work. The terms 'in employment', 'employment' or 'working', as used in this book, refer only to people actually with a job. In the 1971 Census, 37.3 per cent of women with dependent children were actually in employment, compared to 39.2 per cent who were economically active, i.e. 1.9 per cent did not have a job but were seeking one.

3 This halfway point for married women below pension age was passed in 1971 according to General Household Survey data (OPCS, 1979a: Table 4.1) and after 1971 but by 1975 according to Department of Employment estimates (Central Statistical Office, 1979: Table 5.3). The difference in timing is due to the GHS recording rather higher economic activity rates than Department of Employment statistics, the difference being 3.4 per cent for women in 1971 (OPCS, 1973: Table 4.3).

4 One notable exception is a speech made in America in 1978 by Shirley Williams, the then Secretary of State for Education. She spoke of 'the need to establish more fairly the concept of mutual parental responsibilities, fatherhood as well as motherhood. Fathers must be made aware that the job of looking after the family can no longer be left to their wives ... We can use the margin that current tragically high levels of unemployment gives us to make working hours more flexible, to create more short-day and part-time jobs, to reduce overtime, to allow a margin of time off to both parents which can be used when a member of the family is ill. In other words, work should be adapted not just to individuals but also to families.'

2 Parents at Work

1 The General Household Survey provides an analysis of the percentage of women working by number of children and by whether working full-time or part-time, for each year including and since 1971; and an analysis of the percentage of women

working by marital status and age of youngest child, for each year including and since 1975. The report on the 1977 GHS includes more detailed analysis, including the percentage of women working by marital status, age of youngest child and by whether working full-time or part-time; and the percentage of women working by age, age of youngest child and by whether working full-time or part-time.

2 The first published analysis of Census data to show employment rates for women by age of children was in 1961. Estimates of change between 1951 and later dates must therefore rely on 'duration of marriage' as a rough proxy for children's age, e.g. a majority of the children of mothers married 15–19 years are likely to be at secondary school, though some will only be at primary school.

3 This also holds true if the comparison is confined to married women below retirement age.

4 The 1971 GHS employment rates were slightly higher than those found in the 1971 Census, the figures for married women being 42.3 and 40.6 per cent respectively (OPCS, 1973: Table 4.6).

5 The difference in proportions reporting hours and earnings is most probably explained by self-employed women not working regular hours.

6 1961 figures are from the Census, in which people were defined as 'part-time' if they considered themselves to work 'less than the normal hours of employment'. The part-time figures for 1961 consist of all people who defined themselves as part-time plus those who defined themselves as full-time but worked thirty hours a week or less. 1971 and 1977 data, from the Census and GHS respectively, include in part-time employment anyone working thirty hours or less a week (except in the GHS, where teachers and lecturers are considered to be in full-time employment if they work twenty-six or more hours a week).

7 There are no comparable post-1971 figures for *mothers*. Table 1 combines 1974 and 1976 GHS data from the recent report on children with working mothers by the Central Policy Review Staff (1978a). The two years have been combined to even out fluctuations which seem more likely to be due to sampling factors than actual changes between the two years. The 1971 data are taken from the Census.

8 The average hours of lone mothers were longer, over 30 hours a week (see page 47).

9 The average hours of lone fathers were similar, at 41 hours a week (see page 48).

10 There were no comparable data for non-manual workers. Willmott and Young's study shows that the higher the social class, the

longer the annual holiday entitlement.

11 Shiftworking is less common in non-manufacturing industries, but there are no comparable figures for this sector.

12 In the ten years 1968–78, the number of women exempted from the Act prohibiting women in manual occupations in factories from working nights increased from 7,768 to 61,120.

13 Factory Acts also prohibit women in manual occupations in factories from working on Sundays and after 1 p.m. on Saturdays, unless exemption orders have been obtained.

14 'Miscellaneous services' covers a wide range of service industries, including catering, hotels, leisure and entertainments, laundry and cleaning, motor repairs and garages, hairdressing, and private domestic services.

15 In April 1974, average (median) gross earnings for full-time workers were £44 for men and £25 for women (Central Statistical Office, 1975: Table 5.16).

16 120p per hour is equivalent to just below £50 per week, the amount needed in 1977 to keep a family with two children at Supplementary Benefit level.

17 The NES, on which these rates are based, may understate the problem of low pay among part-time workers, since the Survey does not include people whose earnings are below the tax deduction limit; the Government estimates that about one in five part-time workers are thereby excluded.

18 The rise in births from 1977 to 1978 was 4 per cent. There were large increases in illegitimate births and in births to remarried women, which between them accounted for 36 per cent of the total increase: births to women in their first marriage increased less markedly (Central Statistical Office, 1979: Table 2.14).

19 The 1961/71 comparison is based on 'Social Economic Group' classification, which divides occupation into seventeen groupings. The comparisons in the next paragraph are based on the 'Social Class' classifications, which use six occupational classifications – I (Professional), II (Managers, employers), IIIN (Skilled non-manual), IIIM (Skilled manual), IV (Semiskilled manual), V (Unskilled manual).

20 The survey also shows higher economic activity rates than those reported in the 1971 Census; for mothers of pre-school children, for instance, the rate is around 35 per cent, compared to 20 per cent in the Census.

21 The relationship between family income, excluding wife's earnings, and wives' employment rates seems not to hold for low-income families *where the husband is not employed*. Wives of unemployed husbands are less likely to be employed themselves, as are wives whose husbands are sick, especially those whose

illness is long-term and who are not seeking work (see page 53).

22 The exact questions asked were:

Study 1 – 'Would you, on balance, prefer to stay at home and not work or do you/would you prefer to go out to work?' (Hunt *et al.*, 1973).

Study 2 – 'Apart from the money would you prefer not to work or would you want to work anyway even if it were not necessary?' (for employed mothers) *and* 'Would you like to be able to go out to work if you could make satisfactory arrangements for child whilst working?' (for non-employed mothers)(Bone, 1977).

Study 3 – 'If you had more money coming into the family from another source, would you still go out to work?' (for employed mothers) *and* 'Would you like to go out to work now or later?' (for non-employed mothers)(Moss and Plewis, 1979).

3 Employment Prospects and Equal Opportunity

1 The Manpower Research Group (MRG) at the University of Warwick was formed in 1975 and is engaged upon a programme of research financed by the Manpower Services Commission. This chapter draws upon the analysis of female employment prospects, presented in the second medium-term assessment of employment prospects, recently prepared by the MRG (Lindley, 1980). Unless otherwise indicated, the views expressed in this chapter are those of the author and should not be attributed to the Manpower Research Group or the Manpower Services Commission.

2 The New Earnings Survey, conducted in April each year, consists of a sample of approximately 170,000 employees. In 1974, reorganisation of local government and the National Health Service led to a fall of between 17 and 26 per cent in the response rate from establishments in these sectors (parts of industry orders 25 and 26). This does not appear to have had any impact upon the comparability of the information for the years shown in Table 11. In 1975, the sample selection procedure was revised and now excludes persons whose weekly or monthly earnings are below the tax deduction limit. This change could account for a *decrease* in the proportion of part-time females of between two and three percentage points between 1974 and 1975, in industry orders 1, 23, 25 and 26.

3 This estimate must be treated cautiously, for the GHS does not clarify the phrase 'earlier than intended' nor is the interpretation of what constitutes a 'suitable arrangement' for child care made clear. The estimate does not imply that the female labour force (married plus non-married women) would necessarily increase by 7 per cent simply if more child care was made available. The

child care might not be deemed 'suitable' and 'earlier than intended' might mean in three years' time rather than in four years' time. The information does give some idea, though, of the future work intention of mothers and the constraints imposed upon their decision-making by the need to look after children.

4 This section gives brief details of the MRG *standard view* employment projection by sex. For further details, including industrial, occupational and regional tabulations of employment prospects, see Lindley (1980).

4 Managing Work and Family Life: A Comparative Policy Overview

1 The interrelationship of work and family life has received increasing attention in recent years. For some discussion of the issues, see, for example, Kanter (1977a) and Kamerman (1979).

2 Other aspects of the 'work and family problem' include the negative consequences for the family of father (male) unemploy-ment – or of mother (female) employment. This chapter focuses on the policy measures instituted in various countries directed at some aspect of the work and family intersection. I do not discuss here, except very briefly for the USA, the ways in which families have adjusted to the demands of the work world when both parents – or a sole parent – works. In particular, I do not review the very extensive and important research on changes in the division of labour within the family and time allocation in the household, when parents work.

3 For those who are interested in this subject, the most significant comparative study is by Alexander Szalai (1972). The most definitive work on the United States is by John Robinson (1977).

4 Among these countries are several of the Eastern European countries and all the Nordic countries (Sweden, Denmark, Finland and Norway). There is a discussion beginning in France and the USA.

5 For a review and analysis of comparative trends, see OECD (1979). There are those in Britain who would disagree, but the dominant international view is that this trend will hold up.

6 For a detailed report on how families manage work and family life in one US community, see Kamerman (1980).

7 Some of the substantive material in the remainder of this chapter is available in much more detail in Kamerman and Kahn (1980).

8 The term 'national child-care policy' is used here to mean an explicitly announced national policy to provide certain benefits and services for children. Countries may develop such policies as a sub-category of their family policies (more broadly defined than just services for families and children), as in, for example,

France, Sweden and Hungary, or as a specific policy focused on children, as in the West German decision to expand kindergartens to serve 75 per cent of the age group three to six within a specified time period.

9   Although there is a growing trend to supplement paid post-childbirth leaves with unpaid leaves, such a benefit does not provide a real alternative for most families. Clearly such leave involves an economic penalty for families even though it may offer some relief from work pressures for a limited group. In some countries this entitlement to an unpaid leave is for women only; in others, such as France, Norway and Sweden, it is for either parent, and ranges from one to two years after the end of the paid post-childbirth leave.

10   The *complément familial* is a categorical, income-tested family allowance, established in 1978 to replace five previous such allowances. Those now replaced include the mother-at-home allowance (for families where the mother was not in the labour force), the single wage earner allowance (for families with only one wage earner), and the child-care allowance (for families with a lone parent who is employed, or two working parents). In effect this benefit, provided to families with earnings under a specified ceiling and with at least one child under age three, or three or more children, assures these families of an income supplement regardless of the labour force status of parents, which they can use as they wish.

11   For some discussion of this concept, see Kamerman and Kahn (1980).

12   The US child-care tax credit is a credit against an individual's (or couple's) personal income tax. It is available to families with a lone parent or two parents in the labour force (or in full-time education) who would not be able to work without arranging for the care of a child. The credit is equal to 20 per cent of the cost of such care, or a *maximum* of $400 per year for one child or $800 for two or more children. In 1978 over $700 billion in tax revenue (covering about four million children in 2.5 million families) were foregone in providing this credit. Family child-care expenditures can be for group care (nursery school, day-care centre), family day care, in-servant care, or care by a relative. There are no data evaluating the type of care purchased with these funds.

13   There are also non-work and non-family activities such as community and leisure activities which adults may wish to particpate in. However, I am assuming that when children are young, these are foregone. Their significance emerges later and is not discussed therefore in the context of the work–family crunch.

14   Compared to such countries as France, West Germany and the US, the UK has a very high rate of part-time employment among

women, although nowhere near as high as the Swedish rate of close to 50 per cent. The situation in Britain is exacerbated, however, by the fact that most part-time jobs are low-wage jobs and are also not covered by statutory or occupational benefits.

15 There is no direct causal pattern between female labour force participation rates and provision of out-of-home child-care services. Indeed, in some countries causation appears to have run the other way.

16 As part of this goal, Sweden has taken the lead in encouraging men to participate more actively in parenting and family life, women to participate more fully in the labour force and both to be more active in the life of their local communities.

17 Furthermore, there is no evidence that indicates negative consequences for children of mothers working. On the contrary, there is growing evidence that suggests positive consequences for many children as well as women. For the best, and most recent review of this research, see Hoffman (1979).

18 Indeed, much of the comparative literature thus far has focused on how women manage work and family lives, rather than the relationship between work and family life for all adults. There is, however, a significant comparative literature dealing with the 'Women and Work' problem. Among the best sources are: Fogarty, Rapoport and Rapoport (1971); Scott (1974); International Labour Organisation (1974, 1976, 1978); Cook (1975); Department of Employment (1978b); Nelson (1978). Some discussion of this broader topic can be found in Rapoport and Rapoport (1978a, b).

19 In identifying the need for a broader and more coherent policy perspective with regard to the relationship between work and family, I am really urging an approach that has been described elsewhere as 'family policy as perspective' (Kamerman and Kahn, 1978). Growing concern for improving the quality of life in advanced industrialised countries emphasises the need for a new criterion to be added to existing concerns with poverty, inequality and social justice in our social policy debates. The consequence for family wellbeing, broadly defined, could provide such a criterion which would cut across several major policy domains. This use of 'family policy' is illustrated by some of the current Swedish debate. Needless to say, this approach does not imply a family or children's ministry, but rather the application of the criterion of family wellbeing to many domains.

5 Statutory Maternity Leave in the United Kingdom: A Case Study

1 The national insurance maternity allowance is a flat-rate weekly

cash benefit, payable for a total of eighteen weeks, starting at the eleventh week before the expected date of birth. Maternity allowance is paid at the same level as unemployment benefit and, as with unemployment benefit, eligibility is dependent on paying or being credited for national insurance contributions for a period. Until 1977, married women in employment had the option of paying a special low-rate 'married woman's stamp' which excluded them from entitlement to maternity allowance, unemployment benefit and other benefits associated with the payment of NI contributions, but since that date only married women who were already registered for national insurance contributions and who have chosen to maintain their 'married woman's option' have been excluded. Women are also entitled to an earnings-related supplement to their maternity allowance if their earnings were high enough in the tax year to which the supplement relates. This supplement is normally paid from the start of the third week of any claim.

2   There were 27 women MPs in the 1974–76 Parliament.

3   W.W. Daniel has been commissioned by the Department of Employment to investigate knowledge and experience of the statutory maternity pay and maternity leave provisions among women who have given birth and their employers. V. Rowlands is conducting a study along similar lines in Northamptonshire for the EOC/SSRC Joint Panel on Equal Opportunities.

4   The figures given in the report of the IRS survey do not distinguish between women who exercised a statutory right to reinstatement and/or pay and those who, although they were excluded from statutory entitlement, took advantage of their employers' own schemes.

5   The EOC has in fact jointly sponsored Valerie Rowland's research (see note 3).

6   The Stance of Britain's Major Parties and Interest Groups

1   The basic demands of the women's liberation movement are: equal pay now; equal education and job opportunities; free twenty-four-hour nurseries; free contraception and abortion on demand; financial and legal independence; an end to discrimination against lesbians and a woman's right to define her own sexuality; and freedom from intimidation by threat or use of violence or sexual coercion, regardless of marital status, and an end to all laws, assumptions and institutions which perpetuate male dominance and men's aggression towards women.

2   The Directive, now agreed, will come into effect in stages up to 1985.

Bibliography

ADAMSON, J. (1979) *An evaluation of Maternity Pay and Leave and its Effect on Working Mothers,* dissertation for Master's Degree, University of Sussex.

ALFRED MARKS BUREAU (1975) *Survey of Fringe Benefits for Office Staff,* London: Alfred Marks Bureau

ANDERSON, M. (1973) 'Family, Household and the Industrial Revolution', in ANDERSON, M. (ed.) *Sociology of the Family,* Harmondsworth: Penguin Books

BAILYN, L. (1971) 'Career and family orientations of husbands and wives in relation to marital happiness', *Human Relations,* 23, 97-113

BALLARD, R. (1981) 'South East Asian Families in Britain', in RAPOPORT, R.N., FOGARTY, M. and RAPOPORT, R. (eds), *Families in Britain,* London: Routledge

BANFIELD, F. (1978) 'The 1971 Census; Voluntary Survey of Incomes', *Populations Trends,* 12, 18-21

BARRON, I. and CURNOW, R. (1979) *The Future of Micro-Electronics,* London: Frances Pinter

BEENSTOCK, M. (1979) 'Do U.K. Labour Markets Work?' in CENTRE FOR ECONOMIC FORECASTING, *Economic Outlook 1978-82,* Vol. 3, Nos 9 and 10, London: London Business School

BELL, R.Q. (1972) *Virginia Woolf,* London: Paladin

BERGER, M., FOSTER, M. and WALLSTON, B.S. (1978) 'Finding Two Jobs', in RAPOPORT, R.N. and RAPOPORT, R. (eds), *Working Couples,* London: Routledge

BERNARD, J. (1972) *The Future of the Family,* New York: World

BEVERIDGE, W. (1942) *Report on Social Insurance and Allied Services,* Cmd 6404, London: HMSO

BILLER, H. and MEREDITH, D. (1974) *Father Power,* New York: David McKay

BONE, M. (1977) *Pre-school children and the need for day-care,* London: HMSO

BOSWORTH, D. and DAWKINS, P. (1979) *Female Patterns of Work and Associated Remuneration, Facilities and Opportunities,* mimeographed research report to the EOC/SSRC Joint Panel on Equal Opportunities

BOTT, E. (1957) *Family and Social Network,* London: Tavistock

BOTT, E. (1971) *Family and Social Network,* 2nd edition, London: Tavistock

BRITISH INSTITUTE OF MANAGEMENT (1973) *The Management Threshold,* London: BIM

BRITTON, M. (1975) 'Women at Work', *Population Trends*, 2, 22-25
BROWN, G. and HARRIS, T. (1978) *Social Origins of Depression: A Study of Psychiatric Disorders in Women*, London: Tavistock
BRYSON, R., BRYSON, J., LICHT, M. and LICHT, B. (1976) 'The professional pair: husband and wife psychologists', *American Psychologist*, 31, 10-16
BUTLER, N., OSBORN, A., DOWLING, S. and HOWLETT, B. (forthcoming) *Britain's Five-Year-Olds*, London: Routledge
CAMBRIDGE ECONOMIC POLICY GROUP (1979) *Cambridge Economic Policy Review*, No. 5, Cambridge: Department of Applied Economics
CAMPBELL, A., CONVERSE, P.E. and RODGERS, N.L. (1976) *The Quality of American Life*, New York: Russell Sage Foundation
CAMPBELL, B. and CHARLTON, V. (1978) Work to Rule, *Red Rag*
CENTRAL POLICY REVIEW STAFF (1975) A Joint Framework for Social Policy, London: HMSO
CENTRAL POLICY REVIEW STAFF (1978a) *Services for Young Children with Working Mothers*, London: HMSO
SOCIAL POLICY REVIEW STAFF (1978b) *Social and Employment Implications of Micro electronics*, London: CPRS
CENTRAL STATISTICAL OFFICE (1975) *Social Trends 6*, London: HMSO
CENTRAL STATISTICAL OFFICE (1978) *Social Trends 9*, London: HMSO
CENTRAL STATISTICAL OFFICE (1979) *Social Trends 10*, London: HMSO
CENTRE FOR ECONOMIC FORECASTING (1979) *Economic Outlook, 1978-82*, Vol. 3, Nos 9 and 10, London: London Business School
CERC (1979) *Incidence D'un Second Salaire sur les Ressources de la Famille*, Paris: CERC
CHEN, E. and COBB, S. (1960) 'Family Structure in Relation to Health and Disease, *Journal of Chronic Diseases*, 12, 544-67
COHEN, G. (1977) 'Absentee husbands in spiralist families: the myth of the symmetrical family', *Journal of Marriage and the Family*, 39, 595-604
COOK, A. (1975) *The Working Mother*, New York State School of Industrial and Labour Relations: Ithaca
COOPER, D. (1970) *The Death of the Family*, New York: Pantheon
COOPERSMITH, S. (1967) *Antecedents of self esteem*, San Francisco: Freeman
COSER, L. (1956) *The Functions of Social Conflict*, London: Routledge
DANIEL, W. (1978) The Effect of Employment Protection Laws in Manufacturing Industry, *Department of Employment Gazette*, June 1978, 658-661
DANIEL, W. and STILGOE, E. (1977) *Where are they now? A follow-up Study of the Unemployed*, London: PEP
DAVIE, R., BUTLER, N. and GOLDSTEIN, H. (1972) *From Birth to Seven: Second Report of the National Child Development Study (1958 cohort)*, London: Longman, for National Children's Bureau

DEPARTMENT OF EMPLOYMENT (1971a) *New Earnings Survey,* (1970) London: HMSO

DEPARTMENT OF EMPLOYMENT(1971b) *British Labour Statistics, Historical Abstract, 1886-1968,* London: HMSO

DEPARTMENT OF EMPLOYMENT (1973) Part-time Women Workers, *Department of Employment Gazette,* November 1973

DEPARTMENT OF EMPLOYMENT (1974) *Employment Protection Bill: Consultative Document,* London: HMSO

DEPARTMENT OF EMPLOYMENT (1975a) *Department of Employment Gazette,* January 1975

DEPARTMENT OF EMPLOYMENT (1975b) *Department of Employment Gazette,* December 1975

DEPARTMENT OF EMPLOYMENT (1977a) 'New projections of the future labour force', *Department of Employment Gazette,* June 1977, 587-92

DEPARTMENT OF EMPLOYMENT (1977b) *Department of Employment Gazette,* June 1977

DEPARTMENT OF EMPLOYMENT (1978a) *Family Expenditure Survey, 1977*

DEPARTMENT OF EMPLOYMENT (1978b) *Women and Work: Overseas Practice,* London: HMSO

DEPARTMENT OF EMPLOYMENT (1979a) *New Earnings Survey, 1978, Volume E,* London: HMSO

DEPARTMENT OF EMPLOYMENT (1979b) *Department of Employment Gazette,* July 1979

DEPARTMENT OF EMPLOYMENT (1979c) *Department of Employment Gazette,* January 1979

DEPARTMENT OF EMPLOYMENT (1979d) *New Earnings Survey, 1978, Volume F,* London: HMSO

DEPARTMENT OF EMPLOYMENT (1979e) Small Firms Experience of Employment Legislation, *Department of Employment Gazette,* July 1979, 652-653

DEPARTMENT OF EMPLOYMENT (1979f) *Proposed Amendments to the Employment Protection Legislation: Working Papers,* London HMSO

DEPARTMENT OF EMPLOYMENT, DEPARTMENT OF EDUCATION, HOME OFFICE (1973) *Equal Opportunities for Men and Women: Government Proposals for Legislation,* London: HMSO

DEPARTMENT OF HEALTH (1968) *Circular 37/68*

DOUGLAS, J.W.B. and BLOMFIELD, J.M. (1958) *Children Under Fives* London: Allen & Unwin

ELDER, G.H. (1974) *Children of the Great Depression; Social Change in life experience,* Chicago: University of Chicago Press

ELIAS, P. (1980) 'Labour Supply and Employment Opportunities for Women', in LINDLEY, R.M. (ed.) *Economic Change and Employment Policy,* London: Macmillan

EQUAL OPPORTUNITIES COMMISSION (1978) *'I want to work . . . but what about the kids?'; day-care for young children and opportunities for working parents,* Manchester: EOC

EQUAL OPPORTUNITIES COMMISSION (1979a) *Health and Safety Legislation: Should we distinguish between men and women,* Manchester: EOC

EQUAL OPPORTUNITIES COMMISSION (1979b) *'I want a baby ... but what about my job'; a study of current maternity rights and their effects on equal pay and equal opportunities,* Manchester: EOC

EQUAL OPPORTUNITIES COMMISSION (1979c) *'With all my goods I thee endow ... except my tax allowance': response received by the EOC to Consultative Document on Income Tax and Sex Discrimination,* Manchester: EOC

EVERSLEY, D. and EVANS, A. (1976) 'Demographic Change and the Demand for Housing', in BUXTON, M. and CRAVEN, E. (eds), *The Uncertain Future,* London: Centre for Studies in Social Policy

FEIN, R.A. (1974) 'Men and Young Children', in PLECK, J. and SAWYER, J. (eds), *Men and Masculinity* Englewood Cliffs, N.J.: Prenctice-Hall

FERRI, E. (1976) *Growing-up in a One-parent family,* Slough: NFER Publishing

FOGARTY, M., RAPOPORT, R. and RAPOPORT, R.N. (1976) *Women and Top Jobs: An Interim Report,* London: PEP

FOGARTY, M., RAPOPORT, R. and RAPOPORT, R.N. (1971) *Sex, Career and the Family,* London: Allen & Unwin

FONDA, N. (1976) 'Managing Maternity Leave', *Personnel Management,* January 1976, 28-32

GALES, K. and MARKS, P. (1974) 'Twentieth-century trends in the work of women in England and Wales', *Journal of the Royal Statistical Society,* A, 137, 60-74

GALLUP POLL (1979) 'Work and Mothers Study', unpublished tables of survey conducted for *Woman's Own*

GEORGE, V. and WILDING, P. (1972) *Motherless Families,* London: Routledge

GHS UNIT (1978) 'Changing Circumstances of Women 1971-76', *Population Trends,* 13, 17-22

GIBSON, H. and BARKER, T. (1979) *Macroeconomic projections and policy, CEP79/5,* mimeographed report from the Department of Applied Economics, Cambridge

GINSBERG, S. (1976) 'Women, Work and Conflict', in FONDA, N. and MOSS. P. (eds), *Mothers in Employment,* Uxbridge: Brunel University

GOLDTHORPE, J., LLEWELLYN, K. and PAYNE, C. (1980) *Social Mobility and Class Structure,* London: Oxford University Press

GOLDTHORPE, J. *et al.* (1969) *The Affluent Worker: Political Attitudes and Behaviour,* London: Cambridge University Press

GOWLER, D. and LEGGE, K. (1981) 'Dual Worker Families' in RAPOPORT, R.N., FOGARTY, M. and RAPOPORT, R. (eds), *Families in Britain,* London: Routledge

GREENBERG, M. and MORRIS, N. (1974) 'Engrossment; the newborn's impact upon the father', *American Journal of Ortho-psychiatry,* 44, 520-31

GREENHALGH, C. (1977) 'A Labour Supply Function for Married

Women in Great Britain', *Economics,* 44, 249-65

GRONSETH, E. (1957) 'The impact of father absence in sailor families upon the personality structure and social adjustment of adult sailor sons', in ANDERSON, N. (ed.), *Studies on the Family* Vol. 2, Gottingen

GRONSETH, E. (1978) 'Work Sharing: a Norwegian example' in RAPO-PORT, R.N. and RAPOPORT, R. (eds), *Working Couples,* London: Routledge

GUTTENTAG, N. and SALASIN, S. (1975) *Women, men and mental health,* paper given at the Aspen Conference on Women, August 1975

HAAVIO-MANNILA, E. (1972) 'Cross-national difference in adoption of new ideologies and practices in family life, *Journal of Marriage and the Family,* 34, 525

HALSEY, A. (ed.) (1972) *Trends in British Society Since 1900,* London: Macmillan

HAMILL, J. (1978) *Wives as Sole and Joint Breadwinners: Government Economic Service Working Paper,* 13, London: DHSS Economic Advisers' Office

HESS, R. and HANDEL, G. (1959) *The Psycho-social Interior of the Family,* Chicago: Aldire Press

HOFFMAN, L. (1974) 'The effects of maternal employment on the child –a review of the research', *Developmental Psychology,* 10, 204-28

HOFFMAN, L (1979) 'Maternal Employment 1979', *American Psychologist,* 34, 10, 859-865

HOFFMAN, L. and NYE, F. (1974) *Working mothers,* New York: Jossey-Bass

HOFFMAN, L. and NYE, F. (1978) *Working mothers,* 2nd edition, New York: Jossey-Bass

HORNER, M. (1971) 'Fail: Bright Women', in THEODORE, A. (ed.) *The Professional Woman,* Cambridge, Mass.: Schenkman

HUGHES, M., MAYALL, B., MOSS, P., PERRY, J., PINKERTON, G. and PETRIE, P. (1980) *Nurseries Now,* Harmondsworth: Penguin Books

HUNT, A. (1968) *A Survey of Women's Employment,* London: HMSO

HUNT, A. (1975) *Management Attitudes and Practices Towards Women at Work,* London: HMSO

HUNT, A., FOX, J. and MORGAN, M. (1973) *Families and Their Needs,* London: HMSO

HURSTFIELD, J. (1978) *The Part-time Trap,* London: Low Pay Unit

IFF (1978) *Shiftwork in Manufacturing Industry, GB,* London: IFF Research Ltd

INCOMES DATA SERVICES (1973) *Maternity Leave: Study 58,* London: IDS

INCOMES DATA SERVICES (1976) *Child Care at Work: Study 129,* London: IDS

INCOMES DATA SERVICES (1977) *Maternity Schemes: Study 150,* London: IDS

INCOMES DATA SERVICES (1979) *Maternity Cover and Child Care: Study 191,* London: IDS

INDUSTRIAL RELATIONS REVIEW AND REPORT (1980) The IRRR Maternity Leave Survey, *Industrial Relations Review and Report,*

Nos. 217 and 218

INKELES, A. (1960) 'Industrial Man: the relation of status to experience, perception and value', *American Journal of Sociology,* 66, July 1960

INSTITUTE OF PERSONNEL MANAGEMENT (1974) *Special Leave Allowances,* London: IPM

INTERNATIONAL LABOUR ORGANISATION (1974) *Equality of Opportunity and Treatment for Women Workers,* Geneva: ILO

INTERNATIONAL LABOUR ORGANISATION (1976) *Women Workers and Society,* Geneva: ILO

INTERNATIONAL LABOUR ORGANISATION (1978) *Employment of Women with Family Responsibilities,* Geneva: ILO

JACKSON, B. and JACKSON, S. (1979) *Childminder,* London: Routledge

JOSHI, H. (1978) *Secondary Workers in the Cycle: Married Women and Older Workers in Employment: Fluctuations, 1961-74: Government Economic Service Working Paper 8,* London: DHSS Economic Advisers' Office

KAMERMAN, S. (1976) *Developing a Family Impact Statement,* New York: Foundation for Child Development

KAMERMAN, S. (1979) 'Work and Family in Industrialized Societies', *SIGNS (The Journal of Women in Culture and Society),* Vol. 4, No. 4, Special Issue on 'The Labour of Women: Work and Family'

KAMERMAN, S. (1980) *Parenting in an Unresponsive Society: Managing Work and Family Life,* New York: Free Press

KAMERMAN, S. and KAHN, A. (eds) (1978) *Family Policy: Government and Families in Fourteen Countries,* New York: Columbia University Press

KAMERMAN, S. and KAHN, A. (1980) *Child Care, Family Benefits and Working Parents,* New York: Columbia University Press

KANTER, R.M. (1977a) *Work and Family in the United States,* New York: Russell Sage Foundation

KANTER, R.M. (1977b) *Men and Women of the Corporation,* New York: Basic Books

KELLMER-PRINGLE, M. (1974) *The Needs of Children,* London: Hutchinson

KOHN, M. and SCHOOLER, C. (1969) 'Class, Occupation and Orientation', *The American Sociological Review,* 34

LAND, H. (1978) 'Who cares for the Family?', *Journal of Social Policy,* 7, 257-284

LASLETT, P. (1971) *The World We Have Lost,* London: Methuen

LAYARD, R. *et al.* (1978) *The Causes of Poverty: Background Paper 5, Royal Commission on Distribution of Income and Wealth,* London: HMSO

LEETE, R. (1978a) 'One parent families: numbers and characteristics', *Population Trends,* 13, 4-9

LEETE, R. (1978b) 'Adoption trends and illegitimate births, 1951-77',

Population Trends, 14, 9-16

LEETE, R. (1979a) *Changing patterns of family formation and dissolution in England and Wales, 1964-76,* London: HMSO

LEETE, R. (1979b) New directions in family life, *Population Trends,* 15, 4-11

LEETE, R., and ANTHONY, S. (1979) 'Divorce and Remarriage: a record linkage study', *Population Trends,* 16, 5-11

LEICESTER, C. (1977) *Unemployment 2001 A.D.,* Brighton: Institute of Manpower Studies

LEICESTER, C. (1978a) 'Recruitment in the '80s', *Personnel Management,* April 1978

LEICESTER, C. (1978b) 'Future Employment Trends', *The Planner,* July 1978

LEICESTER, C. (1978c) *Manpower Policies for the 1980s?* Paper presented to the Manpower Society Conference, 'Manpower in Europe and the UK: contemporary experience', London, 21-22 September 1978

LEIGHTON, D.C. *et al.* (1963) *The Character of Danger,* New York: Basic Books

LE MASTERS, E. (1957) 'Parenthood as crisis', *Marriage and Family Living,* 19, 353-5

LINDLEY, R.M. (ed.) (1980) *Economic Change and Employment Policy,* London: Macmillan

LOMAS, G. (1975) Race and Employment, *New Society,* 32, 413

MARSH, A. (1979) *Women and Shiftwork,* London: HMSO

MAYALL, B. AND PETRIE, P. (1977) *Mother, minder and child,* Slough: NFER

MILL, J.S. and MILL, H.T. (1869) *The Subjection of Women*

MILLER, D. and SWANSON, G. (1958) *The Changing American Parent,* New York: John Wiley

MINISTRY OF HEALTH (1945) *Circular 221/45.*

MORRELL, J. (1977) *2002: Britain Plus 25,* London: The Henley Centre for Forecasting

MORTIMER, J. (1977) *Dual Career Families – a Sociological Perspective,* paper presented at symposium on The Two-Career Family, sponsored by the Andrew W. Mellon Foundation, Minnesota, 1977

MOSS, P., TIZARD, J., and CROOK, J. (1973) Families and their Needs, *New Society,* 23, 638-640

MOSS, P. and PLEWIS, I. (1979) 'Young Children in the Inner City', an unpublished report to the DHSS on the Thomas Coram Research Unit Pre-school Project

NATIONAL BOARD OF PRICES AND INCOMES (1970) *Hours of Work, Overtime and Shiftwork;* Report No. 161, London: HMSO

NATIONAL COUNCIL FOR CIVIL LIBERTIES (1979) *The Shift Work Swindle,* London: NCCL

NATIONAL INSTITUTE OF ECONOMIC AND SOCIAL RESEARCH

(1979) *National Institute Economic Review*, No. 89, London: NIESR

NELSON, A.H. (1978) *The One World of Working Women: Bureau of International Affairs, Monograph No. 1*, Washington: United States Department of Labour

NEWSON. E, and NEWSON, J. (1970) *Four Years Old in an Urban Community*, Harmondsworth: Penguin Books

NORWEGIAN FAMILY AFFAIRS AND EQUAL STATUS DEPT (1978) *Family and Child Policy in Norway*, Oslo: Family Affairs and Equal Status Dept

PAHL, J. and PAHL, R.E. (1971) *Managers and their Wives*, London: Allen Lane

OAKLEY, A. (1972) *Sex, Gender and Society*, London: Maurice Temple Smith

OAKLEY, A. (1974) *The Sociology of Housework*, London: Martin Robertson

OAKLEY, A. (1981) 'Conventional Families', in RAPOPORT R.N., FOGARTY, M. and RAPOPORT, R. (eds) *Families in Britain*, London: Routledge

ODEGAARD, V. (1936) 'Emigration and Mental Health', *Mental Hygiene*, 20, 4

OECD (1978) *Equal Opportunities for Women*, Paris: OECD

OECD (1979) *Economic Outlook: No. 25*, Paris: OECD

OPCS (1973) *The General Household Survey: Introductory Report*, London: HMSO

OPCS (1978) *One parent families in 1971 and 1976: OPCS Monitor FM2 78/2*, London: OPCS

OPCS (1979a) *General Household Survey, 1977*, London: HMSO

OPCS (1979b) General Household Survey, 1978, *OPCS Monitor GHS 79/1*.

OPCS (1979c) Divorces, 1977, OPCS Monitor FM2 79/1

OPPENHEIMER, V. (1974) 'The Life-Cycle Squeeze: the interaction of man's occupational and family life cycle', *Demography*, 11, 227-245

ORDEN, S. and BRADBURN, M. (1968) 'Dimensions of marriage happiness', *Journal of Sociology*, 74, 715-31

OSBORN, A. (1975) *The Day Care of Children Under Five in the City of Westminster*, London: Westminster Social Services Department

PEDERSEN, F. (1976) 'Does Research on Children reared in Father Absent Families yield information on Father's influences?', *The Family Co-ordinator*, 25, 459-464

PILLING, D. and KELLMER-PRINGLE, M. (1978) *Controversial issues in child development*, London: Paul Elek

PLECK, J. and SAWYER, J. (eds) (1974) *Men and Masculinity*, Englewood Cliffs, N.J.: Prentice Hall

POLACHEK, S.W. (1975) 'Discontinuous Labour Force Participation and its Effects', in LLOYD, C.B. (ed.), *Sex, Discrimination and the Division of Labour*, New York: Columbia University Press

PORTNER, J. (1979) *Impacts of Work on the Family,* for the Minnesota Council on Family Relations

POWELL, D. and DRISCOLL, P. (1973) 'Middle-class Professionals face Unemployment', *Society,* 10, 18-25

RAPOPORT, R.N. (1970) *Mid-career development,* London: Tavistock

RAPOPORT, R.N., RAPOPORT, R. and STRELITZ, Z. (1975) *Leisure and the family cycle,* London: Routledge

RAPOPORT, R.N., RAPAPORT R. and STRELITZ, Z. (1977) *Fathers, Mothers and Others,* London: Routledge

RAPOPORT R.N. and RAPOPORT, R. (1975) 'Men, Women and Equity', *The Family Co-ordinator,* 24, 421-2

RAPOPORT, R.N. and RAPOPORT R. (1978a) *Dual Career families Re-examined,* London: Martin Robertson

RAPOPORT, R.N. and RAPOPORT R. (1978b) *Working Couples,* London: Routledge

RAPOPORT, R.N. and RAPOPORT R. (1978c) 'Dual Career Families: Progress and Prospect', *Marriage and Family Review,* 1, 5, 1-12

READING, B., MORGAN, N. and COCKLE, P. (1979) 'Doing with Deficits', *Guardian,* 15 October

REDICAN, W.K. and MITCHELL, G. (1972) 'Male parental behaviour in Adult Rhesus Monkeys', paper presented at the Annual Meeting of the Western Psychological Association, Portland, Oregon

RENSHAW, J. (1976) 'An exploration of the dynamics of the overlapping worlds of work and family', *Family Process,* 15, 142-65

ROBINSON, J.P. (1977) *How Americans Use Time,* New York: Praeger

ROSS, H. and SAWHILL, I. (1975) *Time of Transition: the Growth of Families headed by Women,* Washington: The Urban Institute

RUTTER, M. (1968) 'Concepts of autism: a review of research', *Journal of Child Psychology and Psychiatry,* 9, 1-25

RUTTER, M. (1972) *Maternal Deprivation Reassessed,* Harmondsworth: Penguin Books

RYPMA, C.B. (1979) 'Biological Basis of the Paternal Response', *The Family Co-ordinator,* 25, 335

SANDERS, D. (1979) 'Fair Care for Children and a Fair Deal for Mum', *Woman's Own*

SCOTT, H. (1974) *Does Socialism Liberate Women?* Boston: Beacon Press

SEEAR, N. (1981) 'Families and Employment', in RAPOPORT, R.N., FOGARTY, M. and RAPOPORT, R. (eds), *Families in Britain,* London: Routledge

SEIDENBERG, R. (1975) *Corporate Wives – Corporate Casualties,* New York: Anchor (Doubleday)

SHAEVITZ, M. and SHAEVITZ, M.H. (1979) *Making it together as a two-career couple,* Boston: Houghton Mifflin

SHANKLAND, G., WILLMOTT, P. and JORDAN, D. (1977) *Inner*

    London: Policies for Dispersal and Disposal, London: HMSO
SIMPSON, R. (1978) *Day Care for School Age Children,* Manchester:
    Equal Opportunities Commission
SMEE, C.H. and STERN, J. (1978) *The Unemployed in a Period of High
    Unemployment: Government Economic Service Working Paper Bill,*
    London: DHSS Economic Advisers' Office
SMITH, D. (1976) *Facts of Racial Disadvantage,* London: PEP
SNELL, M. (1979) The Equal Pay and Sex Discrimination Acts: their
    Impact on the Workplace, *Feminist Review,* 1
SOFER, C. (1970) *Men in Mid-career: a study of British Managers and
    Technical Specialists,* London: Cambridge University Press
STONEMAN, P. (1975) 'The effect of computers on the demand for labour',
    Economic Journal, 85, 590-606
SUNDBY, D. (1980) 'Dual-career couples', in DERR, B. (ed.), *Organ-
    isations and Careers,* New York: Praeger
SWEDISH INSTITUTE (1980) *Child Care Programs in Sweden,* Stock-
    holm: The Swedish Institute
SWEDISH MINISTRY OF HEALTH AND SOCIAL AFFAIRS (1979)
    Financial Assistance to Families with Children, Stockholm: Ministry of
    Health and Social Affairs
SZALAI, A. (1972) *The Uses of Time,* The Hague: Mouton
TRADES UNION CONGRESS (1977) *A Charter for Women at Work,*
    London: TUC
TRADES UNION CONGRESS (1978) *A Charter for the Under-Fives,*
    London: TUC
WALKER, K. (1979) Paper presented at the Annual Conference of the
    National Council on Family Relations, Boston
WALKER, K. and WOODS, M. (1976) *Time Use: a Measure of Household
    Production of Family Goods and Services,* Washington: American Home
    Economics Association
WEISSMAN, M. and PAYKEL, E. (1974) *The Depressed Woman,* Chicago:
    University of Chicago Press
WILENSKY, H. (1968) 'Woen's work, economic growth, ideology and
    structure', *Industrial Relations,* 7, 235-48
WORKING FAMILY PROJECT (1978) 'Parenting', in RAPOPORT,
    R.N. and RAPOPORT, R. (eds), *Working Couples,* London: Routledge
YANKELOVICH, D. (1974) 'The meaning of work', in ROSOW, J. (ed.),
    The Worker and the Job, Englewood Cliffs, N.J.: Prentice-Hall
YARROW, M. *et al.* (1962) 'Child-rearing in families of working and non-
    working mothers', *Sociometry,* 25, 122-40
YOUNG, M. and WILLMOTT, P. (1973) *The Symmetrical Family,* London:
    Routledge
YUDKIN, S. and HOLME, A. (1969) *Working Mothers and their children,*
    London: Michael Joseph
ZILL, N. (1978) *Divorce, Marital Happiness and the Mental Health of
    Children,* Report prepared for NIMH Workshop on Divorce and Children,
    held at Bethesda, Maryland, 7-8 February, 1978

Index